The Production Manager's Toolkit

The Production Manager's Toolkit, Second Edition offers an up-to-date, comprehensive introduction to a theatrical and special event production career for new and aspiring professionals, given by expert voices in the field.

The book discusses management techniques, communication skills, and relationship-building tactics to become effective and successful production managers. With a focus on management theory, top production managers provide insights into budgeting, scheduling, meetings, hiring, maintaining safety, and more. Through interviews and case studies, production management techniques are explored throughout various entertainment genres, including theatre, dance, opera, music, and special events. The second edition includes all new case studies, new chapters, and updated content throughout, showcasing a continued progressive approach to the job and the field.

Filled with references, tools, templates, and checklists, *The Production Manager's Toolkit* is an invaluable resource for students of Production Management, Events Management, and Stage Management courses, as well as new and aspiring professionals.

The book includes access to a companion website featuring downloadable paperwork and links to other useful resources such as unions, venues, and vendors (www.routledge.com/cw/gillett).

Cary Gillett has worked as a production manager and stage manager in the Maryland/ Washington DC area for over two decades. Cary is currently the General Manager of the MD/DC branch of the events and AV production company CMI. In addition, she has worked as a production manager for the Baltimore Center Stage, the University of Maryland in College Park, the Round House Theatre, the Potomac Theatre Project, and the Helen Hayes Awards, celebrating theatre in the Washington DC area. She is an adjunct professor at the University of Maryland in College Park, Howard Community College, and an annual visiting professor at the National Academy of Chinese Theatre Arts in Beijing. Cary serves as a board member of the United States Institute for Theatre Technology (USITT) and is the chair of the Inclusion, Diversity, Equity, Access and Social Justice committee.

Jay Sheehan has been overseeing the production management and stage management areas of the School of Theatre, Television and Film at San Diego State University for 23 years, and was the recipient of the USITT Wally Russel Award for Outstanding

Mentorship in 2022. In addition to teaching stage management, production management, event planning, and live concert production, he also created and leads the Certificate in Entertainment Management Program.

He is a 30-year member of Actors' Equity and spent his early career at the Old Globe Theatre in San Diego. Jay has also held positions including Director of Production and Operations for the San Diego Symphony and for House of Blues, where he oversaw all operational aspects of the 20,000-seat Amphitheatre in Chula Vista, California. Jay currently serves as the Director of Concert Operations for the Richter Entertainment Group, an independently owned live entertainment company that has been producing events internationally since the early 1990s. He is also the owner of his own production company, Cue One Productions, whose event list includes the NFL Super Bowl and Major League Baseball's All-Star Game Special Events. He also produces many charity galas and corporate events across the United States.

The Focal Press Toolkit Series

Regardless of your profession, whether you're a Stage Manager or Stagehand, The Focal Press Toolkit Series has you covered. With all the insider secrets, paperwork, and day-to-day details that you could ever need for your chosen profession or specialty, these books provide you with a one-stop-shop to ensure a smooth production process.

The Lighting Supervisor's Toolkit
Collaboration, Interrogation, and Innovation toward Engineering Brilliant Lighting Designs
Jason E. Weber

The Assistant Lighting Designer's Toolkit, 2nd edition
Anne E. McMills

The Projection Designer's Toolkit
Jeromy Hopgood

The Scenic Charge Artist's Toolkit
Tips, Templates, and Techniques for Planning and Running a Successful Paint Shop in the Theatre and Performing Arts
Jennifer Rose Ivey

The Costume Designer's Toolkit
The Process of Creating Effective Design
Holly Poe Durbin

The Literary Manager's Toolkit
A Practical Guide for the Theatre
Sue Healy

The Production Manager's Toolkit, 2nd edition
Successful Production Management in Theatre and Performing Arts
Cary Gillett and Jay Sheehan

The Voice Coach's Toolkit
Pamela Prather

For more information about this series, please visit: https://www.routledge.com/The-Focal-Press-Toolkit-Series/book-series/TFPTS

The Production Manager's Toolkit

Successful Production Management in Theatre and Performing Arts

Second Edition

Cary Gillett and
Jay Sheehan

Routledge
Taylor & Francis Group

NEW YORK AND LONDON

Cover image credit: © Shutterstock

Second edition published 2023
by Routledge
605 Third Avenue, New York, NY 10158

and by Routledge
4 Park Square, Milton Park, Abingdon, Oxon, OX14 4RN

Routledge is an imprint of the Taylor & Francis Group, an informa business

First edition published by Routledge 2017

Library of Congress Cataloging-in-Publication Data
Names: Gillett, Cary, author. | Sheehan, Jay, author.
Title: The production manager's toolkit: successful production management in the theatre and performing arts/Cary Gillett and Jay Sheehan.
Description: Second edition. | New York, NY: Routledge, 2023. | Series: The Focal Press toolkit series | Includes bibliographical references and index.
Identifiers: LCCN 2022037662 (print) | LCCN 2022037663 (ebook) | ISBN 9780367406356 (hardback) | ISBN 9780367406363 (paperback) | ISBN 9780367808174 (ebook)
Subjects: LCSH: Theater–Production and direction–Handbooks, manuals, etc. | Performing arts–Production and direction–Handbooks, manuals, etc.
Classification: LCC PN2053 .G53 2023 (print) | LCC PN2053 (ebook) | DDC 792.02/32–dc23/eng/20220818
LC record available at https://lccn.loc.gov/2022037662
LC ebook record available at https://lccn.loc.gov/2022037663

ISBN: 978-0-367-40635-6 (hbk)
ISBN: 978-0-367-40636-3 (pbk)
ISBN: 978-0-367-80817-4 (ebk)

DOI: 10.4324/9780367808174

Typeset in Times NR MT Pro
by KnowledgeWorks Global Ltd.

Access the companion website: www.routledge.com/cw/gillett

Table of Contents

Acknowledgments   ix

Foreword – First Edition   xv

Foreword – Second Edition   xvii

Introduction   1

PART ONE   **5**

Chapter 1:   Communication   7

Chapter 2:   Relationships   21

Chapter 3:   Management Techniques and Theory   31

Chapter 4:   How to Be an Anti-Racist Production Manager   41

PART TWO   **47**

Chapter 5:   Planning and Scheduling   49

Chapter 6:   Meetings   65

Chapter 7:   Money and Budget   75

Chapter 8:   Hiring and Casting   89

Chapter 9:   Safety   107

PART THREE   **123**

Chapter 10: Theatre   125

Chapter 11: Opera   137

Chapter 12: Dance   147

Chapter 13: Rock and Roll   161

Chapter 14: Symphony Music   189

Chapter 15: Presenting   199

Chapter 16: Co-Productions   213

Chapter 17: Touring   227

Chapter 18: Special Events   239

IN CONCLUSION   **265**

Chapter 19: Pathway Toward a Career in Production
                Management   267

Chapter 20: Balance   279

Index   287

Acknowledgments

UNITED STATES INSTITUTE FOR THEATRE TECHNOLOGY (USITT)

We would not know each other let alone have written this book if it was not for the USITT annual conference. We owe a debt of gratitude to our amazing network made possible by USITT. Specific thanks to David Grindle, Michael Mehler, Deb Acquavella and Tina Shackleford, among many others. If production management is your chosen path you must go to this conference! The possible growth and networking is endless!

INTERVIEWS

This book would not have been possible without the wisdom and experiences of those we interviewed. The process of interviewing for this book was the most enjoyable part for us. Talking for hours with fellow production managers about what we do and why we do it. It was inspiring to say the least and we are better production managers and people due to these conversations. For the second edition, we know this had to continue so we reached back into the network of amazing production managers and others in the industry whose voices we felt needed to be in this book.

FIRST EDITION

Jesse Aasheim
Kasey Allee-Foreman
Tom Bollard
Linda Cooper
Jamila Cobham
Rosie Cruz
Robert Drake
Vinnie Feradou
Kimberly Fisk
Eric Fliss
William Foster
Ken Freeman
David Grindle
Harris Goldman
Ben Heller
David Holcombe
Paul Horpedahl

Yvonne Kimmons
Joel Krause
Neil Kutner
Liza Luxenberg
Nancy Mallette
Anne E. McMills
Lee Miliken
Ouida Maedel
Christy Ney
Rick Noble
Glenn Plott
Scott Price
Karen Quisenberry
William Reynolds
Michael Richter
Jennifer Ringle
Abby Rodd
Bronislaw Samler
John Sanders
Carolyn Satter
Paige Satter
Jenn Schwartz
Perry Silvey
Richard Stephens
David "dstew" Stewart
Doug Taylor
Dixie Uffleman
Tracy Utzmyers
Jill Valentine
Deb Vandergrift
Mike Wade
Drew Wending
Jamie Whitehill
Rebecca Wolf

SECOND EDITION

Itzel Ayala
Lawrence Bennett
Veronica Bishop
Heather Rose Basarab
Drew Cady
David Chan
Cody Chen
Jared Clarkin
Autumn Coppaway
Parker Detchon
Molly Dill

Joseph Futral
Miguel Flores
Anna Glover
Laura Glover
Jon Harper
Frank Hamilton
Duane Lester
Matthew F. Lewandowski
Katie McBride-Muzquiz
Herman Montero
Tajh Oates
Bettina Hahn Osbourne
Shannon Pringle
Jaqueline Reid
Kelsey Sapp
Paige Satter
Juan Torres
Michael Walsh

PHOTOS AND IMAGES

We offer gratitude to those who provided images, templates, and photos for the book:

Richard Anderson
David Andrews
Stan Barouh
Gary Beechey
Lawrence Bennett
Brianne Bland
Tom Bollard
Mark Campbell
Parker Detchon
Kimberly Fisk
Bill Geenen
Zachary Z. Handler
John Holter-McCoy
Paul Horpedahl
Ryan Knapp
Lynn Lane
Cheryl Mann
Matthew Matulewicz
René Milot
Chris Oosterlink
Shannon Pringle
Jay Sheehan David "dstew" Stewart
Richard Termine
Ruth Anne Watkins
Adam Zeek

A special thanks to our friend and artist Joseph Garcia for designing the interior graphics. We are fortunate to have you with us for the second edition.

OUR EDITORS

The support, inspiration, guidance, and mentorship provided by our amazing technical editors are astounding. A special thanks from the bottom of our hearts to Carolyn Satter and David Stewart (first edition) and Shaminda Amarakoon and Deb Acquavella (second edition). And to our Routledge editors – Stacey Walker and Lucia Accorsi – thanks for the guidance and encouragement. We're glad we stumbled into your booth at USITT all those years ago!

SPECIAL THANKS FROM CARY GILLETT

Thanks to those who trusted I could be a production manager and hired me to do so – Cheryl Faraone, Danisha Crosby, Daniel MacLean Wagner, Linda Levy, and Michael Ross. Thanks also to all the horrible production managers I have worked with and for (who shall remain nameless). You have taught me what NOT to do.

To my current and former students – you inspire me every day to be a better production manager and teacher. Thank you to Scott Kincaid and Dwight Townsend-Gray for forcing me to start teaching production management. Thanks to Michelle Heller and Tarythe Albrecht for providing feedback and support throughout the first edition. And to the members of the Production Manager's Forum Diversity, Equity and Inclusion committee who inspired me to be a better ancestor for the next generation of managers and humans.

A personal thanks to my husband Bill – you are my love, my friend, and my editor. You put it all into perspective. And to Phoenix - I hope you read this someday and are proud of me as I am of you every day.

SPECIAL THANKS FROM JAY SHEEHAN

In addition to those listed, heartfelt gratitude goes to all my mentors that have helped guide and teach me along the way. Their constant, unwavering support will always be cherished.

- In memoriam, to my first mentor, Douglas Pagliotti and the Old Globe Theatre for believing in a young stage manager enough to give me my Equity card.
- To my mother Rose Marie Sheehan, who never questioned my choice to get into "show business."
- To my Uncle Nick Manoy, who taught me to always do the right work for the right reasons.
- To Earl Parish, my stepfather, who taught me perseverance and to always try my best.

- To my brothers and sisters, Tom, Erin, and Michael who were always there to cheer me on during the writing of this book.

- Special thanks to my sister, Kathleen Sheehan, for her editing skills and steadfast encouragement throughout this entire process.

- To all my students at San Diego State University, both past and present, who affect me daily and make me a better teacher, production manager and friend.

- To San Diego State University School Directors, Niyi Coker, D.J. Hopkins, Randy Reinholz and Nick Reid, for believing in USITT and supporting my goals as a mentor.

- To Ally Wood for her assistance and expertise in getting my photos ready for publication!

- To Carolyn Satter, who taught me about relationships, lifelong friendships and where to park trucks.

- To Paige Satter, for her constant wisdom and guidance, especially during the writing of this book.

- And lastly, with special gratitude to my soul mate, Mark Sheehan, my guide, my light, my everything. I could not have done this without you.

Foreword – First Edition

Networking. Communication. Compassion. Risk taking. I learned many of these skills from my parents as they molded me to be a good person, but I also learned a good deal from great friends such as Cary and Jay, the authors of this book. I am a huge fan of both of them and the institute that brought us together, the United States Institute for Theatre Technology (USITT). USITT is indeed my second family; there are my friends that push me to continually learn, to be better, and to believe in myself. The genesis of this book began out of that family.

I earned my BFA in stage management from Webster University. During a meeting with the incomparable Peter Sargent, Dean of Fine Arts, I asked him "where do you see me 15–20 years from now?" He replied, "you will become a production manager." What? Who? What's that? Production management always seemed to be an accidental career for many. Skills honed through many hours in dark theatres and deep conversations with creative types. Disagreements over what we perceived as being "the right way" of doing something. And then, BOOM, someone anointed you as the Person in Charge. So now I'm in charge, now what? Does this new role come with a "how-to" video? Osmosis? A book? Surely there is a book. Wait, you must be kidding me. There are no books? Stage Management? Technical Direction? done. Directing? Done times a thousand. How to manage a production from the 100,000 foot level? Sorry, there isn't a book on this subject...yet...

As an educator for 15 years, I worked to train young managers how to become future leaders. Leadership and management are things that are vital to the health and progress of our industry, but those skills are so rarely taught beyond the primary concepts of stage management. When teaching future production managers, where is it we educators go? Where do emerging production managers turn? How do we find a basic understanding of how to create dynamic teams and deal with difficult conversations? Ask any production manager what they think the best course of training is and you will get varied answers, but the truth of the matter is that there aren't any foundational resources, to begin with. We, as leaders and managers, need to learn how to adapt, not only to the changing landscape of theatre but to management and leadership as a whole. With new trends in leading diverse teams, and how to create more equitable and inclusive workplaces, resources such as this book become even more critical in our continued quest for education and knowledge.

Our theatre world is so much better with this book in it and even better with Cary and Jay at the helm. Read this book. Consume it. And now that you know better, do better.

David "dstew" Stewart

Producer, Inclusive Strategy and Content for Disney Live Entertainment

Partner of Production on Deck

NOTE

1 Quote courtesy of Caged Bird Legacy, LLC.

Foreword – Second Edition

As you'll see in this book, defining production management can vary from industry to industry. Events can range from performing arts to conventions to special events to venue rentals. Although managing an event in concept is very similar, the way an event is managed can differ greatly.

The Production Manager's Toolkit came at a time when there was no guide for teaching the course, no collection of wisdom and insight from leaders in the field, and nothing that described the wide variety of opportunities available to both the entry-level technician and the seasoned professional who decides to move into production management. *The Toolkit* offers information on different career paths available, and case studies from veteran production managers. They collectively focus the spotlight on a profession that is vital to any well-run production.

As you build your career, one of the cornerstones of success will be the relationships you develop. These relationships can become mentors, technical resources, great friends, and creative collaborators. This book is a result of collaboration. Authors Cary Gillett and Jay Sheehan are deeply involved with United States Institute for Theatre Technology (USITT), a volunteer organization that supports people working in the arts and entertainment industry. They had an idea for this project and were able to develop it, starting with connections that began at USITT.

This book is an excellent study of production management. The personal satisfaction we get is when our plans become a reality, the show starts on time, and the audience leaps to their feet. This personal satisfaction is what keeps our passion lit and the thing that we look forward to doing every day. As we look toward the future, there may be some rough waters ahead that all of us will need to navigate through. But, as my colleague David Stewart wrote in the first edition's foreword, I too feel "that we are in good hands with Cary and Jay at the helm."

Carolyn Satter
President, USITT (usitt.org)
Director of Production, San Diego Theatres (retired)

Introduction

WHAT IS PRODUCTION MANAGEMENT?

Production management is viewed by many different people as many different things. Simply put it is the ability to manage a production – from beginning to end. But it's not just the physical production – it's the people, the resources, the facility, the money, the calendar, the temperaments, the list could go on. It is the ability to make sure the project happens on time, on budget, safely and in the end, everyone is still speaking to each other. Production managers take their skills of organization, communication, and strategic planning to provide structure for an idea and make it come to fruition. It may not seem to many as a creative position, but it is truly an art.

So why is it important to learn about production management? The truth is very few of us that find ourselves in this job now started out wanting to do this. Many production managers come to this job via stage management or technical direction and there are even a few who were designers or actors. We are doing a disservice to the production managers of tomorrow if we are not imparting our wisdom to them. Even if they might not know that they are destined to take over our shoes they should be prepared nonetheless. All those in the production emphasis of study (though some could equally argue that performers, directors, and designers would benefit too) should be required to learn about production management and ideally from those who have walked the walk.

HOW THIS BOOK CAME ABOUT

We met in 2013 at the United States Institute for Theatre Technology (USITT) annual conference. As this conference does for many, it connected the two of us based on common interests and areas of focus. We realized that we have similar jobs at similar institutions and that we both had recently started teaching production management. We swapped syllabi, discussed teaching techniques, and then asked the age-old question – "What book do you use?"

DOI: 10.4324/9780367808174-1

Then in 2014 we met again at USITT and the conversation about books quickly commenced again. We must have been pretty vocal about our unhappiness with the texts we were using because one colleague told us to stop complaining and write the book ourselves. Naturally, we laughed – we're not writers! But it got us thinking. A group of us attended a session together later that day and we sat right next to each other taking copious notes on the session (or at least that's what we thought the other was doing). In actuality, we were both composing the table of contents. When we made that realization, we knew our decision was made. We struck while the iron was hot and walked down onto the expo floor to a publisher's booth and said – "we have this idea for a book." And the rest is history.

WHY WE WROTE THIS BOOK

The purpose of this book is to provide a tool to those teaching and studying production management as well as provide those new to the field with resources and ideas. Part I and II of the book focuses on not only the hows of the job (budgets, schedules, meetings) but the whys too (to make artists' and clients' dreams come true). By providing techniques of management, communications skills and tips on building relationships, the entire scope of the job is represented. Part III looks at how to connect the hard and soft skills to the work itself providing a well-rounded view of production management in America by looking at all of the various disciplines in which a production manager works.

Throughout this book you will meet production managers from all walks of life and aspects of the performing arts. We knew the only way to write this book was to connect to the amazing network of production managers in this country and beyond. One thing we hope you will walk away from this book realizing is the power of a strong network and all it can aid you with. Each production manager quoted here has a unique perspective to share and a few great stories along the way too. We hope you enjoy their stories, and ours, as we take this journey together.

THE SECOND EDITION

From the moment we began thinking about the new edition it was clear that we had to keep progressing the field, both in how we talk about production management and whose voices we include. In here you will find all new case studies by spectacular individuals. You will also find new chapters plus new content throughout that showcases a continued progressive approach to the job and the field. We, as writers and managers, never stop growing and learning and we hope this new edition shows that loud and clear.

We began working on the second edition in 2019. When the pandemic hit, we paused, and we reflected. How could we write a book on production management when the field had been all but shut down and the future seemed so uncertain? With the approval of the publishers, we decided to give ourselves and the book some time. When we finally re-started again in 2021, we had both undergone personal challenges and growth (as had so many in our field) and we committed to staying open and honest with each other and our colleagues about what the future held. This book will never include everything there is to know about production management, that is impossible. What it does include are ideas, questions, topics, and (we hope) inspirations for those who want to do this work. We will keep iterating and pivoting to make our work, our lives, and our industry better. Please join us in doing the same.

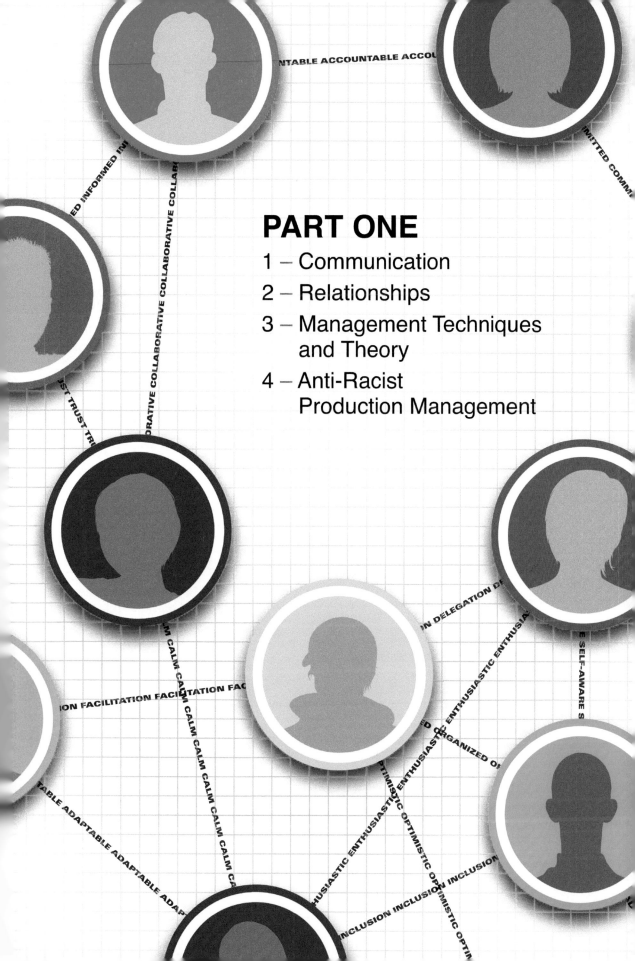

PART ONE

1 – Communication

2 – Relationships

3 – Management Techniques
and Theory

4 – Anti-Racist
Production Management

CHAPTER 1

Communication

> "The single biggest problem in communication is the illusion that it has taken place."
>
> *- George Bernard Shaw*

Impeccable communication skills are a necessity for any production manager. Day in and day out, we are communicating with all sorts of people, using every possible channel such as verbal, face-to-face, non-verbal, electronic, and written. It's important to create expectations for how you will communicate with people and how you expect them to communicate back. Learn who you are working with and tailor your communication plans to their needs and yours. It is key to our work as production managers to communicate clearly and effectively. If we are not communicating well, how can we expect others to do the same? We must lead by example.

In her book, *The Stage Manager's Toolkit*, Laurie Kincman offers three words as "key elements of successful communication" – *tactful, timely*, and *specific*.

- To be *tactful* is to pay attention to what you are saying and doing and how it affects other people. Try not to upset or offend those you are communicating with.

- Communication is most effective when it is *timely*. If someone poses a question to you, get back to them as quickly as possible, or you risk sending a message that communication with them is not important. A good rule of thumb is to get back with a response within 24 hours. If the answer to a question is not yet known, you should at least respond with an update that you are working on it.

- Be *specific:* choose your words carefully so as not to confuse or complicate the situation.

> *"[These words] demonstrate respect for both the production and the personnel and will enable [you] to facilitate creativity and collaboration in a highly successful manner."*

Kincman advises.[1]

DOI: 10.4324/9780367808174-3

To complement these elements we, the authors of *The Production Manager's Toolkit*, offer up three more communication words – *respectful, empathetic,* and *genuine*.

- *Respectful* communication is reciprocal. If you respect the other person and what they are saying or asking, they will respect you in return.
- Communication that is e*mpathetic* speaks to every person's need to be understood. Take a moment to put yourself in someone's shoes to truly understand what they feel and what they are experiencing. It will enable you to connect with them and their situation in a meaningful way.
- To be *genuine* is to be honest, to yourself and others. Many people can tell if someone is not genuine, and this can lead to distrust.

In his book, *The Four Agreements*, author Don Miguel Ruiz encourages us to be impeccable with our words.[2] Only speak the truth, and if you speak, know that you have made a promise to make it true. Next time you are speaking with someone, keep this in mind and pay attention to what you are saying and promising. Going back on your word, no matter how miniscule, could have a dramatic effect on the relationship you are building. Your word is your vow.

FACE-TO-FACE COMMUNICATION

In a world of increasing electronic communication, study after study has proven that the most productive and successful system of communication is face-to-face. Having the ability to give and receive full focus and attention is the best way to demonstrate that you are interested and engaged in the subject and in the person. The three major benefits of face-to-face communication are non-verbal communication, immediate feedback, and paravocalics (the changes in tone we give our voices). Here are a few pointers for good face-to-face communication:

- Eye contact: Look into the other person's eyes when you speak to them. By engaging in this way, you connect deeply to the person speaking and are able to create a connection vital for good understanding.
- Listen, don't just hear: To hear someone is to recognize the words they are saying. To truly listen is to understand what drives their need to speak, what concepts are being conveyed, and the emotional content of these messages.
- Smile: Dale Carnegie, in his book *How to Win Friends and Influence People*, states that "actions speak louder than words, and a smile says, 'I like you. You make me happy. I am glad to see you.'"[3] People want to be liked, and a smile is an easy way to show this.
- Take your time: Just because the person is standing right in front of you does not mean you need to give an immediate response. It's perfectly acceptable to delay the response: "Thank you for bringing that to my attention. I need to look into that more and get back to you." Then make sure that you do. Remember what *The Four Agreements* teaches us – your word is your vow.

BODY LANGUAGE AND NON-VERBAL COMMUNICATION

Albert Mehrabian, a researcher in the field of body language, claims that the impact of a person's message is 7% the words they say, 38% how they use their voice when they say it (paravocalics), and 55% what their body says while they talk.[4] Body language is a fascinating and quite daunting field of study; however, there is quite a bit you can pick up on if you know where to look and pay attention. Barbara and Allan Pease offer up three "rules of body language"[5] which can help anyone start to decipher non-verbal clues:

- Read gestures in clusters – Like words, gestures can be strung together to form a sentence. Look at the whole body, not just one element to figure out what is being said.

- Read gestures in context – Someone's gestures are influenced by their surroundings. For example, a person might cross their arms in front of their chest not because they are closing themselves off, but because they are cold.

- Look for congruence – Do the words match the gestures or are they in opposition? Often times a person might say one thing with their words but tell a different story with their body.

> **TIP** – A great way to study body language is to watch people. In a meeting where you are merely a participant or observer, pay attention to the people actively participating. Are their gestures matching what they say? Does one person say they are open to new ideas while tightly crossing their arms across their chest? Does someone agree with another while not making eye contact? What else can you observe?

We should not only be paying attention to people's body language but also their face. The face gives so much away without us even realizing it. Psychologist Paul Ekman has spent his career studying and mapping out facial expressions. He concludes that there are seven emotions with universal signals that cross race, culture, and language – anger, fear, sadness, disgust, contempt, surprise, and happiness. In his book *Unmasking the Face*, he speaks of "micro-expressions," or expressions linked to our emotions that we have no control over: "You feel fear, the expression begins to appear on your face, you sense from your facial muscles that you are beginning to look afraid, and you de-intensify the expression, neutralize it, mask it. For a fraction of a second the fear expression will have been there."[6] By learning to read another person's face, you can truly get a glimpse of what they are thinking.

You must also realize that YOU communicate with your body and face so it's important to take the time to observe your own actions. What is your resting face (your face when you aren't making a face)? Does it look angry or bored? That might give someone the wrong impression. You might need to actively keep a pleasant or

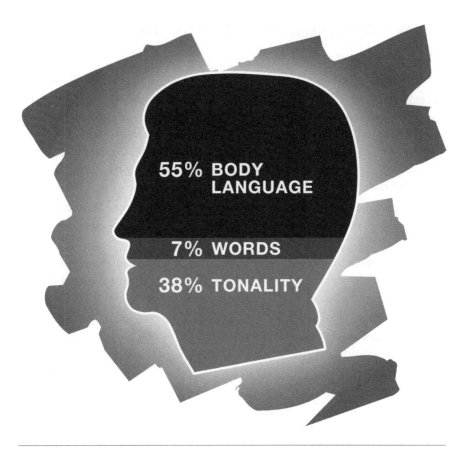

Figure 1.1 The impact of a message.
Credit: Image by Joseph Garcia

engaged look on your face while you are talking with someone. What do you do with your arms while you speak? Are they held tight to your chest or stretched out with fingers crossed behind your head? Whether you realize it or not, you are sending a message. Be conscious of that message.

> **TIP** – Performing artists are quite gifted at reading body language. It makes sense, as many of them make a living using their bodies (and faces) to communicate character, motivation, and story to an audience, so they are often both self-aware and observant of others. Have you ever noticed how hard it is to lie to an actor? Not that you should make a habit of that, of course. They can read your body language and judge if you are telling the truth or not!

Our body language demonstrates how we feel, but it can also inform how we feel. "This is because gesture and emotions are directly linked to each other."[7] Studies have shown that if a person sits with legs crossed and hunched over (low-status position) before an interview, they will feel less good about the outcome than if they stood

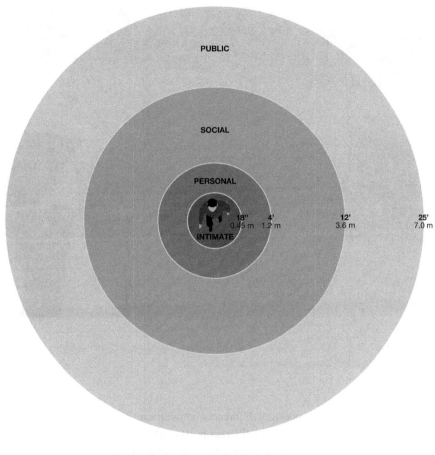

PROXIMITY	RADIUS	
INTIMATE	18"	0.45 m
PERSONAL	4'	1.2 m
SOCIAL	12'	3.6 m
PUBLIC	25'	7.0 m

Figure 1.2

Credit: Image by Joseph Garcia

up, with hands on hips and head held high (high-status position). Sociologist Amy Cuddy covers this and many other fascinating topics in her book *Presence*. If you assume these powerful positions, you can in fact change your hormonal balance to build confidence. She identifies this not merely as "fake it until you make it," but rather "fake it until you *become* it."[8]

Another fascinating concept to consider is proxemics or the study of people's relationship to the space around them. Anthropologist Edward T. Hall divided this study into two concepts – personal space and territory.[9] Personal space is the area around the body that shifts as we do. Each of us has a different expectation of how large that space should be, who can enter it, and when. Personal space can be cultural: There are

Figure 1.3   The College-Conservatory of Music at the University of Cincinnati
Credit: Photo by Adam Zeek, – www.zeekcreative.com

national and ethnic differences and differences between men and women, children and adults, as well as between people in different parts of the country. The territory is the larger space we inhabit such as a room, office, building, etc., and can be considered public, where we have no control over what exists inside of it, or private, where we have all of the control. Understanding another's relationship to personal space and territory can allow for either a positive or negative interaction based on how you choose to exist physically in relation to them.

Consider for example that you enter a rehearsal room to speak with a director. The rehearsal is still in progress, so you enter the space, cross behind the director, stand off to the side far back from them and wait until the break has been called. The rehearsal room is the director's territory, and until the break is called, their personal space should not be affected by others not directly involved in the rehearsal. What if you took a different approach? This time you enter the space, walk between the director and the performers and stand two feet from the director until they choose to acknowledge you. Which option sets up a successful conversation to come?

COMMUNICATIONS BY PHONE

Life is complicated and people are busy, so you can't always meet face-to-face. Communication by phone is the second-best option – you maintain the personal connection, but you are unable to connect with them visually. With no eye contact, facial expression, or body language, you will need to find another way to let your partner know you are engaged. A good technique is to repeat back to them part of what they are saying or paraphrasing what you are hearing so they know you are listening. Listening is still vital here, and so is smiling. You can hear someone's voice when they are smiling and attentive. Remember – paravolics accounts for 38% of the message received.

COMMUNICATION BY VIDEO

In our growing and changing technological world, communication opportunities feel vast and endless. The most recent development in communication technology is video conference. Where once the phone was the only way to connect, the COVID-19 pandemic exploded our use of video so we can both see and hear those with whom we are communicating, be they right next door or across the world. It's important to note that technology is only as good as the people who use it. It's also important to know that technology is not perfect and often fails, but it's not going anywhere so best to learn how to use it and take advantage of what it has to offer. Study the platforms you are using and help others to navigate them.

There is an assumption that video conferencing is as good as in-person communication. This is not true. The barrier of the screen, the time lag, camera shot, microphone, and speaker capabilities all have the chance to impede the communication process. But it is true that you can see the person so having the opportunity to use your body language skills is a bonus and, in many ways, makes this opportunity better than a mere phone call. (For more insight into meetings via video conference, please see Chapter 6 on Meetings.)

WRITTEN COMMUNICATION

When we talk about written communication, unless in unusual circumstances, we usually mean email. Email has changed the way we communicate, and in many ways NOT for the better. The three major benefits of face-to-face communication (non-verbal communication, immediate feedback, and paravocalics) are removed in written communication. Communicating via email is not only impersonal but also less effective, as you remove all context of what you are feeling when you write it. Email is an inaccurate conveyor of tone. Email communications are best for distributing information or to follow up on a conversation that you had face-to-face: "Thanks so much for chatting with me today. Here is a list of the tasks we came up with."

Written communication requires a serious amount of scrutiny on the part of the writer. Once something has been sent, it is out of your control, so take time to choose your words and organize your thoughts. Because we remove the personal connection, it is also necessary to write in a formalized letter style so that our tone is not misunderstood. Unless you are intimately familiar with the person you are communicating with, you should format the email like a letter, with a salutation or greeting, the subject or body of the letter, a closing (i.e., sincerely), and your name.

> **TIP** – Format an email response in exactly the way the person sending you the original email has done. If they have included all the structural elements of a letter, then you should do so too. If they become slightly less formal and remove the greeting or the closing, then it's generally okay for you to do the same. Understand that as a person in a leadership role, you might be looked upon to set the tone in the communication as well.

In a world of ever-changing technology and social networking, our challenges with written communication increase. If email is challenging, texting and instant messenger are worse. Choosing email over a social networking site as the main form of communication is usually the best choice. That's not to say that social networking is bad, but it can blur the line between personal and professional communication, which can be dangerous. It is also important to set expectations for communication tools like text messaging. Who is allowed to send you a text message and under what circumstances? Who do you choose to text, why and when? Not everyone uses the same technology and tools. There are people working in this profession who reject text messages and social media. As stated previously – you must cater the communication to the person who needs to receive it.

> **TIP** – The CC line of emails can be challenging to navigate, particularly in a large organization. Whom you are copying and why takes some thought and strategy too.
>
> *CC stands for carbon copy and refers to copy of a document made at the same time as the original. When communication used paper exclusively, a second piece of paper coated with a pigment (originally carbon) was placed under the original and the pressure of the pen or typewriter would transfer to the bottom sheet thus making an exact copy.*

HOW TO SAY YES!

Saying yes seems like such an easy concept, but to a production manager, it can be quite a challenge. Artists have lots of ideas, many of them going beyond budget allotments and sometimes defying the laws of physics. Our job as production managers is to make our artists' dreams fly, not to shoot them down. By saying no, you can kill the professional relationship, and even worse, you can create a situation where the next time that artist has an idea, they'll do it without including you. So how do you take those ideas and make them a reality? Learn to say YES! Theatre improv artists use the technique of "yes, and" in response to a new idea, never "no, but." You too can leverage this technique with a few easy considerations.

- Resist the temptation to immediately refuse an idea. Even if you know the idea is impossible, give it time. "No" is the easy way out, but not always the smartest.

- Understand the why behind the idea. Engage the artist on a creative level and allow them to explain the concept to you. Most artists are passionate about their ideas and want to talk about them. By allowing them that opportunity, you are cultivating the relationship. Make sure you truly understand what they need. It's possible that a solution will arise that easily meets the needs.

- Challenge the obstacles in the way. Are there other people denying the artist's idea? Talk with these entities and understand the concerns. Often a "no" is merely a way to avoid dealing with a scary or unknown situation.

- Get the facts. Take this opportunity to learn something you did not know. Even if an immediate benefit is unclear, you never know when this information might be useful for a future project.

- Line up the right partners to get the job done. Maybe the request goes beyond the skill level of your team and specialists need to be engaged. Good production managers know their own limitations and knowledge gaps, and they will find the right personnel to support the project.

- Try it. Who knows, it might be the most brilliant idea ever imagined or it might not. Often, you will not know until you try. We learn more from our failures than we do from our successes.

Figure 1.4 If You are not sure you can achieve something – do a test!
Credit: Photo by Ryan Knapp

> "As leaders in production management, we have to be the person to deliver bad news. It's not easy telling people no. Just remember that it's not all "take" and that you must be willing to "give" and make compromises in order to be successful."
>
> - Jay Sheehan

HOW TO SAY NO

Sometimes it is necessary to say "no." Let's explore the best way to do this, save relationships and keep conversations going. In his book, *The Power of a Positive No*, William Ury offers up a description of a "Positive No" as a "*YES! No. Yes?*" The first *YES!* protects your interests; it is the positive reason behind the no. The *No* asserts your power in the situation. The final *Yes?* keeps the door open for future possibilities and therefore saves the relationship.[10]

Here's an example of this technique in action: You get offered a job by a reputable company that you have been hoping to work with, but you are already engaged on another project, and you do not wish to burn a bridge by disappointing the company you are already working for. Your "Positive No" could sound something like this: "Thank you so much for the offer to work with your company. Unfortunately, I am busy with another job at the moment and would not be able to devote the time and effort that your project is due. I hope you will keep me in mind for future opportunities. It would be my pleasure to work with you soon." The "*YES!*" (or the positive reason behind the *No*) supports your best interests while supporting their project. The "*Yes?*" (or the relationship saver) is the connection to future work with that company.

Here is another example: A director requests four new costumes one week before tech. Due to the nature of the costumes, they would have to be completely built, which there is neither time nor money to accomplish. This "Positive No" could be along these lines: "As much as we would like to accomplish your request, we are not in a position to ask our staff to go into overtime to build these costumes, nor can we increase the materials budget to allow for the necessary items. However, we do have a substantial costume stock with many clothes from the same period. Would you like me to set up a time for you and the costume designer to look through them?" Here the "*YES!*" supports your staff as well as your bottom line and the "*Yes?*" allows for a viable option that in the end might prove better than the original request.

The most important key to successful communication is to keep the conversation going. If you immediately end a conversation or crush someone's ideas, you make future collaboration very difficult. Keep the conversation going. You are all on the same train together headed toward the opening of a great artistic endeavor, don't hit the emergency brake if you can avoid it!

DIFFICULT CONVERSATIONS

From time to time, we are required to cope with difficult or challenging conversations, either because of the subject matter or the person with whom you are communicating. This will often be compounded by emotion and feelings of "high stakes." Let's face it; in the performing arts, the stakes always feel high. What is the best way to approach these difficult conversations? Here are some pointers.

- Create a shared pool of meaning. Author Kerry Patterson advises: "When two or more of us enter *crucial* conversations, by definition we don't share the same pool. Our opinions differ. I believe one thing; you believe another. I have one history; you another. People who are skilled at dialogue do their best to make it safe for everyone to add their meaning to the *shared* pool – even ideas that at first glance appear controversial, wrong, or at odds with their own beliefs. Now, obviously, they don't agree with every idea; they simply do their best to ensure that all ideas find their way into the open."[11]

- Keep your emotions out of the way. This is easier said than done but is vital for good communicators. If you have done a good job with your communication, rarely is anyone attacking you personally. They are frustrated about a situation or a piece of news that you had the unfortunate luck to deliver. If someone yells, tell yourself they are yelling TO you, not because of you.

- Allow the other person to express themselves or even vent. Sometimes people just want to be heard, and once they are, they are much easier to reason with.

- Don't feel you have to match their energy. If someone is yelling at you, resist yelling back. Try the opposite and speak quietly or even whisper. Often, this will make the person realize that they are behaving inappropriately.

- Know your triggers. We all have certain things that spark our anger and trigger a fight-or-flight reaction. When you are aware of your instinctual reactions, you can succeed in resisting these urges. SCARF is a great tool created by neuroscientists to assess how people respond to social threats and rewards. It stands for *S*tatus, *C*ertainty, *A*utonomy, *R*elatedness, *F*airness, which are the five domains of human interaction represented in the study.[12] Look for a link to this study and how to assess your own triggers in the companion website for this book!

- Stand your ground. Don't let the heightened emotional situation lessen your scruples. If you believe firmly in something, make that clear. However, keep your emotions in check.

- Give it time. Perhaps a solution does not need to be found immediately. Allowing time or breathing room lets both parties contemplate all sides of the issue and perhaps return to the conversation later with a different perspective. If, however, a resolution is needed right away and time apart is not an option, make the best choice you can. Use your common sense to suggest a compromise.

For many these take time to do well. It's a skill just like anything else. Also, the suggestions offered in this section aren't just applicable to difficult conversations. In fact, the more you use these techniques before difficult conversations, then very likely, the fewer difficult conversations you will need to have.

1. Rational
2. Emotional
3. Stimulus

Figure 1.5   What triggers your stimulus response?
Credit: Image by Joseph Garcia

TOP THREE TAKEAWAYS

- Cater your communication to the person and the situation. Be the one willing to adapt. Chances are you will work with the same people again and again. Make sure that your communications are clear and positive not only for the happiness of your collaborators but also for your own future happiness.

- Pay attention to the world around you. Opportunities to learn more about various ways to communicate are everywhere.

- Don't shy away from challenging moments of communication. In the moment, it might be hard to recognize the benefits, but your patience will be rewarded. No one said the job of production manager was easy, but it can become less challenging the more we find effective techniques of communicating in any situation.

NOTES

1   Kincman, Laurie. *The Stage Manager's Toolkit: Templates and Communication Techniques to Guide Your Theatre Production from First Meeting to Final Performance.* Burlington, MA: Focal Press, 2013.

2   Ruiz, Miguel. *The Four Agreements: A Practical Guide to Personal Freedom.* San Rafael, CA: Amber-Allen Publishers, 1997.

3   Carnegie, Dale. *How to Win Friends and Influence People.* New York: Simon and Schuster, 1981.

4   Pease, Allan, and Barbara Pease. *The Definitive Book of Body Language.* Bantam Hardcover ed. New York: Bantam Books, 2006.

5   Ibid.

6   Ekman, Paul, and Wallace V. Friesen. *Unmasking the Face; a Guide to Recognizing Emotions from Facial Clues.* Englewood Cliffs, NJ: Prentice-Hall, 1975.

7   Pease, Allan, and Barbara Pease. *The Definitive Book of Body Language.* Bantam Hardcover ed. New York: Bantam Books, 2006.

8   Cuddy, Amy. *Presence.* New York: Little, Brown Spark – Hachette Book Group, 2015.

9   Hall, Edward T. *The Hidden Dimension.* Garden City, NY: Anchor Books, 1990.

10 Ury, William. *The Power of a Positive No: How to Say No and Still Get to Yes.* New York: Bantam Books, 2007.

11 Patterson, Kerry. *Crucial Conversations: Tools for Talking When Stakes Are High.* New York: McGraw-Hill, 2002.

12 NeuroLeadership Group. http://neuroleadership.co.in/scarfsolutions/

Relationships

> "We manage things, but we lead people."
>
> - Jack Feivou, Enchant Christmas – Vice President
> of Production & Executive Producer

How do we lead people effectively while at the same time keeping a close watch on the event or production details as required? It isn't easy, yet it is one of the most important tools in the production manager's toolkit-leading people by creating and navigating the various relationships within the production and/or organization. For the production manager to be effective in their position, it is important to have allies and good working relationships with everyone. It's all about relationships. You wouldn't be able to get your work accomplished effectively without having these relationships.

> "To build relationships I create trust—sometimes in a big hurry. To do this I answer questions with considered truth."
>
> - Rick Noble, Director of Production at the
> Perelman Performing Arts Center

DEVELOP TRUST TO DEVELOP RELATIONSHIPS

One important way to create and maintain a relationship is to develop trust; the basis of which all relationships must strive to have. According to author Stephen Covey, "Trust is the glue of life. It's the most essential ingredient in effective communication.

DOI: 10.4324/9780367808174-4

Figure 2.1   Relationships are built with conversation
Credit: Photo by Michael Mazzola

It's the foundational principle that holds all relationships together." Trust must be established, and trust takes believing in your team. There is no one way to create and maintain relationships. You will use various techniques to achieve successful results in your relationship building. The important thing to remember is that every relationship at any given moment or situation can and will be different. Much like a chameleon that must change colors at any given moment in order to survive, so must the production manager be able to change the tone of voice, body language, and message delivery to the various team members on the project.

> **TIP** – Because production management is about people, one way to lead and gain your team's trust is to ask their opinions early in the production process. Having a foundation of trust from which to begin shows the other person that you care about what they have to say.

> "I try to take a human approach. I also try to be honest and straight forward and build a foundation of trust so we can talk about the hard things. Having a foundation of trust to begin from shows the other person that you care about what they have to say."
>
> - Linda Cooper, former Production Manager at the La Jolla Playhouse

LISTEN WITH INTENTION

This simple gesture of listening to others with intention, is exactly what is needed to begin a successful and rewarding relationship. Listening with intention means that your focus is on the other person and your mind is not wandering off halfway through the conversation. Listening with intention means that you don't get distracted when you are in a conversation with someone. Listening with intention means that you put your phone down when someone asks to speak with you, and you give them your undivided attention. We recognize that this is not an easy task to accomplish. All of us are constantly distracted and constantly interrupted. If you do get distracted and start to wonder what the person just said, you'll have to work hard to bring your focus back to the conversation. Use your body language and facial expressions to let that person know that they are being heard. Often, just letting someone's voice be heard is an important first step on the way toward creating trust between the various

1. Ear
2. You
3. Eyes
4. Undivided Attention
5. Heart

Figure 2.2   The Chinese character for "listen" shows us a Holistic approach to the idea
Credit: Image by Joseph Garcia

team members. This is not a simple task, yet this is essential to the very essence of collaboration ... building trust between the production manager and the members of the team. While listening, remember that you will have many opinions and you will have to balance the will of the group and the will of the individual person. Just remember that the production manager should always make sure that everyone in the room has a voice and is heard.

In addition to listening with intention, showing appreciation toward your collaborators can also be a powerful relationship-building tool. This can be appreciation for the work, the challenges they've faced, and the successes they've achieved. Extend this notion to the whole team, and create a culture of appreciation.

> **TIP** – Make words such as "please" and "thank you" a regular part of your vocabulary. The words you speak are as important as the actions you take, and kind words really do go a long way.

> "You should understand what the person brings to the table and always listen to what the other person has to say. Treating people with respect means that you are listening to them and are a willing participant in helping to achieve the production's goals. Listening is an essential objective for you to accomplish and should be a large part of your toolkit."
>
> - David "dstew" Stewart, Producer – Inclusive Strategy and Content for Disney Live Entertainment and Partner of Production on Deck

MEET WITH YOUR TEAM

Another approach toward building a new relationship is to try to find time to meet with your team members individually. This is especially true if someone requests some time with you. Your best response and one that will begin to build the relationship is – "Yes. When?" If you don't try and achieve this, it may come off as if you don't care about the individual's concerns. "Make Time for Others" should be a standard item on the production manager's to-do list.

When you do get some one-on-one time, make sure your office is set up in a way that invites collaboration. Set your desk so it faces the door. You should never have your back to your office door, as this could be observed as a negative part of your management style. As you invite your guest to sit down, perhaps it may be better received to have an additional chair in front of your desk for you to sit in. Having both you and your guest on one side can level the playing field and reduce the power structure and help to get the relationship off to an equal start.

Once you get settled in and ready to begin the conversation, you should always let your guest speak first. Doing so shapes the conversation to follow and keeps the focus on your guest. It's important to not start with what you want to talk about. A simple "How are you" is an effective way to start the conversation.

> **TIP** – Another way to get to know people is to offer to take them for a coffee or lunch. This is another opportunity to have a no agenda meeting. Try to get to know one another a bit. Getting to know people on a personal level is an important step toward building relationships.

UNDERSTAND EVERYONE'S ROLE

How else can a new production manager ease the transition of joining a team that may have been in place for some time? In the case of a touring show, or a presenting organization, the production manager may have to create and maintain relationships with 20–30 different people each week. It takes some special skills and experience for a new production manager to build the trust of the group that they are joining.

One way to quickly gain trust is to understand everyone's role within the production area and know whom you are talking to when you get introduced to people for the first time. Be adept at remembering names. You should know your audience and try to take some time to learn about the people that you will be leading. Reading bios and resumes of the production team prior to meeting them can help you connect on a personal level as well.

> "I try to treat people with fairness, honesty, and respect. I feel that sharing as much information as possible strengthens our team and helps to ensure that everyone is working together toward the same goal."
>
> - Lee Milliken, Production Manager at The Metropolitan Opera

When meeting people in person for the first time, remember that you typically don't get a second chance to make a first impression, so make your first encounter with someone meaningful. Production managers should greet people with confidence that you know what your role is and that you know what you are doing as a production manager. You should greet people genuinely and have an intrinsic charm that allows people to respond back in a genuine manner as well. Your tone of voice and the words you use will be remembered; make them count. Using kind words like please and thank you and greeting people with respect is the first step toward building a relationship. People will respect and admire you if you engage them with knowledge, confidence, and an openness that invites collaborative, congenial working conditions.

> "The first step in good relationship building is going to people, not making them come to you. This is known as MBWA - manage by walking around"
>
> - David Grindle, former Executive Director of USITT

QUIET OBSERVATION

Another way to gain the confidence and trust of your new team is to just sit back and observe the situation for a bit. Don't rush to judgment as you do the observation. Some issues may need to be dealt with delicately, so be careful as you choose your words and tone. Take some quiet time to try and understand the various relationships between members of the organizations. Watch for actions more than words while you observe. It's one thing to say something needs to be done, and another thing to watch it get done. The people that get things done are the ones that you want to align with, so make sure you acknowledge the good work of your team as this is yet another way to strengthen these crucially important relationships.

KNOW THE RULES

For a visiting production manager to be successful they will need the help of their colleagues that run the production areas of the venues. A great way to help this relationship grow quickly is to know the rules of the venue you may be going into. Some of these theatres have an agreement with the International Alliance of Theatrical Stage Employees union (IATSE) and have very specific rules that you must abide by. (For more on unions see Chapter 8, Hiring and Casting.) Before you go make sure you know which contract you will be working under. Your best bet would be to make sure it is discussed during your "advance" phone call with the venue's production manager.

> **TIP** – If it is a union house, make sure you establish a relationship with the union steward and ask to go over the rules of the venue's contract regarding work rules, overtime, and when breaks need to be called. Having this communication with the steward will show that you are interested and care about knowing and understanding how their venue runs.

Additionally, you should study the technical specifications of each venue you go into. Understand that you are a guest in someone else's house, so greet new people with grace and gratitude for the opportunity to work together. Be humble as you meet people, and don't let your ego drive the conversations. Be flexible and adaptable as you shift through the various relationships you are creating and remember that while all relationships are not of equal importance, it IS important to create the relationship in the first place. Some relationships will be an immediate connection with another person, while other relationships will take time and care to create and nurture. Take the time to understand and appreciate everyone's role on the production team.

DON'T TAKE THINGS PERSONALLY

While you may say all the right things and have the right actions of a good leader, not everyone will jump on board your vision. There will be those who disagree with your decisions or policies. There may be those who don't agree with you when you tell people why you can't do a project. There will be those who may have an ulterior motive or agenda within the organization. And there are some people that are just plain difficult people to work with. Just be aware that you will, at times, encounter upset people. You can't expect to sit down with every type of personality and varying levels of passion and get immediate positive results. The most important thing to remember is to not take things personally. While this is difficult to maneuver, it's important to realize that whatever baggage the upset person brings to you, it's usually about them and not you. Remember, you can't make everyone happy all the time. (If you have some challenges with this, check out the book, *The Four Agreements*, by Don Miguel Ruiz.)

> "You must communicate with people as much as humanly possible even if it is to say, 'I don't know anything yet. The more they are hearing from you the more they believe you are on their side, and you've got their back."
>
> - Abby Rodd, Production Manager at Glimmerglass Opera

As you can start to see, the production manager is much more than just a budget manager or acquirer of goods and services. We are also part psychologists, as words like "trust" and "truth" start to become part of our everyday vocabulary. In addition, we must be excellent communicators as well. Communication with others is essential and an additional way of creating and maintaining relationships with your production staff. Your team wants information to do their jobs correctly, and it is the production manager who has the responsibility to give them what they need to do their jobs effectively and efficiently.

> "Random acts of kindness go a long way in maintaining relationships. If my crew needs something to do their job better, I will be the first one to make sure that they have the tools they need to do their work."
>
> - Carolyn Satter, former production manager and President of USITT

Figure 2.3   A hot meal on a long day is always appreciated
Credit: Photo by Ryan Knapp

FIXING POOR RELATIONSHIPS

One thing you will have to contend with at some point in your career is how to fix a poor or broken relationship. This is an important part of the process of listening and learning. Make sure that your ego is not the one setting the course here. To fix a poor relationship, you will have to be honest with yourself about the conflict. Is someone disagreeing about money? Did you perhaps use a tone of voice that someone found uncomfortable? Remember that the production manager CAN and WILL be the cause of stress to some staff or production team members, so be prepared on how you might go about your business.

Think of the acronym FADM when it comes to approaching a challenge

- Face It – Address the issue or problem head-on. Break it down and it will not seem so overwhelming.

- Accept It – Sometimes it is what it is. The scenario is not likely to change.

- Deal with It – Act on the results of steps one and two.

- Move Forward – Don't spend a lot of time rehashing old issues. There is too much work to be done to solve your problem and move forward with the work that needs to get accomplished.

Remember, the best way to fix a problem is to face it head-on and have calm, honest conversations with people. Many conflicts can be resolved in a face-to-face meeting. Don't hide behind emails or text messages as your way to communicate when a personal crisis begins between you and a team member. Take a deep breath and let FADM lead the way toward resolution.

> "Everyone on the team is important."
>
> - Lee Milliken, Production Manager at The Metropolitan Opera

EMPOWER YOUR CREW

As a production manager, no one on your team should be overlooked as far as trying to create relationships and teamwork. While the production manager may not get personally involved in the crew selection (though on some occasions they do), it is important to make sure that you introduce yourself to the various crew positions and

Figure 2.4   Authors Cary Gillett and Jay Sheehan have built their personal and professional relationships over many years
Credit: Photo by Jay Sheehan

make the crew and other pertinent staff feel welcomed to the team. Empowering and showing trust in the show's crew from the first moment of engagement is an important part of the relationship-building process. You wouldn't be able to have a show without your crew. You should make sure that they understand the importance of their work and how much it is appreciated. Kind words can go a long way when it comes time to motivate and encourage. Make a point to get to know everyone. Learn and use their first names when talking to them. It is said that there is no sweeter sound than hearing your own name spoken during a conversation. You should also always say "thank you" at the end of a long day. Being appreciated for the hard work that they do will always be welcomed and respected.

CONCLUSION

There is no one way to create and maintain relationships. You will use various techniques and tools from this book and your own experiences to achieve positive results with relationships and relationship building. The important thing to remember is that every relationship at any given moment or situation can and will be different. Creating and maintaining relationships take hard work and a willingness to work on these relationships daily. Practice making relationships work in your everyday life and you will begin to see how your work will start to get easier and easier each day.

What relationship is the most important for the production manager? The bottom line is that all relationships matter, and you will need to put time and energy into them to make them work. Realizing that everyone on the team is important is another big step in creating and maintaining relationships. You should go the extra mile to make everyone feel important and valued as empowering your team is vital to success. Be kind, treat people with respect, treat people fairly, and keep the lines of communication open. If you can do this successfully, you are on your way to becoming an effective production manager.

TOP THREE TAKEAWAYS

- Trust is the foundation on which relationships are made. There can be no true collaboration without trust.
- Take the time to listen. Most people simply want your ear. Listen with intention so people feel heard.
- MBWA – manage by walking around. Stop in to see your team every so often. It means a lot to those who are working hard when the production manager takes notice of their work.

Management Techniques and Theory

> "I suppose leadership at one time meant muscles; but today it means getting along with people."
>
> - Mohandas Gandhi

To mount a show or an event requires an incredible amount of effort and collaboration from an amazing amount of people. All those various people must be able to work together. The production manager must find a way to effectively manage the people, the workflow, and the project. If you want to be a good manager, you must first be a strong leader. Leadership often includes some if not all of the following, and to varying degrees. Find the combination of these characteristics that is right for you and your team.

- Collaboration: We do not do this job in a vacuum. Working well with others is vital to the success of a production. Sit down at the table with them and be a part of the team. All of us have a lot to contribute to the big picture.

- Communication: You need to be able to speak all languages (set design to the set designer, directing to the director, quick change to the wardrobe crew), and when two of those people can't figure out how to speak with each other, you need to intervene and interpret.

- Listening: Listen, do not just hear what others are saying. Listen to understand, not to respond. Listen with empathy.

- Goal setting: Our goal is opening night. Other, smaller goals must be set in order to reach that main goal. The production manager must set goals and remind people about them to keep everyone focused and productive. Teams go astray when they lose sight of the goal.

- Organization: In thought, in paperwork, and in action.

- Commitment: The production manager should be the hardest-working person on the production team. No one should question their commitment to the project.

DOI: 10.4324/9780367808174-5

- Accountability: Trust is a huge factor in leadership. If your team cannot trust you will get something done, you are in trouble. You must also be willing to take the blame if things go wrong. Own your decisions – you are the one ultimately responsible for facilitating the production.
- Be a people person: Knowledge and interest in people, how they work and what motivates them is key. A good production manager does not sit behind a desk all day but interacts with everyone in the production constantly. Knowing and caring about those people makes that interaction much easier and more meaningful for both you and them.
- Self-awareness: Know when to act and know when to get out of the way. Understand how you best contribute to the project. Know your strengths and limitations.
- Be a good follower: The artistic leadership creates the vision of the production. You must be able to follow their lead and support their ideas. You may also need to explain this vision to others in order for them to be good followers, too.
- Be informed: You need to know what is going on so you know how best to support the process. You need to know a little about every part of the project and every person working on it. You are not the master electrician or the props artisan, but you need to know how those people work and what they must do to get their jobs done.

> **TIP** – The production manager works in service of the production or event. You work for the organization, and you work for your staff, as much as they work for you. By approaching all work from the mindset of a servant leader you allow yourself to put others' needs above your own to change the "I" to "we."

ADAPTABILITY

Being adaptable in today's ever-changing world is one of the most important traits production managers can have. You always need to be ready to change it up at a moment's notice and have a good, positive attitude while you navigate and accept the potential changes that lay before you. It is important to understand that change can often be hard, that uncertainty in life is a given, and that being prepared to adapt is your best option for success.

But what are we really asking when we say, "be adaptable?" It means you should be thinking about how to adjust to changing situations or conditions. It means to be prepared to accept the changes that are out of your control. Being adaptable also means that you are quick to learn new skills and you know how to apply them to the changing environment. But being adaptable also means being resilient and you are able to recover quickly from difficult conditions and decisions that swirl around you. Always remember that for production managers, every day something changes, and every day is a new adventure, and that your success will be determined by how well you can manage these daily disruptions in life while you "embrace the mess" that might be before you.

Be adaptable, be flexible, be resilient, and be open, and willing to compromise. Following these tips should help lead you to success. As Charles Darwin said –

"It is not the strongest of the species that survive, nor the most intelligent that survives. It is the one that is most adaptable to change."

FACILITATION

The production manager has a unique position to advocate for the work of the creative team/producer and for the work of the production staff. In an ideal world, those factions are aligned, but what happens when they are not? Oftentimes, the creative team/producer will request a change or addition that the production staff might not be able to do or want to do. The production manager walks a fine line between art and practicality and must constantly find ways to keep everyone motivated and productive. The production manager is often the one who knows the most about what both sides need and want and therefore is the best equipped to make the final call. Often, sacrifices will need to be made; for example: "We can add the new platform to the set by the first day of tech, but we'll have to delay the installation of the backdrop until the following week."

> "Production managers should learn how to accept responsibility for poor judgement or bad decisions they make. It's amazing how quickly people will forgive you when you own the mistake and say 'I apologize.' Once this happens, the work can quickly resume."
>
> - Jay Sheehan

Figure 3.1 "I Stopped by the Wig Room to Take a Few Process Photos and They Really Needed Someone to Test Fit Wigs on, so I Took a Seat." – Ryan Knapp, Clarice Smith Performing Arts Center
Credit: Photo provided by Ryan Knapp

MANAGING BY WALKING AROUND (MBWA)

One of the best techniques for management is to be around your staff and their work as often as possible. This means you need to get up from your desk at least once a day, if not more, and visit the shops and production offices. These are not official meetings; there is no agenda. This is an opportunity for you to see how people are working. During these short visits, you will be amazed at how many questions or issues can be addressed and solved. University of Oklahoma Production Manager Kasey Allee-Foreman says that walk-throughs are her favorite part of the day. "I love going and checking in, it makes me feel like I am in touch with the whole production. I love giving my staff and students an opportunity to show me what they have done, in their comfort zone." Be careful not to disrupt their work as you walk around. You do not want them to resent your presence by slowing down productivity.

> "A production manager must be exceedingly competent at the technical details and really good in the room with people. You have to be able to do both of those things to succeed."
>
> - David Holcombe, Production Manager
> at Carnegie Mellon University

MANAGING YOUR BOSS

Most of the production managers report directly to an artistic director, a managing director or an executive director or CEO (chief executive officer), or a client. Often, these people are artistically or business-minded, without a background in production. One of the most difficult skills you must acquire is the ability to teach them about what you do (and what your staff does) without offending or upsetting them. You must also understand what is important to them, how they work, and what they expect of you. Help them forward the mission of the organization or the project. Finally, you must appreciate the pressures they are under from those above them (often a board of directors or large funders). Your boss may ask for a one-page budget summary not because they do not trust you but because they are expected to present a budget picture to the board of directors the next day.

> "You must have an artistic sensibility so you can understand where the artistic team is coming from and where they want to go. You have to have a passion for the work."
>
> - Vinnie Feraudo, former Director of Production at Seattle Opera

MOTIVATION

A good manager can motivate their staff toward common goals. In our case, it is the presentation of a new project. One of the best things about working in this industry is our ability to tackle multiple projects and rarely do the same thing twice! The result of this can often be challenging. Going through the same process multiple times each season can feel monotonous. How can you get your staff to break out of a perceived rut? The key is motivation.

In his book *Drive: The Surprising Truth About What Motivates Us*, author Daniel H. Pink dispels the rumor that motivation is caused by rewards such as money and recognition. He argues that true motivation is to allow people the opportunity to have:

- Autonomy: We all have the urge to direct our own lives. As a manager, you must know when to take a step back and allow your employees to work on their own. Guide instead of micro-managing, and they will achieve so much more!

- Mastery: Most people have the desire to improve themselves. Support your staff in professional development. You want them to stay current in an ever-changing technological world and get better at what they do. This will benefit your overall product.

- Purpose: We do what we do in service of something larger than ourselves. Most chose to go into the performing arts because we see a higher purpose in it. People in the performing arts work hard because they are members of a team and because they do not want to let their team down. Promote a team mentality in your workplace, and much of the work will take care of itself.[1]

> "The technical stuff is easy to learn, and it's constantly changing anyway, so you will need to re-learn it. You are dealing with human beings. You have to have empathy for where everyone is coming from."
>
> - Perry Silvey, former Director of Production for the New York City Ballet

PRODUCTION MANAGER AS PSYCHOLOGIST

Any production manager will tell you that their office sometimes feels like a psychiatric practice. Staff, designers, stage managers, and even directors sometimes come to you with their problems (work or personal). All people want is to be listened to. To distinguish between the problem that is expressed (e.g., the set does not do what I thought it would) versus the underlying problem (e.g., I don't trust the set designer) can sometimes be the key to successfully solving the issue. Getting to the root of the issue requires understanding what people need.

Psychologist Abraham H. Maslow's theory of the "Hierarchy of Needs"[2] does a great job of describing what people need. The theory states that all people have needs.

If our needs are met, then we are happy. Our needs are constantly changing and are affected by outside factors. In Maslow's Hierarchy pyramid, the items at the bottom are the most crucial to basic survival. The items higher up cannot fully be achieved until the ones below it are fulfilled. It is believed that to reach a point of true creative ability, one must achieve "Self-Actualization" (the top of the pyramid). This requires that all needs are fulfilled.

Many people cannot meet their needs alone and require outside influences to help them. As a manager, you can provide a great deal toward providing those needs. Here are some examples:

- Physiological needs: By insuring that people are paid on time, you do a great deal toward supporting their basic needs of food and shelter. Advocate for raises or overtime, if applicable, so people can make more money.

- Safety needs: Enforcing and maintaining a safe and healthy workplace is not only critical to physical safety, but it also supports the mental well-being of your staff as well. (See more in the chapter on Safety.)

- Love and belongingness needs: By creating a supportive and collaborative work environment where everyone's opinion is valued and considered, you build a team where people can invest themselves. They feel they belong and their contribution matters.

- *Esteem needs:* Sometimes egos need a little stroking. What's wrong with that? Let your team know how much you appreciate them and how good they are at their work. Not everything needs to be a big victory to deserve a celebration. Look for the small wins!

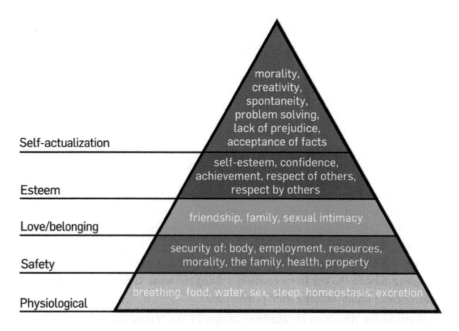

Figure 3.2 Maslow's Hierarchy of Needs

> **TIP** – Do not forget YOU in all this. Sometimes you need help, too. One production manager we interviewed said the most important relationship they had was with their own psychiatrist! We all need a release, especially if you spend all day hearing other people's woes and trying to solve their problems. Look for personal and professional connections to help you stay positive during challenging times.

> "You have to be able to have confidence in yourself and confidence in your team. Trust is a huge part of being successful as a production manager, and if you think it's all about you, we will fail."
>
> - Kasey Allee-Foreman, Production Manager
at the University of Oklahoma

DELEGATING

Many production managers (especially those early in their careers) find delegation very hard. Giving a task to another can often feel like a personal failure to get it done. In fact, the reverse is probably true. By passing a task on to someone you trust, you can ensure that it gets done while you focus on other important things. It takes time and practice, but good delegation is key to success as a production manager. If you struggle with this, it is best to start small. Test the waters by giving someone a small task that you retake if needed. If it goes well, then increase the responsibility and try again.

WORKING ON A TEAM

In most organizations, production management is a lonely, one-person job. Larger institutions that produce large amounts of work choose to hire teams of production managers. If so, there is likely a lead production manager who oversees the other members of the team. The "associate" or "assistant" production managers are given specific tasks such as payroll, timesheets, purchase orders, contracts, calendars, etc. In some cases, they may be given their own shows to manage. In those teams, clear communication is vital. Who is doing what and when? Who is overwhelmed and needs help from another? The worst thing that can happen is when effort is duplicated, or one member is overloaded with work. Regularly meeting as a team is essential to make sure everyone has what they need.

There are two distinct benefits to working on a production management team. The first is the ability to have team members cover for each other so no one person must work all the time. If you are in technical rehearsals for a week, chances are good you can share responsibilities, and everyone can get a night (or day) off. Free time is good for morale. The second benefit is that more voices in the room offer opportunities to generate ideas.

Find team members you trust and respect, engage in conversations about the work and the challenges being faced. Two heads are always better than one. Having a partner or team that can see problems from differing angles is incredibly useful.

> "A key attribute is decision making—sometimes you have to make a decision; it could be right or wrong depending upon the viewpoint. That can be the hardest part."
>
> - Linda Cooper, former Production Manager at the La Jolla Playhouse

NEVER STOP LEARNING

Most of us have learned from a production manager whom we have worked with or who preceded us. Think back to what that person asked for or required from their team or specifically from you. Whether it was good or bad – learn from these memories. Sometimes, we learn great lessons about what not to do by watching someone struggle or fail with a project or a situation. Remember what you wanted from a production manager when you worked for or with them. Give that now to those who work for you. Take each project as an opportunity to learn something that you did not know and, by doing so, continue to grow. It will benefit you and your projects.

Sometime things will not go as planned. Even the best plans are sometimes thwarted by accident or on purpose. The best way to deal with a new problem is to be flexible and patient. The production manager is leading the charge. If you get upset, then it gives others permission to do the same. Review those essential qualities of a good manager – adaptable, calm, organized, self-aware, collaborative, etc. When things go awry, go back to these key words and start again.

> "Learn from your mistakes. They can be your greatest teacher."
>
> - Cary Gillett

TOP THREE TAKEAWAYS

- You cannot think about management without thinking about leadership. Take guidance from this chapter and decide what type of leader you want to be.
- Hone your unique leadership skills to guide your staff, your clients, or your creative team through the next project. What can you bring to the table? When should you get out of the way and let them work?
- Take pride in the leader you are and strive to be. Keep growing.

NOTES

1 Pink, Daniel H. *Drive: The Surprising Truth about What Motivates Us*. New York: Riverhead Books, 2009.

2 Maslow, A. H. "A Theory of Human Motivation." *Psychological Review*, 50 (1943), 370–96.

How to Be an Anti-Racist Production Manager

> "Nobody knows everything, everybody knows something and together we know a lot."
>
> - Mantra from the Equity, Diversity, and Inclusion committee of the Production Manager's Forum

It is important to realize that all structures in the live entertainment industry are inherently biased and, like many systems, steeped in a history of systemic racism and oppression. This chapter is meant to inspire production managers to actively work against these frameworks to progress our field and the people able to do this work. To do this you must acknowledge your own biases and surround yourself with those who can challenge your thoughts and instincts. You must also throw out the concept of "we have always done it that way" and start to rethink how and why certain practices are in place. Don't be afraid to make big changes.

> "The field of production management is changing, and all of our roles are changing with it. As a young production manager, I have to lean into that change. My age is a factor and always on my mind. But we all have a voice, and we must have the confidence to speak our truth."
>
> - Itzel Ayala, Production Manager at The Bushwick Starr

SHOWING UP

Step one is making the decision to do the work. This step requires both bravery and grace, with yourself and with others. It also demands honesty. You must begin the process of acknowledging that you, and those who have come before you, have inadvertently

DOI: 10.4324/9780367808174-6

Figure 4.1
Credit: Photo by Jay Sheehan

contributed to the challenges our industry faces and that you have a lot of learning and unlearning to do. Above all, you must have a strong desire to make a change.

The process will not be easy, and you must find a way to get comfortable with being uncomfortable. Educate yourself on the issues and don't shy away from conversations. Don't fool yourself or others into thinking that you can become an expert in this field, which is impossible. Instead, make it known that you have started the journey, and let it be just that – a journey. Some days will be hard and others harder yet. You will step away from the work at times, and that is okay as long as you eventually return. Begin "speaking in draft"[1] to show yourself and others that you are learning as you go.

One common starting place is with language and terminology. Start gaining familiarity with some of the common terms and research, what they mean, and how they might affect the work of your organization. Here are some concepts to begin with: equity, diversity, inclusion, racism, sexism, ableism, color-blind vs color-conscious, social locations and privilege, use of pronouns, microaggressions, and conscious and unconscious biases. (This is not an exhaustive list, keep researching to learn more.)

Some other starting places you might want to consider are: building affinity spaces and anti-racism/anti-oppression working groups, attending and/or funding others to attend anti-racism/anti-oppression training, hiring consultants to provide organizational assessments and strategies, budgeting with anti-racism/anti-oppression values in mind, and creating group agreements with your team.

DECENTRALIZE LEADERSHIP

Leadership does not mean being in charge, it means guiding the process. Though you as production manager might be viewed as the head of the department or the one who holds the power in decision making, this does not mean you have to do it alone. In fact, you shouldn't. By decentralizing leadership, you acknowledge that you require outside influence to make decisions, and you allow others to join you in the process.

Everyone wants to feel valued and a part of the team. Work hard to create an inclusive work environment where everyone feels comfortable sharing their thoughts and bringing issues to the table. This starts at the top. As a production manager, you need to know that people look to you to set an example. If you show respect for others and their ideas, you will inspire others to do the same.

Start by having an open-door policy where everyone you work with knows they can come to talk to you about anything at any time. You might even want to go a step further and hold open office hours or open meetings where anyone can raise any issue they wish. When an issue is brought to the table, take it seriously and work hard with your team to address it and learn from it. Be open to others' ideas and suggestions. You don't have to have all the answers, nor do you have to do all the work. Share the load and share the process. Show respect and appreciation for the contributions of others.

> "Anti-racism is about pushing past knowing better and instead actively doing better. We must dig deep into ourselves and embrace the vulnerability, humility, and complexity of engaging in this work. Doing this work is building an essential muscle that will grow stronger with effort and time. There is no shortcut to this work, the only way forward is through."
>
> - Catherine Campbell, Director of Production at the Repertory Theatre of St. Louis

STRENGTH IN NUMBERS

Beyond the work you do at your organization or on your various projects, recognize that there is a wealth of knowledge and ability throughout the industry. Make connections with other individuals and groups also doing this work. Go beyond the network of production managers and look to directors, designers, administrators, etc. to find allies and accomplices. Take the opportunity to learn from them and share what you have learned. Learning can take many forms – a book club, podcast listening group, or a formal organization. The work to dismantle oppressive systems becomes more manageable when you are not doing it alone. You can cultivate power and strength by working together.

> **TIP** – Join the Production Manager's Forum (PMF), a nationwide collection of production managers, and then connect with the PMF's Equity, Diversity and Inclusion committee. This group began in 2014 and actively works with the membership of the PMF to progress anti-racist/anti-oppressive ideals across the industry and create spaces for group learning.

ALWAYS PROGRESS FORWARD

Accountability is possible through changing hiring practices and culture, looking at what you program and whom you hire to work on those projects. Ultimately, do that which makes you feel uncomfortable so that others with less privilege don't have to. How can you leverage your privilege to advocate and/or create change for those without? Managers and leaders should endeavor to do more than just listen. We should leverage our positional power to lead conversations, though difficult and uncomfortable.

Once you have found your anti-racist community, use them to encourage you to continue learning. This is a lifelong journey with many bumps to be found along the road. When you fall away from the work, find the opportunity to re-commit. Your allies and accomplices are there to help you, and at times they will need your help too. Find an accountability buddy or two, maybe one inside your organization and another outside. Open an honest channel of communication. Give and receive feedback with grace. Feedback is a gift, and accountability shows love and appreciation.

CASE STUDY – NO MORE 10 OUT OF 12s

CONTRIBUTOR – TAJH OATES, PRODUCTION MANAGER AT THE ALLEY THEATRE

One of my favorite toys as a kid was Legos. My brother and I used to spend hours building these giant Megazord-inspired creations, and then crash them into each other to see which ones survived the best. I was always fascinated by how even though we were using the same set of Legos each time, we could create vastly different shapes each time. They were typically made up of the similar components–feet, arms, torso, head, weapons, etc. We would use different bricks in different places to change the size and scope, occasionally becoming limited at the end when our pool of Legos was down to a slim selection of what fits and see how we can piece them together.

Much like Legos, calendars and schedules are just arranged blocks of time to assume a general shape. In theatre, we like to think that the schedule that we have been operating off for the past several decades is the only schedule that works. This schedule model was knowingly inhumane, often resulting in staff members working 70–80+ hours a week to make the dream happen. As technicians, our mindset is always to pull it off, no matter how much we have to push ourselves to get there. Around-the-clock work, mistreating our bodies, subsisting off of caffeine, salty snacks, and the occasional nearby takeout – all various components that lead to staff burnout, all for the goal of making the show happen. We've normalized this as part of how our industry has worked. But hear me out – what if we just changed the schedule?

Like many theatres, the Alley Theatre runs *A Christmas Carol* every holiday season. Despite the show being the same show every year, COVID pushed us into producing a different version of *A Christmas Carol* – a live adaptation of our previously virtual offering. However, given our model, we gave it the same amount of rehearsal time that we would have given our annual, well-seasoned *Carol*. The shorter rehearsal period combined with a myriad of other factors led to us realizing that the remount schedule was not going to be enough rehearsal time before we got into tech.

Figure 4.2 David Rainey (Scrooge) and Todd Waite (Jacob Marley) in the Alley Theatre production of *A Christmas Carol*
Credit: Photo by Lynn Lane

Prior to the pandemic, the thought of changing the schedule would seem unheard of. However, with the push for "No More 10 out of 12s" and other calls for improved work/life balance, we had already started changing our schedule. We had removed 10 out of 12s, set a standard span of days for rehearsal to end by 6:30 pm, and had gone to a five-day work week while in the rehearsal hall. If we needed more time, we could have simply overridden these new policies and say that we tried. As an organization, we chose to stand by our commitment, which meant that it was up to us to start getting creative with the schedule. Previously, changing the schedule would have had a strong pushback of "we won't have enough time." With the precedent of having already changed our schedule this season and seeing that the show still opens, we were able to shift the question to "how can we make sure that we have enough time?"

If we needed more rehearsal time, that meant that it had to come out of our tech time. While losing tech time isn't the most ideal option, the tradeoff is finding out ways to not need as much tech time. What work can we do to get ahead where we can? The key became information and communication, which is up to a collaborative process shared between the production manager, the stage manager, and the director. By creating a strong work list of all the things that need to get done, it allows for the entire department to figure out how we can accomplish all the other priorities. Sometimes, it meant having to work out of sequence, or working through without an actor or with placeholder cues while we were still building. We were able to bring the designers in early to be able to focus.

The process was a bit chaotic and required us to be flexible and adaptable – the exact skillset that separates theatrical artists from anything else. Instead of trying to stick to a schedule that didn't work, we adapted to one that did work. We also did it while making sure that our production staff got days off, weren't working continual 14-hour days, and everyone was out of the building before midnight. We found that it was a lot easier to discuss our options at a 9:30 pm production meeting instead of a midnight production meeting like we used to. And, most importantly, the show still opened on time. We were even able to lose most department coverage after the first preview.

Just like Legos, calendars can be broken down into components, moved around, and rebuilt to be a stronger shape. You could always default to building it the same way every time, but what happens if you move things around? You can always crash it into the old model and see which one is more stable. You can even learn that some new parts aren't as stable as old parts – that's okay. Not every change is going to be perfect, but the only way to improve is by at least making the commitment to try and change. You'd be surprised at what discoveries you may find.

Now we must start unpacking the fact that the entire plot of *A Christmas Carol* is about not working over the holidays and spending time with your family, yet the ones running *Carol* are often the ones not spending time with their families. Baby steps.

NOTE

1   This phrase was coined by Nicole Brewer in her Anti-Racist Theatre Trainings. For more information on these trainings please visit — https://www.nicolembrewer.com/

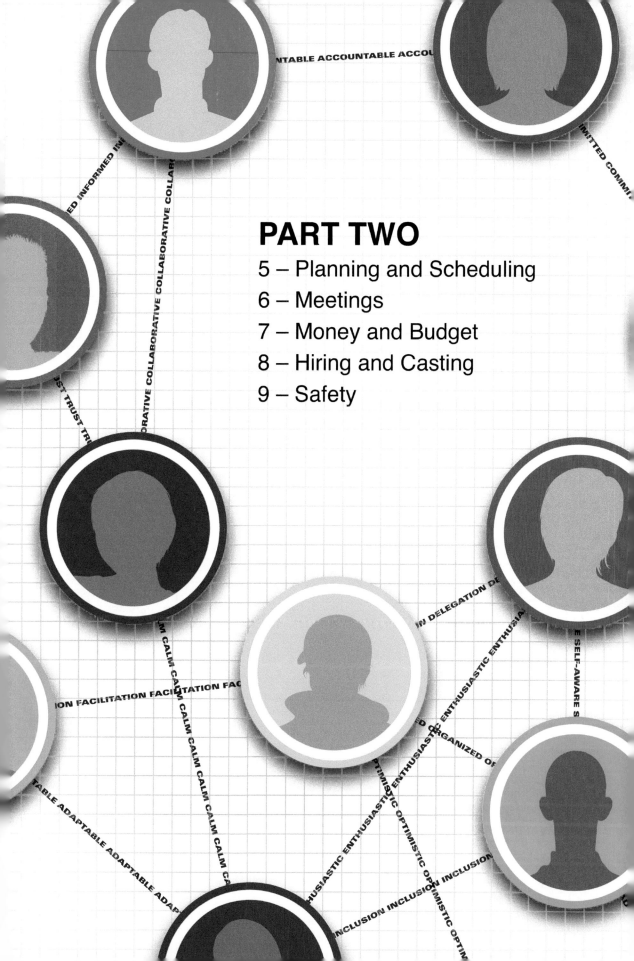

PART TWO

5 – Planning and Scheduling
6 – Meetings
7 – Money and Budget
8 – Hiring and Casting
9 – Safety

CHAPTER 5

Planning and Scheduling

> "In any one five-minute period, you need to be thinking of what's happening now to the next five years ..."
>
> - Perry Silvey, former Director of Production
> for the New York City Ballet

Shows and events do not come together overnight. They require special long-term planning and scheduling to make them successful. Depending upon the type of project, the planning may start six months to five years in advance. This chapter will help you through the steps of planning a single show/event or a whole season.

THE ROLE OF THE PRODUCTION MANAGER IN SEASON SELECTION

Every organization is different, and therefore their approach to selecting the work will also differ. Whether it is one performance or a series of events spanning a few months, there is likely a process by which those events are selected. If you are lucky, the organization values the input of the production manager and invites you to the table. If such an invitation is offered, do not turn it down. If by chance you work for a producer who would rather shut their door and not open it again until the projects have been chosen, then you might have your work cut out for you. Nevertheless, find a way to insert yourself into the process. The outcome can only benefit you, your staff, and the organization.

By being a part of the season selection process, production managers have a chance to comprehend the ideas as they are developing. They can add production insight and start to prepare for how they will be produced. It is a wonderful way to connect with the artistic leadership of the organization by understanding what types of projects they want to do and why. You can bring a large amount of knowledge and forethought

DOI: 10.4324/9780367808174-8

to the season consideration that many others cannot. Production managers have an intimate understanding of how projects come together and the necessary resources. If a project is being considered that is way outside the means of the organization, it is best to speak up early rather than coping later with a decision that is not implementable. This is not to say that the production manager's job here is to shoot ideas down, quite the opposite. Bringing challenges to the forefront allows them to be considered and hopefully solved. Perhaps a show requires more cast, crew, and designers than any you have previously produced – that means more money. The solution could be that the overall season is reduced by one project to accommodate for these additional costs, or more money needs to be raised.

If you are a member of the season selection process you must be informed, which means doing the work. This begins with reading the proposals or scripts, seeing performances elsewhere that are being considered, doing research on previous productions of these shows, and talking to people who have worked on them. Careful consideration of each project is necessary. Here are some questions you should ask:

- How many people will this project take to produce (directors, designers, cast, crew, etc.)? Who is being considered to fill these positions?

- Will this project fit into our standard production period? (Think about the time it will take to build, rehearse, tech, etc.)

- What are the design elements, and how large or small are they? (Will a unit set suffice, or will the set need to show multiple locations? How many total costumes are required?)

- What is the time period of the show? (Finding and/or building period items can be more costly.)

Figure 5.1 Baltimore Center Stage's Pearlstone Theatre
Credit: Photo by Bill Geenen

- What special rehearsal requirements might be necessary? (Example: Does the cast need to learn to roller skate or play the banjo, or both?)
- Will the show have specific community outreach attached to it?

VENUES

Along with the selection process, one must also consider where these projects will be presented. Different venues have different opportunities and challenges.

- Proscenium theatre: Since the 19th century, this has been the most typical location to produce a show. Most Broadway and regional theatres still use this type of venue. The benefits are plentiful – lots of options for backstage storage (be that in the wings, traps below the stage, or fly loft), the audience location is predetermined and therefore does not require much attention (other than sightlines), lots of options for special effects, etc.
- Flexible theatre: A black box or other flexible theatre space does not have permanent seating, so they can be configured in any way of your choosing (as long as it meets the approval of your Fire Marshal see the Safety chapter). You could choose a proscenium type configuration or maybe go with three-quarter thrust, arena, or alley. One challenge to consider is labor and time, as it will take both to set up the venue as you wish.
- Non-theatrical venue/found space: Any space can become a performance venue – the lobby of a building, an art gallery, a hotel ballroom, or a tent in someone's backyard. One big challenge with these venues is that none of the "normal" theatre areas or equipment exists and will need to be created – dressing rooms, backstage space, control booth, positions from which to hang lights and speakers, etc. You also need to give thought to the audience experience. Where do they enter/exit? Where do they sit? Or do they sit? Where do they go to the bathroom?
- Outdoor venue: Who says it has to be inside? Plenty of organizations produce outside in the summer months. Outdoor venues can vary from proscenium type theatres with permanent seating and a roof (or sometimes no roof) to a hillside or parking lot with nothing permanent other than what you choose to provide. The biggest challenge by far with outdoor venues is the weather. It is very unnerving to have this very large element of the experience completely out of your control. Contingency plans should be considered from the beginning of the project – what do we do if it's too hot, or too cold, or raining? Often, an alternate indoor location is a good backup plan. Another big consideration with an outdoor venue is the schedule. If you perform at night, then you will need to have technical rehearsals occur then as well. Some outdoor venues plan overnight electrics calls to get the lights focused.

Other important things to consider regarding the venue:

- Does your organization own this venue? Do you already have approved access? Will you be required to rent it?
- Are you sharing this venue with others during any part of the process?

- How old is the venue? Has it been properly kept up?

- Is the venue already outfitted with seating, lights, sound equipment, etc., or will you need to provide those things?

- How much time will you need in the venue? (See MANAGING THE SCHEDULE later in this chapter.)

- Does the local Fire Marshal need to approve how the space is set up or being used?

- Will you need to acquire any permits to use the venue?

- If you are outside, are there any curfews or decibel limits to be aware of?

SCRIPT/PROJECT ANALYSIS

Once the project has been selected, it is helpful to do a detailed analysis. This allows you to understand everything this project will require and help you to plan out the budget and schedule. If there is a script, that is the best place to start. Here is what to look for:

- People
  - Creative team requirements: director, choreographer, musical director/conductor, designers, writers
  - Support staff: fight choreographer, intimacy choreographer, dialect/vocal coach, movement coach, accompanist
  - Stage management: stage manager (SM), assistant stage manager (ASM), production assistants
  - Cast requirements: gender, age, skillset
  - Production staff requirements: set, paint, props, costumes, lights, sound, projections, etc.
  - Crew requirements: backstage, wardrobe, hair and make-up, lighting, sound, projections, etc.
  - Live music/musicians
- Design elements
  - Set/paint/props
  - Costumes/wigs/make-up
  - Lighting
  - Sound/music
  - Projections/video
- Special considerations
  - Effects: flying, fire, water, fog, haze
  - Children and/or animals

What if there is no script? Sometimes there is not, because it hasn't been written yet or the project will be devised. Maybe all you have is a list of characters and a synopsis, or maybe you don't even have that. The best thing to do here is assume the worst-case scenario – lots of people and lots of stuff. It's important to start having conversations with the playwright, director, or choreographer as soon as possible so you can know the direction the show is headed. It's always best to stay ahead of the game, but sometimes you just have to keep up. For a project such as this, you might need to schedule your time in the rehearsal room, so you are part of the development process.

RIGHTS AND PERMISSIONS

Before deciding upon a specific show or project, it is important to find out if you can get the rights to produce it. Any published script will require permission from the publisher. Here are a few of the biggest theatrical rights houses at present: Dramatists Play Service (www.dramatists.com), Concord Theatricals (www.concordtheatricals.com), and Musical Theatre International (www.mtishows.com). Their websites will walk you through the process of getting the rights to produce their shows. The rights houses will need you to provide information about your organization and your plans to produce the show. Common required information includes ticket prices, expected box office revenue, venue capacity, dates, and a number of performances. It might not fall to the production manager to wrangle the rights, the general manager, or managing director might do this instead. Make sure you are clear about what your organization's protocols are.

If a show is not published, rights are often still necessary but need to be acquired directly from the playwright, librettist, composer, or their representation – agent, lawyers, etc. If a show is being created by your organization, the question of rights will be determined by the content. If it is unique material generated by the company, then you do not need to gain any permission. If, however, it is based on an existing story or uses content from another source (song, movie, book, etc.), then permission is needed. These permissions will require you to track down the publisher, agent, or other representatives. A good way to start is an internet search of the title to see if you can find who owns the rights to the content. Then you will need to find the right contact person for that organization. It's best to start this process early, as you never know how long it will take. Your project is usually not a priority for them. You will need to ask early and often.

Once rights have been secured, you will be required to pay royalties. This could be a flat fee or a percentage of the box office or both. Every rights house is different, it's best to do your homework when applying for the rights, so you are aware of costs and procedures for payment. The more popular the show, the more expensive the royalties. Musicals are notoriously expensive, sometimes costing thousands of dollars for just a few performances, whereas straight plays that have been in circulation for a few years might only cost a few hundred dollars. If you are working in an academic environment, the costs can sometimes be less, though not always.

Gaining the rights to produce a show does not allow you to do whatever you wish with it. Making changes to published material is not allowed without permission. If you wish to adapt the script or to cast it non-traditionally, it is best to ask permission first (not forgiveness later). Rights houses have been known to shut down production when they discovered that these types of adjustments had been made without their knowledge. It is also illegal to photocopy a script without permission. Most rights houses will require you to purchase or rent the exact amount of scripts, librettos, or scores you will require to produce the show. A rental package will need to be returned in the condition it was received, or fees will be charged.

Works that fall into the category of public domain do not require rights. Determining whether a work is part of the public domain is a complicated process, as there are many rules and laws about copyright, and most differ from country to country. Here are a few basic public domain rules:

- All works published in the United States before 1927 are in the public domain.

- Many works published in the United States from 1927 to 1963 are also in the public domain, as new laws about renewal went into effect after that time.

- Most countries follow an international copyright treaty known as the Berne Convention that was put into effect in 1886, which requires copyright protection on all works for at least 50 years after the author's death.

It is important to understand the Fair Use Privilege, as well, as it is another way to use materials without obtaining copyright. This can be helpful if you are looking to use clips of videos or songs, short length of text, etc., to make a larger and original artistic work. The challenge here is the vague nature of the law and how people may interpret it differently.

WHEN IS USE A FAIR USE?

The following four factors must be considered to determine whether an intended use of a copyrighted work is fair use:

- The type of work involved
- The amount and importance of the materials used
- The purpose and character of the work
- The effect of the use upon the market for the copyright work.

These factors are intended to be a highly flexible set of general guidelines. The courts do not apply them in a mechanical or numerical way. For example, not all factors are equally important to every case and it's up to the courts to decide what weight to give them. This makes determining whether a use is fair use is a highly subjective and unpredictable exercise.

- Excerpt from Stephen Fishman's *The Public Domain: How to Find & Use Copyright-free Writings, Music, Art & More* [1]

TIP – When in doubt about copyright – talk to a lawyer!

SHOW TREATMENTS

Now that the season has been selected, the production staff will want to know more about the projects you will be producing. The production manager should plan to create "treatments" for each project that include the details that most people will want to know. These treatments should include the creative team on the production as well as details on casting, venue, rehearsal/tech/performance dates, unique production challenges, and often, a synopsis if it is not a well-known show.

SHOW TREATMENT EXAMPLES:
THE MATCHMAKER

by Thornton Wilder
Directed by Paul Allen
October 11–19 in the Trey Theatre
Setting: 1880s NYC
Cast size: 16

Description: Old merchant hires a matchmaker to help find him a wife and ends up marrying her in the end.

MOLIERE IMPROMPTU

Translated and adapted by Rinne Groff
Directed by R. Wilson Matthews
November 8–16 in the Cradle Theatre
Setting: Versailles, 1665
Cast size: 13

Description: Moliere and his troupe in rehearsal are surprised by an unannounced visit by the King, who demands performance. Done in Commedia dell'Arte style.

Other items of note: Masks will be designed and built.

MANAGING THE SCHEDULE

The production manager is the ultimate project manager and makes sure things happen on time. When the curtain rises on opening night, the show must be ready. But the path we take to get there can be rocky and winding. How do you ensure that it will all eventually come together?

- Planning: Take the time well ahead of the project to lay out the ideal scenario. This may be one month to five years in advance, depending upon the complexity of the project. Think about the various stages that will need to occur (design, cost out, build, rehearsal, tech, previews, etc.) and how long each stage will take. If you are unsure of the process or necessity of time, then ask others or do some research. Each project will be different and might require new information.

- Communicate: Make sure everyone is on the same page with the plan. Share calendars, meet with groups and individuals, and go over the plan so they understand both how we will reach our goals and why our goals are important.

- Be flexible: Things will go wrong. Even our best planning will be interrupted by a shipment delay, a mistake, or a last-minute design change. Look back at the plan and re-evaluate. What parts of the process could be compressed to find the additional time? What parties can work simultaneously to cut down on time? There are some things we can control and some we can't – flexibility means understanding the difference.
- Look at the budget: Money can often save time. Maybe something can be jobbed out instead of being built in-house. Many arts venues will allow items in their stock to be rented or borrowed: sometimes individual items, but in some cases entire sets or collections of costumes or props.
- Keep moving forward: Momentum can be stifled if you are not careful. Sometimes you need to assist with a decision or insist that one is made so things can progress.

CREATING THE SCHEDULE

The nice thing about producing shows and events is that there is no guessing at the date when the project needs to be completed. Be it a single event or a show that runs for months, we all know that it needs to be ready by opening night. In order to create the most effective schedule, you should start with the opening and work backward. The next two questions to ask are about time: How much time do we need, and how much time do we have? If you are lucky enough, the answer to these two questions will match, but that is rarely the case. Due to budget or venue availability, you may have to make accommodations to make the schedule fit into a specific timeframe. A common shift recently in professional theatre has reduced the number of weeks of rehearsal from five down to four or sometimes even three weeks. This change has been made for monetary reasons and does prove challenging for the director and performers. Any sacrifice you make will affect someone. You, as production manager, will need to weigh the options and come up with the schedule that serves the overall production best. (For calendar examples and templates please visit the companion website.)

DEADLINES

Lots of information will be required from individuals to make a production come together – scripts, designs, casting, etc. An important part at the beginning of the planning process is to determine the deadlines. It is best for the production manager to make the first draft of the deadlines based on what they know of the season, workload, and time frame. Once the draft is done, it can be shared internally with the shop heads and artistic leadership/producers for feedback. Once the deadlines are set, they need to be communicated to the people who are expected to meet them. Depending upon the items and the people involved, further negotiation might be necessary. However, once the deadlines are final, everyone needs to stick to them.

It is best to have multiple steps to the deadlines. Let us take a costume design as an example. Once the director and designer have met and discussed the concepts, a "preliminary" deadline should occur to allow everyone to touch base and check to see if their ideas are aligned. Often, there will be additional work on the part of the designer, and a "final" design conversation will need to take place. The next step is a "hand-off" deadline where the costume design package is handed over to the costume shop for work to begin. Typically, the shop will "cost out" the package (more on this see Chapter 7, Money and Budget), and if it is not achievable within a given budget, a "revision" of the package will also be requested. All of the phases (preliminary, final, hand-off, and revisions) should have deadlines before the entire production process begins. Further deadlines might be necessary, as well. If the costumes are being built, then certain fabrics and accessories will be due from the designer. If it's a new work and casting decisions are decided later in the process, you might need a deadline for final casting so the costumes can be completed on time. As you can see, it can be a complicated process, and deadlines help to keep it on track.

Of course, unforeseen things happen; we need to remain flexible, and contingency plans may need to be developed. If, after a costume deadline, an unexpected script revision changes the necessities of the costumes (or any other aspect of the show), then we will have to make some hard choices. Do we make the changes and push back the final deadline? Do we choose not to accept the new script version because the changes requested are not possible? Or do we meet somewhere in the middle? The art of compromise is one of the production manager's essential skills.

PRODUCTION MEETINGS

The best way to check in on the progress of the team and ensure deadlines are met is to schedule production meetings around those deadlines. A production schedule can be extremely complex, so looking for moments of intersection can be very helpful. If you know a particularly challenging deadline is approaching, call a production meeting to check in with everyone and see how things are going. Perhaps challenges can be solved all together, or if not, at least you have a heads up that this deadline might not be met. (For more see the chapter 6 on Meetings.)

REHEARSAL SCHEDULE

In most cases your stage manager and director will take on creating the rehearsal schedule. However, the stage manager might not start until a week before rehearsals begin, so you may need to have a hand in crafting the basic schedule until they join the project and fill in the details. The first thing to determine is when rehearsals will begin. You may need to decide how many weeks you can afford to hire your performers. Once the start date is set, you'll need to figure out what times rehearsals will occur and when there will be time off.

If this is a union show, there is guidance found in the union rules. The Actors' Equity Association (union of actors and stage managers in the United States) has very specific rules for how many hours per day and week can be rehearsed and how many hours there must be between the end of one rehearsal and the beginning of the next. One day off per week is the norm, and often this falls on Monday. Don't feel obligated to work the number of days or hours the union requires if the project does not need

A Midsummer Night's Dream   Rehearsal Calendar

Sunday	Monday	Tuesday	Wednesday	Thursday	Friday	Saturday
SEPTEMBER						**1**
2 Rehearsal 10am-4pm	**3** Labor Day ACTOR DAY OFF	**4** Rehearsal 5:30pm-10pm	**5** Rehearsal 5:30pm-10pm	**6** Rehearsal 5:30pm-10pm	**7** ACTOR DAY OFF	**8** Rehearsal 10am-6pm
9 Rehearsal 10am-6pm	**10** Rehearsal 6:30pm-10pm	**11** Rehearsal 5:30pm-10pm	**12** ACTOR DAY OFF	**13** ACTOR DAY OFF	**14** Rehearsal 5:30pm-10pm	**15** Rehearsal (Stage) 10am-6pm
16 Rehearsal (Stage) 10am-6pm	**17** Rehearsal (Stage) 5:30pm-10pm	**18** Rehearsal (Stage) 5:30pm-10pm	**19** ACTOR DAY OFF	**20** Tech Rehearsal 5:30pm-10pm	**21** Tech Rehearsal 5:30pm-10pm	**22** Tech Rehearsal 10am-10pm
23 Tech Rehearsal 10am-8pm	**24** ACTOR DAY OFF	**25** Dress Run 5:30pm-10pm	**26** Dress Run + Photos 5:30pm-10pm	**27** Opening Night Show 7:30pm Reception	**28** Show 8pm	**29** Show 2pm Show 8pm
30 Closing Night Show 2pm	**Notes:** Only the fairies are required to attend **aerial** and **dance** rehearsals. Aerial rehearsals will be held at Joe's Movement Emporium					

Ruth Anne Watkins, Stage Manager   Updated: 8/4/2012 (RAW)

Figure 5.2   Rehearsal calendar example
Credit: Provided by Ruth Anne Watkins

it. Too often we allow the maximum hours allotted to guide the schedule. The union created this rule to protect its members from being worked too many hours. There is no penalty for working less. Contemplate this as you plan your schedule and don't forget to consider the humans doing the work. Some producing organizations are starting to look at five-day work weeks for rehearsals (as opposed to six) and considering if long tech days are actually a good use of time.

There are other factors that can inform the rehearsal schedule. The rehearsal venue might impact scheduling. It might be that your rehearsal space is also a classroom used during the day, so it is only available in the evenings. You may also have to consider artist conflicts when days off and daily hours are determined. Like any schedule, it is a puzzle and may require prolonged consideration before a final version is complete.

Many producing organizations have come together to do away with 10 out of 12 technical rehearsals. (Means that the actors work 10 hours out of a 12-hour time span with a 2-hour break.) All others involved would end up working much longer hours. At the publishing of this book, there was a "10 out of 12 working group" leading the charge. Their work can be found here – https://nomore10outof12s.com/. And visit the companion website for links to panel discussions on this topic and more.

BUILD SCHEDULE

Trust in your shop heads to get the build schedule created. Your technical director, costume shop manager, head electrician, scenic charge, props artisan, and other department heads will be able to advise the best course of action for their respective shops. The design of the show is the primary guide for the build schedule. Often, certain items will have to be created first, as other items build upon or relate to them. Labor is the next big determining factor. Working with the shop heads and/or crew chiefs to figure out how many people you have and how long it will take them to complete the necessary tasks is a complex puzzle. Finally, we need to know when the items need to be delivered to the stage so they can be used for technical rehearsals or possibly even before.

Many production managers do not have their own staff and shops and are often required to bid out items to be built. Many commercial scenic and costume shops exist throughout the country. You will also find individual artisans willing to be hired for a single job or project – such is often the case in props and costumes. The advantage you have with these types of entities is that you get to determine the time and the money that can be allocated and then look for the right person who can deliver what you request. (More about bidding to outside vendors see Chapter 8, Hiring and Casting.)

LOAD-IN SCHEDULE

The load-in schedule is one big puzzle. Each shop will need time to get their part of the show into the venue, and the production manager (with some careful consideration and knowledge) must orchestrate it all. Again, your shop heads will provide the most useful information about loading in, so trust them to give you guidance. It may sometimes be necessary for you to weigh in and advise or decide between competing priorities. The design of the space or show will be the best starting place for this schedule. One element might need to be installed first because another element may block access once it is installed. For example, it's often common to start with light hang in the theatre so the electricians have a clear stage to fly in the linesets used for electrics or maneuverer ladders or lifts around the space without having to worry about the set. However, light focus cannot occur until the set is in place, so that will have to occur later in the schedule. Often, elements will cross over between departments and will require multiple steps and personnel, a TV monitor, for example, that lives attached to the wall of the set. The scene shop may need to install the wall first before the video department can install the monitor, but the scenic artist has to come back and finish the paint job once the monitor is in. The bottom line is that the elements in the venue should be complete by the time technical rehearsals occur.

TECH SCHEDULE

The tech schedule is best broken down into four phases – rehearsals onstage, technical rehearsals, dress rehearsals, and notes periods.

- Rehearsals onstage: Whenever possible, try to give the performers and director and/or choreographer time in the space and on the set before tech begins. This time is invaluable and can save time later in tech. It's nice to begin the first rehearsal onstage with a walk-through guided by the technical director or stage manager. This way, the performers get a chance to ask questions and understand how things were meant to be used. In an ideal world, the performers would have enough time onstage to space through the show, restage any necessary sections, and get a full run-through in before tech.

- Tech rehearsals: This is where we add all the pieces together – lights, sound, costumes, automation, video, performers, etc. It is often described as the most inefficient and frustrating part of the process. Everyone is together in the room working on their aspect of the production. Everyone more than likely thinks their aspect is the most important. To determine how much time tech will take requires an understanding of all the elements being put together. (A show with one set, no quick changes, and no video will take a lot less time to tech than one with four sets, thirty quick changes, and three projectors.) Another important element to understand is how the tech will be run. Will there be a paper tech, where the director, designers, and stage manager sit down and talk through the whole show and all its cues? Will it be a cue to cue, where each section of the production with lighting, set, or sound cue in it is worked, but then sections without cues are skipped? Will you dry tech everything first without performers and then attempt a run? Every show will require something different. The stage manager is ultimately responsible for running of the tech but you as the production manager need to understand and support all of the plans.

- Dress rehearsals: This is where the full show with all its elements is run through in order, preferably without stopping. Everyone learns a lot from doing the show in real-time (stage managers, crew, performers, designers, directors/choreographers), so having at least a couple full-dress runs before you have an audience is very important. Make sure there is time to do so in the schedule. Often, one of these dress rehearsals is when production photos are taken. It's important everyone knows this is coming so they can do their best to get everything completed in order to have the best photos possible.

- Notes period: This is the time the designers and shop staff take to refine the work and make fixes or changes based on what has been discovered during tech and dress. The notes period overlaps tech/dress, occurring at times when the venue and production elements are not in use for rehearsal. In the case of scenic, paint, lights, sound, and video, these notes will need to take place in the venue, making for a complicated scheduling puzzle. Part of the production manager's job during the tech/dress period is to create a schedule for the next day based on the desires, needs, and priorities of each person. It's important to understand who can work together and who needs the venue to themselves. Oftentimes, notes will not all get accomplished and will be pushed to the next day because time ran out.

Figure 5.3 A view of the tech tables from above
Credit: Photo by Ryan Knapp

STRIKE SCHEDULE

It is important to know in advance how much time you have in the venue following the final performance. This will not only help you to plan the strike schedule but may also inform how much stuff you can put in the venue, to begin with. If you only have four hours post-show for strike versus four days, that will drastically change the scope of the physical production. If the production has a long run, you can wait until after the opening to begin the strike planning, but if it is a one-night event, you'll have to be thinking about the strike at the same time as you are planning everything else. Similar to the load-in schedule, you will need to take guidance from your shop heads and crew to figure out the best way to get everything out. Some items might need to be struck first to ease the exit of others.

DOES THE SHOW HAVE A FUTURE?

Hopefully, you will know well in advance if the show will have future performances either at your venue or another. However, it is possible to find out after the strike that the show will be remounted in a future season. In any case, preparation of show paperwork and proper archives is always necessary. In most cases, the stage manager for the show will be expected to turn in their production book, which contains all the information about the show from the blocking to the cues. The production manager should make sure this book is turned over in a timely fashion and double-check that it includes all necessary elements. In addition to the info from the SM, it's important to collect all the design paperwork (plans, renderings, lists, etc.) as well as any schedules, contact sheets, and other paperwork you created. In the end, a full package of anything and everything to do with the show should be archived to help a future production.

If you know in advance that the show will be moved or remounted, then it's important to make sure the physical production remains intact, is properly stored, and is able to be transported. If the production move is happening shortly, it might fall to the production manager to plan for the storage as well as the transportation of the items. It's important to communicate the post-show plans to your team so that items can be engineered and built to come apart and be put back together easily as well as fit into the mode of transportation. Storage and transportation cost money, so it's imperative that funds be allocated toward this as soon as possible. Finding the proper storage and transportation can take time, so the sooner you know about this possibility the better!

MANAGING THE PHYSICAL RESOURCES

Whether it be lumber, tools, light boards, speakers, couches, or petticoats, each item we use needs to be managed and cared for. This becomes doubly important if you have very few resources or an abundance of them. Creating a system where you can track what items you have is a critical step toward success. If you are lucky enough to have the money and space to house a large stock of proper-ties, you should take the time to inventory and log what you have so items can be properly found and used when needed. If you do not know what you have, chances are good you'll buy something a second time without realizing it and waste money.

Figure 5.4
Credit: Photo by Bill Geenen

TIP – Invest in the upkeep of your equipment, be it a table saw or a sewing machine. This will cost less overall than constantly needing to replace them. Create a schedule where items are serviced and cleaned. Ideally, this would be in the off-season when the tools are not in use. Make sure you budget for this maintenance.

TOP THREE TAKEAWAYS

- Seeing a production from its inception all the way to completion can be a very fulfilling experience. Time, preparation, and careful thought are the keys to success. It's never too early to begin to plan your next show or event.
- Stay flexible – your careful planning will often need to change. Keep those plan Bs (and Cs) in the back of your head in case they should be needed!
- You are not alone. Use your team and your network to help you craft the best schedules possible.

NOTE

1   Fishman, Stephen. *The Public Domain: How to Find & Use Copyright-free Writings, Music, Art & More.* 3rd ed. Berkeley, CA: Nolo, 2006.

Meetings

The true test of a production manager is how well they can facilitate a meeting. A good production manager can do it with a calm demeanor, in an acceptable amount of time, cover all that is necessary and keep everyone focused on the task at hand throughout. No one ever wants to feel that their time is being wasted or that their topic has not been given its proper attention. This is even more important at the end of a long day or week.

TYPES OF PRODUCTION MEETINGS

A production meeting is meant to be an opportunity to get all the participants on a show or event in the room to discuss relevant topics that affect more than one or two people. Every production manager you speak to and every project you work on will have a different set of meetings that they require, so there is no definitive list. You will often see something resembling the following:

- A concept meeting: This is usually the first meeting where the director, choreographer or client explains their idea for the show or project.
- A preliminary design meeting: At this meeting, the designers or production staff present to the director or client what they propose based on the concept and their research of the subject matter. Often a discussion between the two parties will take place, hopefully resulting in a unified approach as the project continues.
- A final design meeting: The design is finished and approved by all involved. This meeting precedes the build process.
- A cost out meeting: Once the design is finished, we need to make sure it is affordable so the production staff will cost out each element, and, when we are over budget, a meeting might be necessary to make cuts or adjustments.
- A pre-rehearsal meeting: If you are working on a show that has a rehearsal period, it is always smart to meet as a group prior to the rehearsals to make sure everyone is on the same page. Oftentimes, this is the first meeting the stage manager will attend.

DOI: 10.4324/9780367808174-9

- During rehearsal meetings: Rehearsals are well underway, and the technical rehearsals will begin soon. Load-in is either about to start or in process, so this is a perfect time for another connection. These meetings could be weekly, if that feels appropriate, or spaced out throughout the rehearsal process.

- Post-tech meetings: After every tech and dress rehearsal, a production meeting takes place to wrap up the notes and activities of the day and then plan for the schedule and priorities of the next day.

- A debrief meeting: Many organizations will call a meeting after the show has been completed to reflect back on the process and learn from what occurred. This is common in an educational setting and also with events that will happen again.

> **TIP** – Start the first meeting with values – What do you and your organization value? What do your collaborators and clients value? By starting with these topics your process is guaranteed to move smoother. Make the collaboration about the people, the process, and the journey, not the final product.

SCHEDULING THE MEETING

Finding the perfect time for a meeting can be the most challenging part. Many production managers say they spend more than a quarter of their time getting the right people in the room for a conversation. Here are a few tips to ease this task:

- Acquire as many participants' schedules in advance as you can.

- Determine preferred meeting times for participants.

- Be flexible with your time. Move things around to accommodate others. There is a lot of goodwill that can come with that.

- Use technology! There are great, free online scheduling tools that are incredibly convenient and easy to use. The possible problem with using an online scheduling service is there will always be participants who cannot figure out how to use it. You will have to be patient while you work to accommodate those individuals.

- Acknowledge that you might not be able to get everyone together. If that is the case, let those who cannot make it know that the meeting will be recorded and/or notes will be taken and distributed.

Once you have the time set – communicate it! Send everyone the details of the meeting. If you can, create an online calendar appointment and invite everyone to it. Finally, send a reminder as the meeting approaches – at least one week before the meeting and then another reminder the day before.

> **TIP** – Time is money. Have you ever calculated the cost of a meeting? Think about everyone who you have required to be there and what an hour of their time costs you or your organization. Is it money well spent?

Figure 6.1 Charlie Mingroni and Jay Sheehan planning concert details for Live Art in Richmond, VA

Credit: Photo by Melissa Grove

HOW TO PREPARE FOR THE MEETING

Adequate preparation for the meeting is extremely important. Production meetings tend to be filled with passionate people who often have radical ideas that require large agendas. With many passionate participants at the same meeting, you need to be prepared for wherever the conversation may go. It is impossible to be prepared for everything, but the more you attempt to be prepared, the easier and more productive the meetings will be.

There are two critical tasks that must occur before the meeting for the correct agenda to take shape. Step one is to have a generic agenda already pre-planned for your current point in the process.

If it is the first production meeting where the director presents his or her concept, the agenda might look something like this:

- Introductions
- Organizational values
- Director presents concept to group
- Open conversation for questions/discussion
- Next steps
- Remind next meeting date
- Discuss what is due at that meeting

If it's the last production meeting before tech, it probably resembles something closer to this:

- Upcoming important dates
- Area updates
- Costumes/hair/wigs/wardrobe
- Electrics
- Paint
- Props
- Scenic
- Sound/music
- Stage operations
- Video
- Load-in/tech questions
- Review load-in/tech schedule
- Strike schedule

Once the generic agenda is complete, the next step is to take time to connect with every meeting participant to find out what topics they need on the agenda. This can be done via email or phone, but in person is always best. This helps you set the agenda as well as judge the emotional temperature of the soon to be face-to-face participants. Say, for example, that a big topic that will affect multiple people is on the agenda. Whom does this topic affect? What will their reactions be? Should this have come up before now, and will this frustrate people? Is this upcoming meeting the right forum for this conversation? Maybe not. It is perfectly within the production manager's right to hold off on bringing up a topic to the whole production team if they think it will cause unhelpful issues. The production manager should consider priming the conversation by talking with participants prior to the meeting so that they have more time to consider the issues before attending the meeting. Know the people you are working with; know what they need. Once the agenda is set, send it out to the meeting participants. This should happen ideally 24 hours in advance of the meeting. This is also a great last-minute reminder that the meeting is coming up!

PREPARING THE ROOM

Preparing the room may seem a trivial task, but it is not. People have a physical and emotional reaction to spaces, how they are lit, how they are arranged, etc. Give yourself adequate time before the meeting to prepare the space. Are there enough chairs, and can they be arranged so that everyone can see everyone else? Is there a computer and screen/projector set up for the agenda to be displayed or to connect via video with a member of the team who cannot be physically present? Where will you sit? Do we need documentation to refer to – schedules, set drawings, costume renderings, etc.?

> **TIP** – Lighting matters! Consider the lighting options in your meeting room with intention. Is there natural light that can be utilized? Are the lights at a level that everyone can see? Is there a non-fluorescent option to provide?

WHEN THE MEETING CANNOT BE IN PERSON

It is ALWAYS preferable to meet in person, but that is not always possible, and sometimes you need to sacrifice meeting in person in order to keep meetings timely. If someone cannot attend in person, the next best option is to meet with the rest of the team in person and have the missing person join remotely. If, however, no one can meet in person, as is often the case when working with out-of-town artists or people with demanding schedules, then embrace unfavorable circumstances and have everyone meet remotely.

MEETING VIA VIDEO CONFERENCE

Technology is amazing and getting better and more versatile every year. Only ten years before the creation of this book, there were no affordable and accessible video conference options for theatres. Today, we have services such as Zoom, FaceTime, and Google Meet and the COVID-19 pandemic has expanded our reliance and comfort on these platforms. Although these services are amazing in how they can create connectivity, they are only as effective as how they are used and the people who use them.

> "I once did a series of video interviews to weed through a large group of potential candidates. I was shocked at how few of those being interviewed paid attention to how they presented themselves on screen. Everything from lights shining behind the person so they were in shadow the whole time to one person who Skyped from a phone and gave me an upward view of their face. Only one interviewee took the time to set up the shot. On top of that, she was three hours ahead of my time zone and got up early so that for the 9 a.m. interview (6 a.m. her time) she was awake and prepared. For this, and for many other reasons, she got the job."
>
> - Cary Gillett

If a video conference is necessary, make certain to give yourself adequate time to test the equipment and the platform you are using. Can you get everyone into the meeting? If not, the meeting will likely be more effort than it is worth. Once the technology allows everyone to join effectively, the meeting should be run as any other meeting. Special attention should be paid to make sure everyone has opportunities to comment when necessary. It's a good idea to call out people by name to allow them an opportunity to speak. Often, people on a video call are multitasking and their focus is not entirely on the call. Keep an eye out for this and encourage everyone to give their full attention. Keeping the meeting moving and honoring the time you allotted will help.

> **TIP** – Hybrid meetings (with some people in person and some people virtual) are often used and very challenging. If you must meet this way, pay close attention to how everyone can see and hear the same things. Positioning of cameras/displays in the room is going to be vital. And make sure you have a decent speaker phone in the room where you are meeting.

FACILITATING THE MEETING

Start on time and make it clear to everyone that you plan to do so. Respect other people's time and expect them to respect yours. If someone is late – call them and find out how soon they will arrive. Begin the meeting at the agreed-upon time even if you are missing people. You may have to jump around on the agenda to make sure not to cover items critical to the missing person. If someone arrives late, acknowledge it, quickly catch them up and move on.

If it is the first time this team is meeting, it is important to start with a round of introductions (including names, pronouns, and positions on this project) so people can put names to faces and understand everyone's role in the process. It might be able so useful to remind everyone of the purpose of the meeting and established goals and values for the project and/or organization. Then, clearly relate the agenda you will be following for this meeting. For example: "We will begin by checking in with each production shop, then discuss any outstanding notes from the rehearsal reports, review the tech schedule and then open the floor for any additional topics." Hopefully, participants will have already related to you what they hoped to see on the agenda, but at this time you should ask if there are any missing topics for the agenda. If participants add topics, you must quickly decide if they are to be inserted into this agenda or whether that topic should be set aside until you have had a chance to speak with this participant or for a more appropriate meeting to come.

> **TIP** – Start with asking the director or producer of the project to speak first and share any updates, questions, or concerns that need to be addressed. Then end the meeting with the stage manager to make sure all relevant topics have been covered. This will book end the meeting nicely.

Then the meeting takes off. The production manager's job is to keep things on track. There is an agenda for a reason. Here are some additional tips:

- Stay engaged throughout the meeting. If the person leading the meeting is not paying attention, then no one else will. Utilize active listening and only talk when necessary.

- Stick to the agenda as much as you can, but also be flexible enough to recognize that an important topic may arise that needs to be allowed into the agenda immediately. Let new topics in, but don't let them monopolize the conversation.

- Dissuade side conversations that will inevitably come up. Remind people to stay focused on the main topic. You never know what comment or idea might affect someone else in another area. Make sure everyone is included in the conversation.

- Look for opportunities to suggest a breakout session after the meeting: "It seems that a new drawing of the scenery masking will be necessary. Let's plan to have the set designer, lighting designer, technical director and master electrician stick around after the meeting to discuss. If anyone else feels strongly about being a part of that conversation, you are welcome to stay." This help keep the meeting on track and allows you to respect people's time.

- Keep an eye on the clock. If the meeting is scheduled for an hour—keep it to an hour, even if that means cutting a topic from the agenda. For example, maybe it would have been great to talk everyone through the tech schedule, but you are going to email it to everyone after the meeting is over, so, if necessary, we can remove it from the agenda. It is also okay to remind people how much time is left and to encourage the conversation to move on to other topics. In the event that the meeting needs to run long, give everyone as much warning as possible. You will need to gauge who can stay and who needs to go. Perhaps a participant only needs to make a quick phone call to arrange to stay later.

- Make sure everyone who needs or wants to talk can do so. This may mean calling on people who have not spoken to make sure they have space to speak. It can also mean making sure others don't dominate the conversation and take up too much space and time in the meeting. If someone says "nothing for the group" don't be afraid to encourage them to share their thoughts or notes even if they think the group does not need to hear them. Sometimes this comment is appreciated from the efficiency perspective, but it can be problematic from the collaboration standpoint.

- Listen for the questions not being asked that need to be – and then ask them. You don't need to have all the answers. Sometimes, just need to ask the right questions.

- Pay attention to the emotional temperature of the people in the room. Is everyone relaxed and joking, or is there tension in the air? What is their body language saying? What is causing that tension, and can it be resolved? Perhaps a director is being pushed to make a decision, and they are clearly not comfortable doing so right now. Yes, it would be ideal if we had the answer now, but it would be more ideal if the director did not erupt in anger. In this case, the phrase you should become familiar with is "I think we can table this decision right now. Can you get back to us by tomorrow with your choice?"

> **TIP** – It is not given that the production manager will always run the meeting. In some cases, a stage manager, producer, or even director will step up to take that role. Taking a backseat is not a sign of weakness but, often, just the opposite. If you do not take a passive role in the meeting, you can still have a great impact. Regardless of the leader, it is still your responsibility to make sure notes are compiled, distributed, and followed up on.

FOLLOWING UP

Someone should be taking notes at the meeting. These notes are as much for the people who could not be present as they are for those who were. It is possible that, three days later, the items we discussed will be forgotten. Ideally, the note taker is not the production manager who is running the meeting. You can run a meeting and take notes, but it is extremely difficult and should be avoided. The stage manager or assistant stage manager would be good options for note-takers. After the meeting, the production manager should review the notes to make sure they are accurate and easy to read. Then the notes should be distributed to everyone or placed in a mutually accessible place such as the shared cloud storage site for the show.

Meeting notes should include the following:

- Who was in attendance at the meeting
- Where and when it took place
- Information about the next meeting (if known)

Detailed notes of what was said (these notes should be organized by production area for easier referencing later). For example:

SCENIC

- Some of the elements are hopefully climbable.
- The director would like to use the set as a percussion instrument, possibly using microphones.

PROJECTIONS

- Each character having their own graffiti or written signature projected as each character is introduced to the audience.
- We'll need at least one actual television on stage, portraying the way so many people received information about the events.
- What are the rights surrounding the news video clips?

COSTUMES

- Police will wear gas masks, but not necessarily all the same.
- Actors are barefoot for most of the show, at some point the police will put boots on.
- The director stressed the need for simplicity.

LIGHTS

- How comfortable is each character being in the spotlight? How are the spotlights different?
- Light will be used to create a foreground/background, telling the audience what to focus on, even if no one leaves the stage.

After the notes go out to the team, then the real follow-up work begins. It would be great if, after sending out the notes, all the answers to questions magically happened, but this is unlikely. Continuously follow up with individuals to make sure that progress continues to be made. Make sure the director who promised a choice by tomorrow delivers and that the production staff follow up on their updates too. Hopefully, the follow-up from the first meeting is done by the next meeting, but, if not, make sure those topics are top on the next agenda!

> **TIP** – Ask for feedback about your meeting facilitation abilities so you can get insights from everyone you engage with. A good production manager keeps improving and gets better at what they do and how they do it.

Figure 6.2 Scenery walk thru
Credit: Photo by Ryan Knapp

WALK-THROUGHS/SITE VISITS: "THE ROVING PRODUCTION MEETING"

Many times a production meeting may take the shape of a "roving" meeting. These types of walk-throughs are more common for corporate theatre and special events, but many times in the performing arts you may also have the need to move about the venue or shop. (For more details on the site visits see Chapter 18, Special Events.) The roving production meeting can be helpful for many, as physically seeing the space can help directors, designers, technicians, and event planners work more efficiently. Conduct this meeting like you would any other type of production meeting – keep an eye on the time and keep the agenda handy. Many times, as the group moves from place to place, side conversations begin to happen without you realizing it. Before you know it, many people in the group are having private discussions that really should include everybody. As the production manager, you are responsible for keeping the sidebars to a minimum and keeping everyone focused.

TOP THREE TAKEAWAYS

- Production management is a collaborative art, and meetings sustain the life of collaborations.

- Arranging and facilitating successful meetings is one of the most essential ways to achieve project success.

- A successful meeting is yours for the taking. Do not forget to check out the companion website for meeting agenda examples and other useful information.

Money and Budget

> "Theatre can be good, fast, cheap—pick any two."
>
> - Old theatre proverb

One of the key functions for most production managers is the creation and management of the production budget. Your immediate supervisor, whether it is a producer or client, will expect you to have intimate knowledge of the elements of the production and stay within the allocated funds for the project. This chapter will explain where funds come from and where they should go, as well as techniques for tracking money and managing changes.

INCOME SOURCES

Before you can decide how much money to spend on an event or production, you must first know how much you have. Funding for any performing arts organization comes from a variety of sources, and accounting for these funds is critical for effective budgeting. Organizations describe this income differently, but generally, the presenting industry has titled these funds Earned and Contributed. Here are examples of both:

- Earned
  - Box office revenue: This is the money generated from ticket sales. In most cases, these funds only account for a portion of the amount needed to run an organization. Some box offices will add ticketing fees to the cost of admission, which is also a revenue generator.
  - Ancillary income: Some organizations have items for sale in their lobby before, during, and after events such as concessions and merchandise. These are funding sources as well, though likely very minor to the overall financial health of the organization.

DOI: 10.4324/9780367808174-10

- Contributed
  - ○ Grants: The two most typical types are grants from the government (local, state, and federal) and private corporations. These funds typically require an extensive application process, and you must report specifically on how the money was used. Many grants stipulate exactly how this money is to be spent.
  - ○ Donations: Money can also come from private sources such as individuals or small companies. Unlike grants, there is no application process, but they require much work to secure. For this reason, organizations that need donations to operate will often need a staff of people to develop this income – hence, this staff is usually called the development team. The donor pool for any organization is an important one to foster. The funds they contribute can be critical to the success of the organization.
  - ○ Fundraisers: The development team may also decide to hold large events for the sole purpose of raising money. These could be gala celebrations with a healthy ticket price and/or auctions where donated items are auctioned off and all proceeds go toward the organization.

> **TIP** – Do not underestimate the value and work of the development team. They raise the money! If they reach out to you for assistance in showing donors the production side of things, find ways to collaborate with them as you would any other director/design team. Most people who donate to arts organizations do not know what is behind the scenes and allowing them a peek can be a valuable move.

UNDERSTANDING THE OVERALL BUDGET

In most organizations, there are different budgets for the different departments. Take a producing opera, dance, or theatre company, for example, they have multiple departments, all with their own budget – production, marketing/public relations, facilities, development, business, etc. The production manager will only be responsible for the production department's part of the budget.

The person who decides the overall budget is most likely the producing or managing director of the organization, or client if it is a special event. They will likely begin the budget planning conversation as such – "What amount do you need to produce this season/show/event?" or "This is the amount we have allocated for you to produce this season/show/event." Let us look at these scenarios in detail:

- When the overall budget is requested: If you are asked to provide your own overall budget, it's best to create a budget that is reasonable but achieves the shows/events you plan to produce. If you request too little, you might get what you ask for and then find it challenging to work within a constrained budget. If you ask for too much, you might demonstrate that you are insensitive to the financial constraints of the organization and find it difficult to have your budget requests fully funded in the future. Once you have submitted your request, be ready to justify your budget with specific data and artistic information to explain why you made certain budget choices.

- When the overall budget is prescribed: If you are given a specific budget amount, take that amount and make it work. However, it is in the best interest of the organization that the shows/events be successfully achieved. If the prescribed budget is too small, then you need to say something. It's possible negotiation of more money or fewer projects might be necessary.

It is important to clearly understand what is expected to be in your production budget rather than another department's budget within the organization. Here are a few examples of items that might shift between budgets depending upon the organization: Staff salaries and fringe benefits (health, pension, social security), professional development (training/classes for the staff), travel/transportation/vehicles, archival photography/videography, and office supplies.

> "They are not my numbers; they are THE numbers. Don't get defensive."
> - Glenn Plott, Former Director of Production at Cincinnati Opera

CREATING THE PRODUCTION BUDGET

The truth is budgeting for shows and events is a catch-22. You need to create the budget before you create the show, sometimes before you even know what the show is going to be. All production managers are in this same boat, and, luckily, the more you do it, the easier it becomes. Here are some guidelines to help you if it is your first time through the process.

The production budget should include at minimum the following items:

- Artist fees: If you are working with unions, the artistic fees will be easy to determine, as they are based on the union minimums. The minimum is what you are required to pay for each position. However, this does not preclude you from paying more. As people work their way up in this business, they expect more compensation, especially if they have worked at the same organization many times. You may be asked to budget before roles are cast and creative teams are put together. Start with the union minimums as your baseline, but it's a good idea to put in a little more money to give you some wiggle room for negotiating fees. Understanding the specifics of the labor agreements that you are working with is a huge asset. Do your homework. (See Chapter 8, Hiring and Casting for more on unions). If the artists belong to a union you will also be required to make health and pension contributions as well as some other fees directly to the union.

- Producing rights costs: This will include royalties, purchasing scripts, music package rentals, etc. (Check out Chapter 5, Planning and Scheduling for more details.)
- Supplies: Scenery, paint, props, costumes, hair/wigs, make-up, lights, sound, video/projections, and stage management. (Each area of production should get a budget line for each show/event.)
- Labor: Often you need to bring people in beyond the full-time staff to complete the work, or maybe you have no full-time staff, so all you have is overhire workers. These people can serve as run crews, carpenters, electricians, costume stitchers, etc. (See Chapter 8, Hiring and Casting for more contemplations about labor costs.)
- Rentals: You might need to rent equipment or supplies from other people or companies to achieve the visions of the project.
- A contingency fund: The artistic process of creating productions and events is often complex and must plan for many variables. At least a small percentage of the budget (usually 5–10%) should be held for initially missed costs or emergencies.

How do you determine the budget amounts? This is the toughest part of the budgeting process and requires a significant amount of work. You need to do some in-depth research on the shows/projects/events that are planned and figure out what/who is required and what it's going to cost. Sometimes this information is easily found. If you are producing a show held by a major rights house, you can find out exactly how much you should budget for the rights (see Chapter 5, Planning and Scheduling). Some large opera and ballet companies will rent an entire show package with scenery, props, and costumes for a set fee.

Do not create budgets by yourself. Your production staff is a necessary resource for you, as they know exact material and labor costs, and they will know what needs to be built versus what can be purchased, rented, or borrowed. You also need to collaborate with the creative lead on the project to understand the scope and scale this is being anticipated, as that will drive costs. The production schedule (how much time you will have to mount the project) will factor in greatly as well. Do not underestimate the value of your professional network, either. If you are producing a show that another theatre has recently done, call their production manager and inquire about their costs. If you are working with a new designer, find a production manager who has recently worked with that person. By doing so, you can learn how big (or small) they tend to design, and then, hopefully, you can anticipate their funding needs.

No matter how much research you do, however, sometimes you must guess. Try to make those guesses as educated as possible, based on what you know about the artistic process and what you have learned from your sources. It is also good if your guesses are based on some amount of historical fact. What was the total budget for your last big musical? That might be a good starting place for the one you are budgeting now.

TIP – Trial and error is the reality of budgeting. You will learn so much about the process once you have been through it a few times. Learn from your mistakes – you will make them; we all do.

Description	General	Show 1	Show 2	Show 3	Show 4	Show 5	Show 6
INCOME							
Production Rental Income							
Co Pro Revenue							
EXPENSE							
Sets							
Build							
Scene Shop Supplies							
Scene Shop Equip. Maint							
Sets Non Cap Equip							
Dumpsters							
Paint							
Paint Supplies							
Transportation							
Subtotal Sets							
Props							
Build							
Prop Shop Supplies							
Prop Shop Equip. Maint							
Props Non Cap Equip							
Subtotal Props							
Costumes							
Build							
Wigs							
Supplies							
Cleaning							
Costume Shop Equip Maint							
Costumes Non Cap Equip							
Subtotal Costumes							
Electrics							
Mainstage Expense							
Electrics Supplies and Lamps							
Projections Mainstage							
Projections Supplies and Lamps							
Equip Maint							
Electrics Non Cap Equip							
Subtotal Electrics							
Sound							
Mainstage Expense							
Supplies							
Equip Maint							
Sound Non Cap Equip							
Subtotal Sound							
Music Expenses							

Figure 7.1 Budget template
Credit: Cary Gillett

Instrument Rental		
Piano Expenses		
Subtotal Music Expenses		

Co-Pro Expenses

Co-pro expenses		

Stage Management

SM Salary(w. tech bumps)		
SM Overtime		
ASM Salary (w. tech bumps)		
ASM Overtime		
Prod Asst Total		
SM Health		
SM Pension		
SM FICA		
SM UN		
SM WC		
New Media Fee		
SM Travel		
SM Expense		

Subtotal Stage Management		

Prod Mgr Expense

Prod Mgr Care & Rec		
Prod Mgr Supplies		
Prod Mgr Shipping		
Prod Mgr Travel		
Subtotal Prod Mgr Expense	-	-	-	-	-	-

Prod Other Expense

Production Vehicles		
First Aid and Safety		
Stage Mgmt Supplies		
Production Storage		
Subtotal Prod Other Expense		

Tech OH & OT

Technical Overhire		
Technical Overtime		
Tech OH/OT Taxes		
Tech OH/OT SUI		
Tech OH/OT WC		

Subtotal Tech OH & OT		

TTL PRODUCTION ACCNTS

Designers

Media Fee		

Figure 7.1   *(Continued)*

USA Pension & Welfare		
Designer Shipping		
Designer Meals In Transit		
Subtotal Designers		
Set Design		
Set Designer Fees		
Set Designer Travel		
Set Designer Expense (incl asst)		
Subtotal Set Design		
Costume/WigDesign		
Costume Designer Fees		
Costume Designer Travel		
Costume Designer Expense (incl asst)		
Wig Designer Fees		
Wig Designer Travel		
Wig Designer Expense		
Subtotal Costume/WigDesign		
Lighting Design		
Light Designer Fees		
Light Designer Travel		
Light Designer Expense		
Assistant Light Design		
Assistant Light Design Travel		
Subtotal LightingDesign		
Sound Design		
Sound Designer Fees		
Sound Designer Travel		
Sound Designer Expense		
Composer Fees		
Composer Travel		
Subtotal Sound Design		
Projections Design		
Projections Designer Fees		
Projections Designer Travel		
Projections Designer Expense		
Subtotal Projections Design		
Total Designers		
Grand Total		

Figure 7.1   *(Continued)*

PAYING PEOPLE THEIR WORTH

A large challenge for any production manager is paying people what their time and effort are worth. Most of us did not choose this business to become rich, but we all hope to make a living. It is very easy to take advantage of someone's desire to work on a specific project or with a certain company. It is true that some will agree to work for nothing or next to nothing, but that does not make it appropriate. A good production manager should try not to allow this to happen. The smaller the theatre, the smaller the budget, and the more likely you will have to ask people to work for a small amount. If you are in this situation, own it and be honest with the people you hire. Work hard to give them compensation in other ways – comp tickets, travel support, goodwill, on-time payment, a reasonable work schedule, etc. And next time you hire them – try to give them a raise.

Understanding what the living wage is where you work can provide guidance on how much to pay people and when to consider paying them more. See the companion website for more information.

> **TIP** – Budgets tell a story. Example #1 – Elements that are important to the organization show up in the budget and are not hidden. Example #2 – If you spend more on materials than you do on the labor you are sharing a value of stuff over people, whether you intend to or not. When you budget, consider the story you are telling those who work with you on the project.

COMMUNICATING THE BUDGET

Once the budget is finalized, you will need to communicate it to your various production team members. At a minimum, the budget needs to get to the creative team (the people making the ideas) and the production staff (the people implementing the ideas). It is best to communicate the budgets as soon as possible so everyone knows what framework they are working within. If the budget is not set before the conceptual process begins, make it known when the budget will be finalized and roughly what amounts they might be dealing with. Be transparent – do not play games or hide things. Have open communication with everyone involved.

A clearly laid out and easy-to-read document is the best way to communicate the budget numbers. Your organization might have a prescribed template, but if not, you have some creative license here. A spreadsheet format (such as Excel) can be a good option to consider.

> **TIP** – A solid understanding of money and accounting is incredibly helpful for a production manager. If budget accounting is not your forte, you need not give up on production management; however, you should attempt to improve your skills. Talk to your director of finance or business manager to understand how they think about the finances and the budget. You can also take a class in accounting at your local community college or find an online course. The truth is that anyone can benefit from additional financial know-how.

MANAGING THE BUDGET

Once the budget is finalized, much of the work is just beginning. Hopefully, by this point in the book, you realize that the work of the production manager is to manage the ever-changing demands of production and to be flexible and considerate in finding solutions. In most situations, the budget is set before the project has begun, which means that the educated guesses you made will soon prove either right or wrong, and you will need to respond.

As the designers and director for a production complete their conceptual work, the discussion of money will arise. There are some designers who are good at designing within a budget, but others will design what they feel is best for the show and then adjust if necessary. At the completion of the design phase, your production staff will need to do what is called a "cost out" to determine what it will cost to achieve the production as designed. If it's over budget, you have some work to do with the creative team. Some options include asking if they will accept less expensive options, if elements could be cut, revising the design, or finding more money. Additional funds could come from another show that was under budget, another budget line in the same show that is unneeded, or your contingency fund. Before you work with your numbers this way, make sure it's something the organization is okay with. Many producers and clients are okay with "vertical budgeting," or moving funds from one budget line to another within the same project or season; however, some are not, and moving money requires approval from above.

Set expectations with those who will spend production funds (staff, designers, outside vendors) on what is an acceptable range for the final expenses. 10% under budget and 1% over budget is a good rule of thumb. If someone thinks they will be under or over more than that, they should be proactive and inform you as soon as possible. Being aware of financial problems early will allow more time to find better solutions. If scenery is forecasting being significantly under budget and costumes is forecasting an overage, then maybe shifting money from one budget line to another is a good course of action. You could also use your contingency here.

What if the budget you created is not sufficient for the production? Here is where a positive, respectful relationship with your budget collaborators will be beneficial, as you will need to approach them to discuss options. Requests for more money will likely be met with questions such as "why are we over budget?" or "how can you make sure this does not happen again in the future?" Come prepared with these answers. For example: "When we budgeted for the set last spring, the cost of steel was cheaper than it is now. We had no way of knowing it would climb so quickly. We can either add money to the budget to complete the show as designed or re-design the show. Though possible, a re-design at this point may cost us additional labor, as we're getting close to load-in, so my suggestion is we stick with the original plan and find the money for the more expensive steel. In the future, I have asked the scene shop to assume more expensive materials from the beginning to avoid this happening again."

TRACKING THE BUDGET

Before you start spending funds, understand the required reporting rules for your organization. Will you need to prepare monthly budget forecasts? Or file end-of-the-year fiscal reports? For many, the end of a season and the end of the fiscal year are the same. Make certain your production heads clearly report their spending, so your reports can be easily and properly prepared. Some organizations choose to have a form filled out before and/or after each expense. This process may seem burdensome, but

Tartuffe: 2951940 - 3952						
Expenses $ 7,223.76						
Allocation $ 8,000.00						
under/(over) $ 776.24						
date	merchant	item	what was it for	debit	credit	notes
27-07-2015	The Clarice	General Hardware	Floor and Sculpture	$ 727.77	$ -	
11-06-2015	A & M	MDF	Floor and Sculpture	$ 896.00	$ -	Split w/Large storage Shelving
12-08-2015	1000Bulbs	6" and 12" Plastic Globes	Chandelier	$ 947.55	$ -	
28-07-2015	Amazon	3" White Plastic Globes	Deck	$ 17.87	$ -	Split
28-07-2015	Amazon	3" White Plastic Globes	Deck	$ 53.61	$ -	
28-07-2015	Vector Art 3D	Flourishes	Screens	$ 35.00	$ -	
29-07-2015	Home Depot	1/2" EMT and 1/2" ply	Chandelier	$ 566.40	$ -	Split w/ IA, Dance
05-08-2015	Fisher	Foam and Lu	Screens	$ 464.10	$ -	Split w/ APP
10-08-2015	Home Depot	Plywood	Shrine	$ 134.94	$ -	SPLIT w. SS and IA
12-08-2015	Home Depot	molding	shrine	$ 50.70	$ -	
14-08-2015	Rosebrand	Muslin	Screens	$ 564.88	$ -	Split with Equip Purchase
8-17-15	1000bulbs	6" and 12" Plastic Globes	Chandelier	$ 380.00	$ -	
9-23-15	Foss Manufacturing	Black Damask Fabric	Black Damask	$ 805.00	$ -	
10-1-15	Theatre Services	Custom Curtains	Damask Curtains	$ 760.00	$ -	Split w/Equip Repair ($935.00)
10-09-2015	DS Pipe & Steel	1.5" tube	Chandelier	$ 225.12	$ -	
9-21-15	Amazon	Clear Ball Pit Balls	Chandelier	$ 116.39	$ -	To be returned
28-09-2015	Royal Designs Studio	Damask Stencil	Damask Stencil	$ 273.87	$ -	
30-09-2015	Royal Designs Studio	Damask Stencil Shipping	Damask Stencil Shipp	$ -	$ 74.07	
12-10-2015	1000Bulbs	6" White Plastic Globes	Deck	$ 190.20	$ -	
13-10-2015	Amazon	Credit for Clear Ball Pit Balls	Chandelier	$ -	$ 116.39	
30-09-2015	Amazon	Clear Plastic Ornaments	Chandelier	$ 159.90	$ -	
23-10-2015	McMaster	Magnets	Statue	$ 44.92	$ -	
				$ -	$ -	
				$ -	$ -	
			Sub TOTAL	$ 7,414.22	$ 190.46	

Figure 7.2 Budget tracking document

Credit: Cary Gillett

it can save time in the end when trying to track down expenses and how each expense should be properly categorized. The more money you have, the harder it is to keep track of it all, and the more organized you will have to be.

It is best to track the funds accurately as they are being used. Do not wait until the end to tally the receipts. You need to vigilantly monitor the budget daily to see how money is being spent and to make sure you are not going over budget. Track each line separately for each show/event, rather than as one large production budget. Spreadsheet software can be your friend by providing an easy-to-read and easy-to-use table for your tracking needs. Be sure to know your spreadsheet software well enough to set it up correctly. Accounting errors will cause you incredible pain. Establish with those spending the money a schedule for reporting. Weekly is generally best. Once the updates have occurred, ask them to contact you to let you know it was completed and, possibly, to send you the updated ledger if you do not have access to it yourself.

PURCHASING

There are a few different ways in which money can be spent. Every person and organization will have preferences or specific policies. Here are the types of purchasing you are likely to encounter:

- Accounts: If you purchase often from a distributor or manufacturer, it is a good idea to create an account with them so that your organization can get billed directly. This way, any staff can contact the company and make a purchase without having to make a direct payment. Accounts can sometimes come with a frequent buyer discount, which is always helpful!

- Purchasing cards: Some organizations give staff charge cards. This can be an easy way to spend funds as it gets charged directly to the organization, and it does not need to be requested or reimbursed. Often cards such as these are only utilized by full-time staff. Part-time or seasonal staff might not have this option.

- Petty cash: Cash or a check can be given to an individual before they start spending organization funds, to avoid out-of-pocket expenses. You will need to anticipate the approximate amount that is needed so the petty cash allotment is appropriately sized. The individual who receives the petty cash will need to return receipts and/or cash that equals the amount they were given.

- Reimbursement: In some cases, petty cash is not possible, or it will take too long to process. Another option is to have individuals spend money out of pocket and be reimbursed. This is acceptable if the individual does not mind using their own money. If this type of purchasing is necessary, be sure receipts for reimbursement are submitted immediately. Processing of such reimbursements may take a while, and it is unfair to ask the individual to wait too long. Although necessary in many organizations, it must be said that this type of purchasing is undesirable. Asking employees to make out-of-pocket purchases for organizational projects is basically asking an employee for a short-term, interest-free loan. There is also a terrible chance that the purchase might not be approved by the organization. This could leave your employee financially responsible for something that should be an organizational cost.

Petty Cash tracking

DATE	VENDOR	ACCOUNT/SUB ACCOUNT	DESCRIPTION	AMOUNT		NOTES
7-Apr	Cosi	Hospitality/Crew & rehearsal	Lunch for rehearsal	$	218.06	
14-Apr	Cosi	Hospitality/Crew & rehearsal	Lunch for rehearsal	$	185.43	
21-Apr	Cosi	Hospitality/Monday lunch	Lunch for rehearsal	$	420.41	
2-Apr	Men's Warehouse	Supplies/show costumes	Tuxedo rental	$	40.00	deposit
19-Apr	Men's Warehouse	Supplies/show costumes	Tuxedo rental	$	252.54	balance
18-Apr	Fedex Office	Supplies/production supplies	Script copies	$	91.69	
16-Apr	Staples	Supplies/production supplies	Clipboards, card stock, spray mount	$	96.70	
19-Apr	Giant	Hospitality/Production meetings	Bagels, fruit	$	58.87	
19-Apr	Starbucks	Hospitality/Production meetings	Coffee	$	31.69	
13-Apr	Wegmans	Hospitality/Crew & rehearsal	Water	$	3.17	
21-Apr	CVS	Hospitality/Crew & rehearsal	Paper plates	$	6.40	
20-Apr	Giant	Supplies/production supplies	Script card supplies	$	26.40	
20-Apr	Giant	Hospitality/Crew & rehearsal	Drinks, snacks	$	95.16	
21-Apr	Fedex Office	Supplies/production supplies	paper	$	4.22	
			Total spent	$	1,530.74	
			Original amount of petty cash	$	1,650.00	
			Balance	$	119.26	

Figure 7.3 Petty cash tracking
Credit: Cary Gillett

Not-for-profit organizations qualify for tax exemption on both a state and national level. This allows for purchases to be made without paying sales tax and helps your budget dollars to go further. Check to see if the organization you are working for has this exemption. If so, they will be able to provide you with a tax-exempt card and number which you (and others) will need to use while making purchases. Sometimes a tax-exempt organization will refuse to reimburse sales tax or will subtract any sales tax paid when reconciling receipts and petty cash. If you are tax-exempt, you may need to make sure anyone who makes purchases has a tax-exempt card or else they may end up paying any sales taxes out of pocket!

Figure 7.4 Tax exempt certificate
Credit: Cary Gillett

TOP THREE TAKEAWAYS

- Budgeting is educated guesswork. The more you do it, the better you will get at it.

- Managing the budget is constant work and requires diligence and attention to detail.

- There are a plethora of tools and applications that can help you to track numbers and spending. Check out the companion website for a host of helpful options.

Hiring and Casting

WHO HIRES WHOM?

Every organization is different. In some cases, the production manager will be expected to hire the shop staff and crew, while the responsibility for hiring positions like designers and performers might fall to someone like the general manager or company manager. When you accept a position as a production manager, you should learn quickly what is expected of you with respect to hiring. Some production managers choose to delegate the hiring of personnel for specific production areas to the heads of each area; for example, the technical director hires the carpenters, and the head electrician hires the light board operator. There is no right or wrong way to handle hiring if the result is that the positions get filled and the best people get hired.

HIRING PROCESS

Depending upon your organization, the hiring process might be decided for you. In the case of a university or other large organization, the hiring process is decided by the human resources department or the like. If you find yourself working at an organization like this, the first important step is to research their process and understand how it works and where you as the "hiring authority" fit in. Typically hiring processes are not given the proper time. They are shoved in and around other work and the pressure to fill a vacant position is tangible. Try to find the right amount of time for the hiring process to take place without placing an undue burden on those who might be filling in until the hire is made.

If you are creating your own hiring process, here are some important steps to follow:

- Writing the job description: It is important to create an honest and detailed job description to entice the right people for the job and lay out the job expectations. The job description should include the job functions, how it fits in the organizational reporting structure, the necessary skills (multitasking, good communication,

DOI: 10.4324/9780367808174-11

cultural competency, etc.), the minimum qualifications (three years of experience in the field, etc.), and any preferred qualifications (i.e. certifications, experience with certain types of equipment). Be careful about overly inflating the requirements. This will limit the number of people who will consider applying for the job. It's become more and more common to remove academic degree requirements altogether from job postings or to list "or commensurate experience" alongside such a requirement. If known, you should include the potential start date and the timeframe for how the hiring process will take place. Make sure the job description also contains application instructions and what application materials are expected (cover letter, resume, references, writing sample, etc.)

- You have an opportunity in the job description to present the organization to the job market and let them know not only what type of people you are looking for but also what type of people work there. You can state your values and the commitments you make to your staff. For example, you can say something along the lines of "This is an anti-racist organization; applicants must have experience doing this work or be ready to engage with the work if hired."

> **TIP** – Whenever possible list the salary range in the job posting. It takes out the guesswork for those considering the job and if they can afford to take the job. It also saves time later if you offer the job to someone down the line and they turn you down because the salary is not one they can work with. Some cities and states now require this so check local codes about listing salaries and asking for salary history from candidates before you begin the process.

> "When organizations aren't transparent about salary ranges, it perpetuates the gender wage-gap; discriminates against BIPOC theatre-makers and drives away potential candidates."
>
> - Theatre Communications Group blog post by Teresa Eyring, Executive Director/CEO and Adrian Budhu, Deputy Director/COO

- Creating a search plan: A well-crafted job description is great, but if it doesn't reach the right people, you will likely not get the response you desire. Give thought to the type of people who might desire this job. Is it an entry-level position or an internship? If so, then marketing this job to college students or recent grads might be the best course of action. You also want to make sure to market to a diverse crowd. By diverse, we don't just mean race, gender, or sexual orientation. You should also look for diversity in areas such as the candidates' background, training, skills, or artistic philosophy. Diversity can lead to a greater range of creative ideas.

Stage Left is a professional theatre looking to ignite conversations and imaginations by producing an eclectic season of professional productions across two mainstages through engaging civic programs, and with inspiring education programs.

At Stage Left, we invite each individual to bring the fullness of their identity and lived experience to their work. As an organization, we are actively working to becoming anti-racist in every facet of our practice. Cultural competence, the ability to interact effectively with people across different cultures, backgrounds, and identities, and an understanding of the principles of anti-racism and anti-oppression are a must.

Stage Left is seeking an A2 - Microphone Technician for its upcoming production of *The Mousetrap*.   Contract dates would be August 24, 2022 – September 26, 2022.

Compensation
$22 per hour plus overtime pay for hours worked over 40 hours in a week.

Vaccination status
This position requires working within a 6-foot radius of a group of people. Proof of vaccination is required.

Key Responsibilities
- Setting up the wireless mic system: setting up the receivers, antennas, and packs for the production
- Mic preparation and maintenance: preparing packs, rigging and coloring mics, checking mics with the Audio Engineer, and distributing and collecting packs.
- Assisting performers with mic placement and checking placement consistency throughout rehearsals and performances.
- Monitoring RF levels and audio signal for all performers during rehearsals and performances.
- Troubleshooting any issues with the mics and providing a solution in a timely fashion.
- Assisting with mic placements during any quick changes
- Assisting the A1, Audio Director, and Design Team as needed.

Key Expectations for Job Performance
- Familiar with Shure Wireless System, and Shure's Wireless Workbench program
- Basic audio system knowledge
- Effective and efficient communication skills
- Ability to work effectively and with sensitivity in a team setting with different personality types
- Good time management skills

Required Competencies
- **Problem Solving:** ability to define problems, establish facts, and draw valid conclusions. Ability to report problems for additional help.
- **Communication:** the ability to communicate transparently and effectively across mediums with an emphasis on interpersonal communication.
- **Relationship Management:** excellent social skills with an emphasis on building and maintaining meaningful and reciprocal internal and external and conflict resolution relationships.
- **Teamwork:** the ability to work well as an enthusiastic member of the production team.
- **Cultural Competency:** an understanding and openness to continue learning of anti-racism and anti-oppression principles and practices, and the ability to interact effectively with people of different cultures and socio-economic backgrounds

Application Instructions
Please submit: your resume, a cover letter (in the medium of your choice), and any additional materials you would like for us to review, to productionjobs@stageleft.org. Please include the position title in the subject line. Submissions are reviewed on a rolling basis.

Submission
To help maintain an equitable process, please do not submit unsolicited candidate recommendations or directly contact the organization regarding this position.

Figure 8.1   Job posting example
Credit: Photo by Cary Gillett

- Publicizing the job posting: Once you have identified the populations you want to reach, get the word out! The job market can be a very competitive one, and you want to get your job posting out as soon as possible to catch the best pool of candidates. There are many ways to spread the news – listing it on your company's website, emailing it out to list serves and your own contacts, posting with trade organizations (United States Institute for Theatre Technology (USITT), Theatre

Communications Group (TCG)/ArtSearch, etc.). Social media can be a huge help, as well. Postings can be easily shared among people even if you only post it once. Don't underestimate the power of word of mouth – start talking to every colleague you meet about your hiring needs; you never know who might be listening or who knows whom.

- Recruit! Sometimes it is not enough to post and email the written job description. You might need to reach out to the community and meet people directly and encourage them to apply. Take this opportunity to meet new people and engage with populations that maybe have not been part of your search plans before.

- Putting together a search committee: As mentioned previously, a differing group of voices and opinions can lead to great success. This is certainly true in the hiring process. Many organizations do not utilize hiring committees, though it should be considered by all. Creating a group of people who will read resumes and conduct interviews allows for a varied response to the candidate pool. In addition to that, think about who in your organization will have the most contact with the new hire, and try to include representation from different areas of your organization. You don't want the committee to be too large, as it might be impossible to find consistent meeting times or come to a consensus.

- Reviewing the resumes and creating the short list: This should not be too hard if you have been specific about what you want in the job description. If candidates do not meet the minimum qualifications, in fairness, they should be removed from the list. Sometimes, at this point, it is necessary to trust your instincts. If the candidate has potential because they are qualified and have appropriate work experience, put them on your short list. Meet with your search committee and get their opinions. They might differ from yours, and that is a good thing. Talk about each candidate, and together make the short list of people who will move on to the interview round. You may want to take a moment at this point in the process to talk with a few of the references of those on your short list to make sure they are the type of people you are looking for. See more on reference checking later in this chapter.

- Making an interview plan: If you have a few candidates on your short list (under four) then it is time for in-person interviews. However, if the short list is still a little long, perhaps a round of phone or video conference interviews is the best next step. Once those are done, pare down the list again and set up the in-person interviews. You should consider what you plan to do with the candidate other than meet with them face-to-face. Perhaps a tour of your facilities and/or a meeting or lunch with others on your staff is a good idea. If you are hiring them to conduct a specific type of work, you may wish to see them complete this work or give a presentation. It is important to share the interview plan and schedule with the candidates, so they come prepared.

- Preparing the interview questions: For best comparative data, you should ask every candidate the same set of questions. Devise the questions ahead of time, giving careful thought to what kind of information you need to know. Do not ask questions that can be answered by looking at a resume. Ask questions that give you insight as to how the candidate will work for and with you and your organization/project. You should be aware that it is not appropriate to ask questions of a personal nature that do not have bearing on the job. Topics such as religion, sexual orientation, family, childcare, etc., are illegal to bring up and should be avoided.

- Conducting the interview: If you have thoroughly planned the interview experience and clearly prepared the candidates, the interview should run very smoothly. Make sure to have time for the candidate to ask you questions. They are interviewing you as much as you are interviewing them. The decision to take a new job, especially if it is a full-time job or a relocation, is a big decision. Make sure you take plenty of notes. After only a few interviews, the candidates can begin to run together. Though you should stick to your list of pre-determined questions, do not be afraid to ask follow-ups based on a person's response or work experience. Take time to get to know the candidate. (Check out the companion website for interview and reference check question examples.)

- Checking references: This is an important step that should not be skipped for any reason and could happen at any point in the hiring process, or at a few points. A good interview might only mean that the candidate is good at interviewing and telling you what you want to hear. Talking with people who have worked with and/or supervised the candidate is an important step to understanding how well they will fit in your organization. You should only contact the references they have listed. If you wish to speak with someone of their reference list, you must ask permission first. It's quite possible that the candidate has not told their current employer that they are searching for a new job. You don't want to put the candidate in a difficult position.

- Background checks and drug testing: Certain employers will require these to take place before someone is hired. It's important to make this clear to the applicants early in the process.

- Deciding whom to hire: This can be the hardest step of them all. The final decision on whom to hire should be a careful consideration of all you have gathered about the person – their qualifications, previous work, attitude, personality, work ethic, etc. Again – trust your instincts. Hopefully, the decision will be clear, but if not, don't be afraid to give it some time, and maybe speak to the top candidates again or ask to speak to more references. Don't rush to hire. Bad hire is not only a drain on your organization but might also require you to go back through this whole hiring process again! Once you have selected the person to hire, the process of negotiating the terms of their employment is the next step. More on that later in this chapter.

- Communicating with those not selected: With the success of one candidate comes the necessity of letting others know they were not chosen. If you have had personal connection with a candidate, it is proper to contact them directly to let them know of the choice that was made. The phone is usually best; email is to be avoided. It's important to be honest yet supportive, as this could be hard news for the candidate to receive. If the candidate asks for feedback on their interview or for reasons why they were not selected, be as honest as you feel comfortable being. It's best to keep these conversations short and sweet.

FREELANCE HIRES

Many organizations do not have enough work to justify hiring full-time year-round employees and choose instead to hire part-time employees when extra help is needed. This is the same when hiring positions like designers or crew who are needed for only one show or event. Hiring freelance can be a different process. You are looking for the best person for the job, the one who can accomplish the tasks you need in the time you have allotted. "Fit" within the organization might not be as important, as this person is only expected to be with you for a short period of time. Of course, you want to hire trustworthy, honest people, and you do need to consider personalities that will work well together. However, it's not a long-term hire, so the stakes are different. It may be less important to vet these people in the same way as a full-time employee, with a search committee, presentation, or staff interaction. At minimum, you should expect to see their resume, have a conversation with them (ideally in person) and speak to a reference (or references). Don't hire people if you don't know anything about them!

HIRING VENDORS AND INDEPENDENT CONTRACTORS

If you are a small company without a production staff or you have a large event or production that will require additional personnel, there are many companies that can provide services to you. There are commercial scene shops, as well as lighting, audio/ video, and labor companies. There are also individuals who are "jobbed-in" to build costumes, props, and other specialty items. If you are located in a metropolitan area, chances are good there is help near you. Here are some helpful tips:

- Knowing whom to select: Word-of-mouth is most helpful. Talk to your production management network and find out what companies they have used and if they received positive results. We have included a list of vendors on the companion website that meet our stamp of approval.

- Asking for a bid/proposal: Regardless of whether you work for a large or small organization, it is recommended that you create a request for proposal (RFP). Creating an RFP will help you as you search for what you need from several companies or providers. The RFP details exactly what is needed and the time frame you will need it in. It also spells out who the vendor will report to at your organization and what communication and interaction between your company and the vendor are expected. If the service needed requires the building or installation of an item or system, you will want to include explicit details, which may include drawings or plans.

- Selecting the best vendor or contractor: Once the bids/proposals are in, you'll have to look at each very carefully. Are they able to do what you require in the time frame you need and for the amount you can afford to spend? This is another great opportunity to connect with your production management network and get opinions, especially if they have worked with this company or individual before.

- Following up: once the selection has been made and you have negotiated a contract, you will need to stay in touch with your selected vendor to make sure the work is progressing appropriately. It's likely the work may not happen on your premises, so find opportunities to connect with the vendor and see the progress of the work. You can do this by asking them to stop by with the items and paying a visit to where the service is occurring, or, at minimum, you could ask for photos of the work.

> **TIP** – When possible, support local businesses. Don't rush the process and take time to learn about them. It might be worth it, in the long run spending a little more to hire a company that could use the business and aligns with your values.

CASTING AND AUDITIONS

Not all production managers will be expected to oversee the audition and casting process. In some cases, it falls to a casting director or even a stage manager. However, it is important to know how they are organized and administrated.

Here are the steps to a successful audition process:

- Identifying the type of auditions:
  - Are these auditions for one event or for an entire season?
  - Is it a dance concert, musical, opera or a play?
  - What roles/types of performers are you looking for?
  - Are the auditions open for anyone to attend or by appointment or invitation only?
- Creating the schedule:
  - Who will be auditioning and when are they available?
  - When are you likely to get the best attendance?
  - What venue are you using for the auditions, and when is it available?
- Planning for audition format:
  - Will the auditions be one-at-a-time, or will they be in groups?
  - Should those auditioning come prepared with material or learn material at the auditions, or will there be cold readings?
  - Will there be sides (selections from the script) provided?
  - Are you auditioning for a musical or opera? Will you need to arrange for a piano accompanist?
  - Will there be a dance component? Do you need mirrors in the room? Sound system? Ballet barre?
- Promoting the auditions: Once you have answered the questions above, you can begin to promote the audition. It's best to create an audition posting that includes all of the information – dates, times, locations, expectations, details on the shows, etc. Also, make sure those auditioning know what to bring with them – headshot, resume, dance clothes, sheet music, etc. If there is a script they are expected to read, let them know where they can access it. Once the posting is made, you can begin to circulate it to places where performers will see it – email lists, casting websites, your organization's website, social media, newspapers, post fliers, etc.

SCHOOL of THEATRE DANCE
PERFORMANCE STUDIES

SPRING 2015 THEATRE AUDITIONS

The Human Capacity

Written by Jennifer Barclay
Directed by Michael Dove

AUDITIONS: Sunday, September 21st, 12-3pm in Cafritz Foundation Theatre (2740)
Monday, September 22nd, 4-7pm in Cafritz Foundation Theatre (2740)
CALLBACKS: Wednesday, October 1st, 4-7pm Schoenbaum Rehearsal Room (3732)

Set in East Berlin, both before and after the fall of the Wall, *The Human Capacity* follows the journey of a Stasi officer as he seeks redemption from the woman whose life he shattered. Both torturer and victim find themselves caught in a struggle to reconcile the horrors of their past with their hopes for the future. The play is a searing look into a society and a family in turmoil, and an exploration of the human capacity for cruelty, perseverance and forgiveness.

Prepare:

- 2 minute dramatic monologue

Roles available for 7 performers – 4 Males & 3 Females
Performance Dates: May 2 – May 9, 2015 in the Kogod Theatre
First Rehearsal: March 23rd, 2015

Eligibility Requirements
In order to be eligible to audition for TDPS productions, students must meet the following criteria:
1. Maintain a minimum overall GPA of 2.7
2. Uphold the University Honor Code
3. Be in good academic standing with the University
Being a part of a TDPS production is a privilege, not a right. We trust each student to behave and act accordingly.

What to Bring: Resume and Headshot
Sign-up Sheets: Posted on 3rd floor callboard – across from Schoenbaum (3732)
Script are now on reserve at the Performing Arts Library

Please contact Cary Gillett with any questions or concerns
301.405.1623 or cgillett@umd.edu

Figure 8.2 Audition posting example
Credit: Photo by Cary Gillett

TIP – Take the time to make sure all the postings are correct! It would be unfortunate if you were prepared for auditions on Saturday and the posting says Sunday. It would be equally challenging if your website says the audition started at 12 p.m. and you were planning for 2 p.m.

AUDITION FORM

Name: _____

Address: _____

Phone: _____   Email: _____

Gender: _____   Ethnicity: _____

Union Affiliations: _____

Do you speak any other languages besides English? Yes ☐ No ☐

If so, what language? _____

Do you play a musical instrument? Yes ☐ No ☐

If so, what instrument? _____

Audition Selection: _____

_____

Medical Conditions/Allergies: _____

_____

Do you wear glasses? ☐ contacts? ☐

Are you right handed? ☐ left handed? ☐

Emergency Contact Information

Name: _____

Relationship: _____

Phone: _____

_____

Please list any conflicts you may have from August – October 2015:

_____

_____

_____

_____

PLEASE PRINT NEATLY

Figure 8.3 Audition form example
Credit: Photo by Cary Gillett

- Creating an audition form: You have an opportunity to gather quite a bit of information from those auditioning. Make a form for them to fill out that includes contact information, emergency information, personal information (do they wear glasses, right/left-handed, etc.). This is also the best opportunity to ask about any conflicts they might have for the period of employment.

- Prepping the site for the audition: On the day of the auditions, you should take time before people start arriving to set up the space properly. Outside the audition room, there should be a place for people to check in and drop off their headshot and resume as well as a place for them to sit and fill out the audition form. Inside the room, things should be clean and tidy. There should be a place for those conducting the auditions to sit and perhaps a table at which to jot down notes and an extension cord so they can plug in laptops or other devices. The table should be away from the entrance, so the auditionee can come right in and begin, as opposed to awkwardly crossing past the table to get to their audition spot. Finally, you need a place for those auditioning to perform – dance floor, open space for a monologue, etc.

- Running the audition: Someone needs to greet performers when they arrive, sign them in, and make sure all the necessary paperwork is filled out and collected. This person should also act as a timekeeper to keep the auditions running on schedule. If you are running the audition, speak to the director, choreographer, or whoever is judging the audition about how they would like to administrate the auditions and how best to stay on time.

- Holding callbacks: Often one round of auditions is not enough, and a second round of auditions, termed callbacks, is necessary. To set up the callback, repeat many of the steps above – determine the schedule, figure out what will occur at the callbacks, communicate the plan to those auditioning and judging, set up the room, etc.

- Deciding the cast: Once the artistic team has decided whom they want to cast, the process of negotiating the terms of their employment is the next step.

- Archiving the audition material: When the auditions are over, don't lose track of the valuable information you collected. Headshots, resumes, and auditions forms should be filed away for future reference. The director/choreographer might want copies of them, too.

NEGOTIATIONS

Once the right person for the job or role has been decided, the next step is to hire them. Often, it is the production manager who is responsible for contacting potential hires and negotiating salary and the terms of their contract. Negotiating can be a tricky thing, and some people feel uncomfortable doing it, but it is a normal part of the hiring process and should be embraced. As a future employer, it's important to understand what you have to offer in terms of money, benefits, or incentives before you contact the potential hire. Members of unions (such as the Actors' Equity Association) often have a minimum they must be paid and other fees such as health and pension contributions that are requirements. Do your homework and know what those requirements are before entering the negotiation process. (More on unions later in this chapter.)

The initial conversation with the future employee should include the exact details of the job they are being hired to do – schedule, expectations, outcome, salary offer, and benefits (if applicable). Be prepared for the potential hire to not give you a decision immediately. The recipient might need to consider the offer and talk it over with friends or family. You should expect they will need some time, but you should offer a deadline by when you need a decision. Set a time a few days from the initial conversation when you will communicate again.

The next communication could play out in one of three ways – they accept the terms presented, they decline, or they ask for different terms. If they are looking for different terms, it is usually because they wish to ask for more compensation. Now, it's your turn to decide. Is this person worth the money? Do you have the money to spend? You may need a day or two to make that decision and may have to speak to your collaborators or supervisors about the feasibility of the request. Don't let too much time pass before contacting the potential hire again. When you connect with them, there are the same three options – you agree to the request, you deny the request and choose not to hire them, or you give a counteroffer. The counteroffer should be above your original offer but not as high as their request. Usually, at this point, a decision between both parties can be made, but in some cases an additional round of negotiations is necessary.

If you are hiring artists, you might need to negotiate with an agent or other third party. If this is so, you will not talk directly to the artist; instead, the agent takes the role of the intermediary and will communicate with you and the artist separately. The negotiation process is essentially identical to what was previously described, but you will need to allow more time for the agent to contact the artist, talk over the terms, and then get back to you. Be aware that an agent gets a percentage of the artist's compensation, so it behoves the agent to negotiate for as much money as possible. Do not be afraid to be honest when enough is enough and you have reached the top salary you have available. It is still quite possible that the artist will accept the job.

Money is not the only term that can be negotiated. If the person will have to relocate for this job (permanently or temporarily), then you should discuss such things as additional funds for travel, shipping of personal items, housing, and per diem. You might also need to discuss other things such as vacation days, benefits, parking, and equipment (i.e. computers). Some artists will request a special listing, or billing, in marketing materials and programs.

Favoured Nations (or Most Favoured Nations) is a somewhat common negotiation agreement in which artists request equal terms with any other similar artist on the same production. These terms can be money or other resources previously mentioned. According to the Actor's Equity Association website: "The Favoured Nations rider has been utilized as a tool by an actor and his/her representative to ensure that no one else in the company (primarily, someone having the same stature or playing the same size role) was getting a better deal. It also became a means of allowing an actor who would normally command a large salary to work for a lower salary without cheapening that actor's value. For example, an experienced actor who would normally be paid higher than minimum might choose to do a role in a not-for-profit theatre which cannot afford to pay more than minimum, and by including the Favoured Nations rider the actor, in essence, says to the commercial entertainment world: 'I still don't work for minimum, but in this particular situation I'm willing to as long as I know that no one else is being paid more than I am.'" [1] This clause can also be used by designers.

HIRING CHILDREN

Every state in the USA has different laws on hiring children. If you find yourself with a show or event that requires the use of someone under the age of 18, it's best to begin exploring the process as soon as possible. In most cases, you will need to file an application with the state government justifying why you need to use this person and how you plan to schedule their time and compensate them. The child will not be able to begin working until this application is approved and a permit is secured. Once it is approved, the permit must be kept on-site wherever the child is working in case inquiries are made. Visit the US Department of Labor website for more information – www.dol.gov.

> **TIP** – In some cases, adults working with minors are required to undergo a background check to ensure safety for all involved.

Each state also has different views on the supervision of minors. In some cases, the parents will need to remain on site when the child is working. In other cases, they can be dropped off and left in the care of an employee. It's best to hire a "child guardian" if you are working with one, and especially more than one, child. This person's sole responsibility is to make sure the children do their job and remain safe and engaged. Their job begins where others' jobs end – stage management, company management, wardrobe, hair/makeup, etc. There is no pre-determined ratio of guardian to minors, but many camps require one adult for every five children, so that is a good rule of thumb to follow.

> On Broadway, it is a requirement to hire a child guardian for any show with one or more minors in the cast. These employees are members of Local 764—the wardrobe union. The collective bargaining agreement (CBE) took a year to negotiate and was put into effect in 2012.
>
> - From an interview with Jill Valentine, Child Guardian on Broadway

CONTRACTS AND RIDERS

Once the hiring process and negotiations are done, it's time to build the contract. If the person you are hiring is a member of a union (see more information about unions later in this chapter), you must use the contract provided by that union, which dictates what information you need to include. If the person is not a member of a union, you may create your own contract. Here are some items that should be included and some tips on how to craft the language:

- Information about the company and the person being hired: If your company has letterhead, it should be utilized. If not, make sure you list the organizational details such as name, address, phone numbers, etc. Also include the information of the person being hired. At a minimum, you should include their name and address.

- Terms of service: Include what job they are being hired to do. If it's for a specific show, you should list the name of that show. If applicable, include a detailed list of their job duties. Include when they are expected to report to work for the first time and what other dates they should be onsite, as well as the end date when their services are to be completed. If this is not explicitly known, you can list a date range, but it's best to be specific about what is expected. Include what deliverables are expected of them. In the case of a designer, this might be drawings, renderings, or a model. The more specific you can be with the contract, the more it can help you later if there is a dispute over the job expectations.

- Compensation: List the exact pay breakdown and a schedule for the delivery of payments. The schedule might be specific dates or when certain tasks are accomplished (such as one-third payment upon signing of this agreement, one-third payment upon first rehearsal, and one-third payment upon closing of the production). Make sure to list compensated terms that were agreed on beyond fees, such as travel, housing, per diem, relocation expenses, etc. Make sure to include any other items that were negotiated beyond money, such as complimentary tickets, pension plans, health benefits, billing in publicity materials, etc.

- Future life of the project: If there is a chance that the project could continue past the timeline of the contract, many people will expect a clause called "right of first refusal." This states that if the project is remounted or reconceived, the signee has the right to be asked first to reprise their role/position before others are asked.

> The Actor's Equity Association's League of Resident Theatres (LORT) contract has a right of first refusal clause built in if there is a chance the production could move to Broadway. The contract dictates that if an offer to continue with the show is not made, the actor will receive four weeks contractual salary. The Stage Director's and Choreographer's Society requires a payment of 50% of the original salary if the right of first refusal is not offered.[2]

- Legal language: Many companies and individuals require or request language in the contract dealing with cancellation, arbitration, liability, force majeure, disputes, and termination. All this language is legalese for "protect your backside." No one wants things to go wrong, but sometimes they do, and you will want to agree upfront how those challenges will be handled. With this and any other legal situation, it is best to speak with a lawyer before committing to anything or signing the contract.

- Expectation of when the contract should be completed: In most cases, you want the contract back immediately. If it stays unsigned for too long, that usually means something is wrong. It's best to request the contract back within one week. It's also useful to link the completion of the contract to the first payment, which often encourages its return.

- Signatures: As the creator of the contract, your company should sign first before it is sent off. By doing so, it is saying that you stand behind what is written on the contract and are ready to make a commitment. Make sure you know who in your organization has signing privileges for contracts. You might not have this authority; it could be a producer or artistic director or another person in upper management.

- Riders: A contract rider can be utilized if you need to make an addition to a standard union contract or if a contract has already been signed and something changes.

> The Actors' Equity Association requires riders if you are asking a performer to do something out of the ordinary such as perform nude, do stunts, and/or move scenery. A rider can also be used to agree to additional compensation for situations such as the use of personal clothing onstage or additional duties such as serving as dance or fight captain. Always check the union rulebook to identify what is worthy of a rider and how it should be formulated.

In some situations, you may be on the receiving end of a contract. This is sometimes the case if you employ a company to provide a service or if an individual has their own contract that they request to use. It's important to make sure all the information mentioned previously is included; when in doubt, let your company's lawyer read it before signing it.

UNIONS

There are several unions that production managers may come into contact with as part of their job. Here are brief descriptions of the major ones.

- *Actors' Equity Association (AEA)* is the union of actors and stage managers in the United States. They focus on theatrical stage productions and, in some cases, corporate productions. There is also an Actors' Equity in England, but they are two separate unions. (www.actorsequity.org)

- *American Guild of Musical Artists (AGMA)* is the labor organization that represents opera singers, choral musicians, and dancers, primarily ballet. (www.musicalartists.org)

- *Screen Actors Guild/American Federation of Television and Radio Artists (SAG/ AFTRA)* is the union of performers and personalities in movies, TV, and radio. (www.sagaftra.org)

- *Stage Directors and Choreographers Society (SDC)* is what its title states and is specific to stage performances. (www.sdcweb.org)

- *United Scenic Artists (USA)* is primarily a designer's union, though it does cover certain allied crafts people. Its members work in TV, film, industrials, and special events in the United States. (www.usa829.org)
- *International Alliance of Theatrical Stage Employees (IATSE)* is the "behind the scenes" union and serves stage, TV, and film productions. It covers positions such as stagehands, crafts people, board ops, and wardrobe. Hiring and contracts are broken down into specializations based on skill. As its title suggests, it is a worldwide union. (www.iatse.net)
- *American Federation of Musicians (AFM)* covers professional musicians in the United States and Canada. (www.afm.org)

> **TIP** – Some unions have local offices for different regions. The International Alliance of Theatrical Stage Employees (IATSE) and the American Federation of Musicians (AFM) are two such examples. Make sure you check in with the local offices before hiring members of these unions to understand different rules or regulations they may have and how that could affect hiring and workload.

Note that each of these unions has different agreements depending upon the size and/or location of the producing organization and that the contract requirements will vary based on which agreement applies to your company. Each union has different rules about minimum payments, pensions and health contributions, travel and housing requirements, additional fees, etc. They also have various agreements about working conditions, length of workday, and employment. You will need to research these unions if you foresee yourself working with any of them. Each has a very useful website that can be a great starting point. It's also not a bad idea to call and speak to someone from the union if you have questions. If your company is contracted to any of these organizations, the union contract should be available to you to have as a reference.

At the time this second edition was published, 28 of the 50 United States follow a "right to work" law that gives citizens the right to work for a living without having to join a union. Anyone is free to unionize, but there cannot be collective bargaining agreements and you do not need to join a union to be employed. In these states, some workers choose to join a union, as it offers health and pension benefits as well as a way into the business if they are new to the area. Some production managers say that union labor is often more qualified, so they choose to spend the extra money, as they feel it is worth it. Often shows will be staffed with union and non-union members. Everyone on the backstage crew can work across departments (lights, sound, props, etc.), which is often not the case in a full union IATSE house. The venue can set its own rules about what is and is not acceptable, and you do not need to have a union crew present for every use of the space. For example, you would not need to bring in a union electrician simply to turn on the lights for a tour of the theatre.

> "Collective bargaining is the process in which working people, through their unions, negotiate contracts with their employers to determine their terms of employment, including pay, benefits, hours, leave, job health and safety policies, ways to balance work and family, and more. Collective bargaining is a way to solve workplace problems. It is also the best means for raising wages in America. Indeed, through collective bargaining, working people in unions have higher wages, better benefits and safer workplaces."
>
> - AFL-CIO website
> - https://aflcio.org/what-unions-do/empower-workers/collective-bargaining

PERSONNEL MANAGEMENT

The work of a manager is not done once the person is hired. Part of your management responsibility will require orienting, training, and evaluating your hires, as well as supervising their compliance with employment expectations.

- Orientation and training: An efficient and friendly process for initiating employees will help your organization. Take the time to orient your new staff members to their surroundings. In the employee's first couple of weeks, schedule meetings, lunches, and tours with people whom they will interact with in their position. Meet with new employees on a regular basis during their first few months on the job to talk about their transition. It may also be necessary to put new employees through training sessions. Training can happen right as someone starts or later in their tenure. Make a point to budget for employee training so you are ready to accommodate any need.

- Professional development: Many employees need development to get them to produce at their top potential. As employees grow and thrive in their positions, the overall organization benefits. Look for opportunities to help your employees grow. This could be skill-based classes, certifications, conference visits, etc. Professional development is best when it is encouraged organizationally and tailored to each employee. Include employees in deciding what kind of development opportunity they should engage in. In your budgeting process, make sure funds are available to support development – travel, housing, conference fees, class tuition, per diem, etc.

> "To keep good artisans, you have to make sure they stay current. If anyone on our staff wants to take a class or brush up their skills, we work very hard to support them. We also partner with the union to train people on new equipment, like light boards. It's so important to invest in your local artists and crafts people."
>
> - Tracy Utzmyers, Production Manager at The Muny in St. Louis

- Performance reviews: Some organizations make it a requirement to meet with staff members at certain times of the year to discuss their job performance and to set goals for them in the future. Even if this is not your organization's policy, you should do it anyway. Producing shows and events is time-consuming work, and it is easy to get wrapped up in the tasks at hand. It's very important to take a moment to talk one-on-one with your staff members about how they are coping with their jobs. This is also a good time to share your impressions of their work and interactions with other employees. A great way to begin this conversation is to ask the employee to write a self-assessment. This way, you can see before the meeting what they think of their work and their role in the organization. This can often guide the conversation, especially if assessments differ.

- Resolving disputes: Let's face it. Not everyone will get along. There will be problems between people, and you will need to solve the dispute. It's important in situations like this to remain neutral and hear all sides. Sometimes, you will need to help resolve the dispute by making a decision. Other times, it might be best to get out of the way and encourage the two factions to solve their own problem. Conflict can be scary, and many people fear it. When working with human beings, conflict is unavoidable, so don't avoid it. If you are one who fears conflict, seek some professional development to help you address your concerns.

- Setting policies and procedures: If the positions you hire do the same type of work regularly, it may be important to establish policies and procedures for your company. This is even more important if you work with part-time staff or have a lot of turnover so that everyone working for you knows how things should operate. A policy is a course of action adopted firmly by your group – e.g., "we only use rigging equipment manufactured by these three companies." A procedure is a course of action that we follow – e.g., "we inspect all rigging weekly to determine if it's safe and usable." Firmly setting these may be a group project with your staff. You will want guidance from experts on your staff, and policies and procedures are adhered to better when everyone is invested in their creation and feels that they are necessary. Once policies and procedures are established, you should document them, communicate them, and post them where everyone has access. Nothing is worse than creating a policy and then finding out that it has not been followed because people were not aware of it.

- Comp time: The work we do is rarely 9-to-5. Full-time production staff members are often asked to work odd hours that fluctuate within any given week, depending upon the project and stage of development. The build of a show might be a 9 a.m. to 5 p.m., 40-hour-a-week situation, but technical rehearsals sometimes require up to 80 hours in a week. The concept of compensated time or "comp time" is one that allows salaried employees to balance the time worked in those busy periods with not-so-busy periods. Some organizations establish an official policy on comp time – for example, an hour of overtime worked this week equals an hour you can take off at another point. Some organizations are less strict and consider requests of this nature on a case-by-case basis. Give some thought to how you will handle this with your staff, and clearly communicate any comp time policy.

- Labor laws: United States federal and state governments have workplace laws that cover items such as safety, wages, benefits, protection, leave, etc. If you are unfamiliar with these laws, learn about them. We have included some helpful links on the companion website.

- Working with the human resources department: Some production managers are lucky to work for an organization that has a human resources (HR) manager. Get to know this department well, as you can rely on them for personnel challenges or questions. They will become a necessary ally and invaluable resource for you. Make sure to document any performance reviews and/or disciplinary meetings with employees and file them with the HR department. They keep a file on every employee of the organization.

- Legal issues: If legal issues arise – talk to a lawyer! If topics such as sexual harassment or discrimination come up, or if there is a concern that laws are being broken, talk to a lawyer! You should not attempt to solve these problems on your own. As always, if you don't know something, find someone who does and ask questions.

TOP THREE TAKEAWAYS

- Production managers are only as good as the people on their team.

- The process of filling a position is a lengthy and challenging one with lots of things to consider for both the employer and the candidate. It should not be approached lightly.

- Whenever possible, take your time and make the best choices you can. Trust your instincts and maybe a few tips from this chapter!

NOTES

1   "Are You a Favored Nation?" *Actors Equity*. http://www.actorsequity.org/newsmedia/misc/FavoredNation.asp

2   "Actor's Equity Association League of Resident Theatre Agreement." *Actors Equity*. http://www.actorsequity.org/docs/rulebooks/LORT_Rulebook_13-17.pdf

Safety

> "Safety is everyone's responsibility. It's going to take collective work. Safety needs to be a part of the culture and have a presence beyond just people."
>
> - Anna Glover, David Geffen School of Drama at Yale/Yale Repertory Theatre

The safety, health, and welfare of people engaged in work or employment is the responsibility of the organization in which they work. In performing arts and special events, it is often the production manager's responsibility to oversee this very important area. This doesn't mean it is solely the production manager's responsibility; everyone has a role in safety. Oftentimes, the technical director is involved, overseeing the safe construction of scenery or rigging installations, as well as writing and maintaining the shop manual for the safe use of tools. Other times, it can be a stage manager looking for hazards on and around the stage. The bottom line is that safety is everyone's responsibility, and this chapter will look at the various ways production managers can effectively mitigate the risks and hazards in the work we do.

OCCUPATIONAL SAFETY

One of the main entities that you will have to have a strong understanding of regarding safety is the Occupational Safety and Health Administration (www.osha.gov).

Congress established a law and provided the Occupational Safety and Health Act of 1970. Known as the OSH Act, it was passed to prevent workers from being killed or seriously harmed at work, as workplace conditions were becoming overly dangerous. While it varies from state to state, most states follow the "General Industry Standards 1910" guidelines and you, as a production manager, should familiarize yourself with

DOI: 10.4324/9780367808174-12

Figure 9.1
Credit: Photo by Bill Geenen

that, at the very least. Under this OSH Act of 1970, it is made clear that employers are responsible for the safety and must provide a workplace that is free of hazards for the worker.

The act also created the Occupational Safety and Health Administration (OSHA), which sets and enforces protective workplace safety and health standards. Additionally, OSHA assures safe and healthful workplaces by setting and enforcing standards and by providing training, outreach, education, and assistance. As an additional protection for employees, workers may file a complaint to have OSHA inspect their workplace if they believe that their employer is not following OSHA standards or that there are serious hazards. Employers must comply, by law, with all applicable OSHA standards. Employers must also comply with the General Duty Clause of the OSH Act, which requires employers to keep their workplace free of serious recognized hazards. There are two acts of OSHA that are relevant here. One that says you must provide a workplace free of hazards (such as a theatre scenic unit with multiple levels) and one that says you will keep your workplace (like a scene shop or costume shop) free of hazards and perform regular training sessions for staff and employees.

The fact is that you can't possibly be responsible for keeping EVERYONE safe ALL the time. It is everyone's responsibility. It is also the responsibility of individual to keep themselves safe by not performing unsafe tasks during the course of their time at work! The bottom line is that you, as a production manager, should do everything within your power to assure a safe and healthy working environment.

Figure 9.2   The College-Conservatory of Music at the University of Cincinnati
Credit: Photo by Adam Zeek – www.zeekcreative.com

"Assess everything so you know how to train."

- Nancy Mallette, Senior Director,
Exhibition Engineering at Meow Wolf

ASSESSING

By assessing, you are documenting knowledge, skills, attitudes, and beliefs of situations or circumstances ahead of time. By assessing, you also analyze procedures in place that keep people safe. Before you expose any artist or staff member to the workplace, the law requires that you assess hazards in advance. We shouldn't build a piece of scenery without knowing the risks involved to the actor or crew. That becomes part of the assessment and verification. (You can't wait for someone to get hurt and THEN evaluate whether or not the scenery was safe!) Bill Reynolds, Former Head of Safety at the David Geffen School of Drama at Yale/Yale Repertory Theatre, agrees and says that "by doing the safety inspection of scenery, rigging, etc. we are verifying that the safety concerns at hand have been properly addressed. It really is an ongoing risk assessment that has to happen with all technical managers and the production manager and production stage manager."

Having these items assessed also gives you an opportunity to understand your staff's level of training in current safety standards. Proper staff training gives you the ability to have many sets of eyes looking at a particular circumstance. If someone sees a potential problem, we must train staff on how to mitigate it, which means lessening force or intensity of the situation at hand. The question becomes how to train, document, assess, and mitigate and how to get staff to understand the importance of these tasks mentioned.

TRAINING

One of the biggest jeopardies in a workplace is the people (we CAN hurt each other); therefore, training becomes primary. Not just handing someone a manual but establishing a protocol for safety in all areas becomes the main focal point for the production manager. Having training sessions or discussions on one topic can oftentimes become the launching pad for other discussions on safety. For instance, a safety discussion on hanging scenery can quickly become a training session in using fall protection, or working on an aerial lift platform, or proper ways to lift weights for the fly rail. A discussion of fire extinguishers can become a discussion about having an evacuation plan in place.

There is no single way to do safety training. It is based on the environment and the potential hazards or risks of that particular situation. Staff training in various life-saving techniques can also be a big plus toward achieving your goals with OSHA, which does have some minimum standards in regard to documenting training. Is your staff adequately trained in CPR, first aid, or blood-borne pathogen response? What about your house managers? Your stage managers? Do you have a defibrillator in the lobby? Has the staff been trained to use a defibrillator? The list goes on, and, as you can see, it makes sense from a safety standpoint to have these leadership roles have some type of certification on their resume, especially those that are close to a large public gathering. Senior management should get involved, too, as safety is everyone's responsibility. They can help to decide who gets trained where. Perhaps the technical director is well-versed in first aid and addressing minor cuts and abrasions. Stage management would be best suited with CPR and first aid due to their proximity to the actors and crew. Every scenario will be different, and each circumstance will need to be individually addressed in order to best come up with that plan for OSHA. Plan on assessing your own situation and decide what level of training might be necessary for your venue or company. If you are in an academic situation, perhaps it is time to consider this as part of the academic mission of your school.

Discussions on safety can become an aspect of the educational environment. Reynolds states: "At Yale, the staff that is involved with the production process at the highest level possible should have the training of what is considered 'best practices in the industry.' Stage manager, production manager, producer ... all should be trained in best practices of safety. It becomes part of the curriculum. We do shows as part of our academic mission. We should include safety as part of that. Safety isn't something 'in addition' to what we do. It IS what we do."

DOCUMENTATION

Documentation of training sessions becomes a key factor for the production manager. According to Nancy Mallette, former health and safety manager for Cirque du Soleil, it means everything: "I can't tell you enough how important it is to document what takes place in a training session. If you went over rigging, write down the day and date and what was covered. You should also document the name of the person doing the training and keep it all in a file in case you ever need it for reference."

You must document an injury if they ever happen under your watch as companies with more than ten employees are now required to maintain an OSHA Form 300 (Injury & Illness Log). This law went into effect in 2005 and production managers must contend with having additional, but very necessary, paperwork. Included in the law are requirements for timely reporting (documenting) of work-related hospitalizations and fatalities. Performing arts companies are included in the list of industries that must report an annual OSHA Form 300A, and it must now be submitted through the Injury Tracking Application https://www.osha.gov/injuryreporting for 2022, the reporting window for 2021 data was from January 2 through March 2.

All of this documentation of work can and will become indispensable for you, especially in the case of an OSHA investigation of a work-related injury. Here is an example:

Let's say an actor slips off a step unit and breaks an ankle. OSHA gets involved and will begin an investigation, and you, the production manager, will become a prime candidate for questions. They may ask you something like: "When YOU investigated the accident, what were the findings of the root cause of the injury?" (If you didn't even investigate the accident, it will imply to OSHA that you don't take it seriously, which won't help your cause!) Another investigative question may be "when was the set last inspected, and how did you document that inspection?" Having the inspection reports available in your reference file becomes a huge factor in how OSHA will treat the situation. Mallette agrees and says that "the more documentation you have with someone's signature on it, the more OSHA understands that you are assuming the responsibility of keeping your staff safe."

If OSHA showed up, your documentation should include the following:

- Dates of when the set/stage platform was built
- Photos of the platform and photos of the step off the platform.
- Some documentation on how/why the technical director engineered and built the platform and step the way they did
- Dates of when you trained the actor how to safely step down off the platform
- Dates of when you rehearsed that part of the show (the step down off the platform)

> This is a perfect example of why good, accurate information should be coming out of the stage management department in the form of rehearsal reports or accident reports. Have a discussion with stage management about the importance of documentation. This documentation also proves verification that issues have been discussed.

If you, as the production manager, have all of this information at your fingertips, your interview with OSHA will go better than if you do not. By doing the above minimums, you have shown a willful attempt that you, in advance, care about your actors

Figure 9.3
Credit: Photo by Bill Geenen

and thought about their well-being. Remember, accidents do happen, but OSHA is looking for facts that reasonable precautions have been taken. It is in your power as the production manager to make that happen.

ASSESSING THE SHOPS

What other precautions can we take as production managers to help us show everyone, including OSHA, that you care about your employees? You should start with a self-guided tour. Go watch the costume shop use toxic dyes and other hazardous materials so that you really understand the possible risks involved. Look around when you do this. Is there personal protective equipment (PPE) in the shop? Are proper eye protection and breathing respirators available for the number of staff members involved with the project? What other common-sense precautions can you come up with? How about fire extinguishers near the dye vat in case of an unforeseen fire or small chemical explosion? What about a chemical spill on the floor of the costume shop? As you can start to see, the questions you may be asked by OSHA are many.

Now take a walk around the scene shop and observe the use of power tools, among other activities taking place. Is there a first aid kit in the shop? Check their content to make sure they are properly stocked and that nothing has expired. Is there personal protective equipment (PPE) around the shop? How about eye protection for those using cutting and sanding tools, and is it being worn? Is hearing protection necessary for the use of the tool? If so, are there disposable foam earplugs within reach of the tools? How about people working above ground? Do you know the rules of what height proper harnesses should be worn when working above ground? (Every state may be different, so check your OSHA website.)

The paint shop is another area that needs serious safety attention. OSHA regulations can be very strict with regard to paints and adhesives and other scenic materials. Have the brushes been cleaned or disposed of properly? Is paint being stored properly? What about eye protection and respiratory gear for the painters?

> In some states, like California, merely leaving the lids off the paint can when done can trigger some severe monetary fines. No production manager ever wants to pay a fine to OSHA!

Once you have completed your shop tours, take a moment to reflect on all of the areas where you think you can make improvements to safety or accident reduction. Work with your shop heads to make sure you have the proper equipment in place. If you don't already have a safety manual or "standard operating procedures" (SOP) manual, this may be your opportunity as a production manager to write one with your management staff. As mentioned earlier, safety is everyone's business, and everyone on the production team and in the acting/performing company should be encouraged and allowed to speak up and point out the possible unsafe situations. "See Something, Say Something" should be a standard operating procedure for all projects.

Did a light boom get put in place that wasn't on the ground plan? What about an added piece of masking that wasn't on the ground plan? Working closely with the other departments can help ensure that injuries can be kept to a minimum. You can also help alleviate the number of questions asked in an OSHA interview by doing everything in your production manager superpowers to advance the safety of the various working environments. If you haven't been that involved in safety before, now is your chance to take a leadership role in safety for your company or venue. This could include setting up and chairing a workplace safety committee with a representative from each shop/department.

THE FIRE MARSHAL

A critical component for just about every project will be the relationship with the local fire marshal. The importance of maintaining a great relationship with this person cannot be overstated. They have the authority to call off your event if they see a problem that would compromise the safety of the workers or public audience. They have that power, and they will use it. That said, this relationship is not one to be scared of. You should be confident in your approach to the fire marshal, not scared OR intimidated. Always remember that their job is to protect people. That's it. Help them to do their job by doing a good job yourself. You should plan to meet your fire marshal, if at all possible. Take a meeting when you have a plan in place and are confident that your plan will pass the fire inspection (also called life-safety inspection) or demonstration. However, if you don't have a plan in place, you can start to create and maintain this very important relationship by using your fire marshal as an additional resource to help you develop it. Realize that the more you meet with your fire marshal, the more confidence they are building in you. They develop confidence in your ability to do the right thing and your ability to follow through. They will learn to rely on this follow-through, which only increases trust.

> **TIP** – Become familiar with performance-related sections of the "National Fire Protection Association Code 101" or "NFPA 101":
> - https://www.nfpa.org/codes-and-standards/all-codes-and-standards/list-of-codes-and-standards/detail?code=101
> - Your fire marshals will be checking for compliance with this code in addition to local building codes.

What are some of the things we can do as production managers to create a good working relationship with the fire marshal? The first thing is transparency. You need to let the fire marshal know what you are doing and have openness to the idea that the fire marshal can inspect your show. If the fire marshal is going to get involved with your effect, set, show, etc., at the very least, you should have the following at your disposal:

- Explanation/design of effect being used that triggered the fire marshal call
- Drawings, renderings, sketches of the effect, or scenic piece
- Reports from your technical managers on how the piece was engineered/built
- Documentation on training or training plan for employees

The same would be used for the permit to use an open flame on a set, plus:

- Demonstrate that we know how to use the open flame effect safely
- Document the flame proofing of all soft goods and provide a sample of the materials used
- Discuss and document what risks there are with using the open flame
- Discuss procedures in how we will deal with risks or emergencies
- Document that we have trained the staff or crew in the proper use of flame and fire extinguishers
- Document the schedule of when the effect will be in use

> Open flame is NEVER permitted onstage without the written consent of a fire marshal. You should always check with local fire department authorities in your area.

In some theatrical and special events, especially in hotel ballrooms, you may be required to provide what is called a "fire watch" staff person. Due to the use of haze or fog-producing products during an event, the fire alarm system may have to be turned off. This is an important item for the checklist, as it will oftentimes come with

Figure 9.4 The College-Conservatory of Music at the University of Cincinnati
Credit: Photo by Adam Zeek – www.zeekcreative.com

additional charges to the budget, especially if an actual fire department representative is needed during the entire event. This fire watch person is on hand to specifically watch for hazards and to report a fire, should one break out, as the fire alarms have been turned off.

By having these procedures in place, we can confidently tell the fire marshal, "if something goes wrong, we have a plan in place, and this is our plan." Don't look at the fire marshal as a burden to your creativity, but as a resource. The more you get to know your local fire marshal, the more you will be put at ease that they are not there to interfere but to strictly reinforce standards and procedures that have been proven to save lives.

TIP – Fire marshals often will review compliance with evacuation protocols (making sure exits and egress pathways are to code). This is important in flexible venues (black boxes) where stage/audience configuration is often changing for each show. Understanding minimum requirements for the number and size of pathways, as well as the lighting and signage for pathways, is important at the design phase, not just ahead for the life-safety walkthrough.

BUILDING SAFETY INTO THE SCHEDULE

As a production manager, we are usually the ones responsible for putting together the various schedules. Scenic load-in, light hang, video install, tech, dress … you name it, we schedule it. But how many of you build safety into the schedule? Has this ever been a part of your mindset? If not, it should be. As the production manager, you're responsible for this happening. It is highly unlikely that anyone else will take the initiative to build safety into the schedule.

Take the time to guide your cast and crew on a tour of the theatre or performance space. (Oftentimes, it may not be a theatre!) Introduce everyone on the team and describe to the performers and crew what their roles may be regarding safety at the workplace. On the tour, you should point out where fire extinguishers and/or fire hoses are located and make it clear that there can be no obstructions in front of them. Double check the extinguishers and make sure that they are all up to date and notate when they need to be inspected or replaced. Also, indicate where the fire alarm "pulls" are in case anyone needs to immediately report a fire. We should then acclimate the performers and crew to the various exits, both emergency as well as regular exits. Make sure everyone knows how to get out in case of an issue needing immediate evacuation. While at the performance space, point out any step-downs or platforms that may need to be navigated around. You should then conclude with a fire/evacuation drill. Perhaps it's just before a tech or a dress rehearsal, but you may want to practice making sure everyone knows what their responsibilities are during an emergency.

TIP – If your performance venue has a sound attenuator (one that plays a prerecorded voice or tone during an emergency) play it for the cast and crew, so they know it is NOT a sound cue that is part of the show.

The emergency plan can be a very simple assignment list:

- Stage manager: Assess the situation and make God mic announcement of what to do.
- Asst. stage manager: Call 911 and report the incident giving the EXACT location of the emergency.
- Stage crew lead: Begin safe, calm evacuation of stage personnel – actors and crew.

- Light board operator: Shut down the power.
- Costume crew lead: Communicate the emergency to the costume shop and ensure, if necessary that an evacuation is in process.
- House manager: Begin safe, calm evacuation of the venue.

TIP – If the emergency involves an injury, make sure whoever calls 911 is near the injured person when placing the call. The 911 operator or paramedics may want information about the patient that can only be answered by having the caller be near the injured party. Assign someone to meet the emergency vehicles out front to lead them to the injured person.

You should have an emergency plan in place for everyone involved in the production. Even if that assignment is "get to an exit," EVERYONE involved has an assignment. You need to take the time to assign these positions and take this responsibility as seriously as making crew assignments for the running of the show. Again, every scenario will be different. You will need to assess your situation and make your own list according to your needs and resources.

You should build a mock evacuation into your schedule at least once during your tech/dress rehearsal week. (You should also ignore the sounds of despair coming from the director, who may think you are using valuable rehearsal time for mundane reasons!) If you are willing to try and do this, it really could help alleviate panic during an actual emergency. If everyone knows, at the very least, where they need to be during a crisis, your chances of survival increase immensely.

Accidents and disasters can and are the result of improper planning and poor human judgment, and many accidents are preventable. Take the time to train, document, assess, and mitigate each and every potentially dangerous situation. Take the lead on getting your staff up to date with the best industry practices in safety. By doing this, you will be on your way to becoming a very effective production manager (and a fire marshal's best friend!).

SAFETY LESSONS LEARNED DURING COVID

The job of a production manager is to keep learning, practicing resilience, and constantly adapting to changing environments. The COVID-19 pandemic was an opportunity to do exactly that. In order to stay afloat many organizations had to learn to produce live events (either for a live audience or for a virtual one) in a way that met strict and necessary safety and health protocols. Production Managers were almost always a part of the decision-making process of these protocols and were able to learn and make the necessary changes in order to keep their teams and audiences as safe as possible. Here are some changes production managers saw during this time that we should strongly consider carrying forward:

- Safety personnel: Many performance unions and organizations required the addition of a safety coordinator or manager to work onsite with the production. This person had to be separate from the stage management team and not affiliated with the producers to work and guide autonomously to uphold safe and sanitary conditions as outlined by the unions. Many organizations were forced to bring on a dedicated safety staff member and/or create a safety team or committee where there was none previously.

- Sanitization: Our performance spaces have never been as clean as they were when we started producing during COVID. The increased use of sanitizing wipes, ultraviolet lights, and regularly timed cleaning breaks meant the set, props, costumes, and venues were germ and dirt free.

- Safety meetings: Many producing and presenting organizations began holding regular safety meetings to review the ever-changing union policies, Center for Disease Control and World Health Organization recommendations, and local ordinances. Whether daily or weekly the amount of time spent on this work increased exponentially from before the pandemic. And in some cases, instituted safety into the workflow when it was not there before.

- Safety budget: The constant purchasing of Personnel Protective Equipment (PPE), testing and sanitizing supplies required organizations to rethink their budgeting process and include increased money allocated for safety, or in some cases create a safety budget line.

- Sick and safe leave: While sick days always existed, our industry has been careless with ignoring illness and well-being of our staff and artists. The pandemic forced those feeling even slightly sick to stay home so that they would not infect others. It also reduced the stigma of taking a mental health day, as many of us needed those as we navigated the challenging landscape of the pandemic.

CASE STUDY – *HAMILTON*

CONTRIBUTOR: KIMBERLY FISK, PRODUCTION STAGE MANAGER

One of the curses and blessings of being on the road is that many of your support personnel, such as your production manager or production supervisor, are not in-residence full-time. They often instead work from the company's home base (usually New York City) and visit the tour as needed. This gives someone in the position of production stage manager more responsibility in the immediate decision-making process. In a crisis situation, you rely on both your training for various emergencies (protocols for fire alarms, power outages, earthquakes, etc.) and equally on your previous real-life experiences. So, when a situation presents itself that is not in your cache of "known evils" it can test your mettle.

Figure 9.5   Kimberly Fisk on the set of *Hamilton*.
Credit: Photo provided by Kimberly Fisk

Friday evening, February 15, 2019. It is our 5th performance of our newest company of *Hamilton*, playing San Francisco. This week at the Orpheum Theatre marked our official opening of the tour. We were in the final 3 minutes of the show, which meant the entire cast was onstage for the finale. I was in my office, where we have a monitor of the stage and suddenly, I realized that the cast was walking offstage unexpectedly and then the orchestra stopped playing! The next thing I knew the cast was all scurrying downstairs to the basement, looking terrified. Nobody could answer my question as to what was happening. I now realize it was because they didn't know. And neither did my team of SMs. They knew some sort of distraction had begun in the house and that people were shuffling and yelling.

Somebody said they heard the word "shooter". The next thing we knew, random people began rushing out of the orchestra pit! Audience members from the front rows, in fear, chose to jump 15' into our pit. They landed on instruments and crushed them; they collapsed the percussion booth lid (luckily our Percussionist himself had just evacuated the booth) and were now running wild-eyed backstage. Some were injured from the jump, most were okay, probably from the adrenaline. Now my team was trying to escort patrons out of backstage, gather the cast to assess what we needed to do all while trying to communicate with the FOH staff, who were equally in the dark as to what just happened. Then suddenly the Fire Alarm went off. This was a blessing because we knew what to do in case of a fire alarm! Everybody filed out of the building and gathered at our pre-determined meeting place for a group check in.

All of this happened within a matter of 4 minutes, and it was still unclear as to what set all of this off. And to make matters worse, once the fire alarm tripped there was no longer mass communication either backstage or to the FOH because the alarm overrides the page system. Now my team of stage (and company) managers were strewn throughout the stage door and plaza areas wrangling and calming the cast as we waited for further word from the house. We were eventually told to re-enter, allowed the cast to get out of costumes and they were released. The house had evacuated, more like stampeded, with some injuries and much chaos. Those few who remained outside were told by FOH staff that they should go home. We would not be completing the performance.

It turns out, one medical emergency had ignited a whole string of events that basically created the perfect storm of chaos and panic. Here is what we now know happened:

A young man, sitting with his mother, Orchestra House Right began to have a seizure. His mother panicked and started yelling for help. As other patrons moved in to help her and to carry her son up the aisle to the lobby, the noise distraction had caught the attention of a house employee, who signaled the police officer assigned to the theatre that evening. As the armed officer made his way into the house, somebody spotted his gun and yelled "shooter!" From this point forward, chaos ensued. One more experienced member of our cast told the company to clear the stage, as the cast could see something was happening even if nobody knew what. Now the entire house was scrambling for safety and running to every exit imaginable, including the pit. When this mass exodus began, unfortunately, another patron in the rear orchestra house left began to have another medical emergency, heart-related. She was now collapsed directly outside of one of the main orchestra doors. A few people were trying desperately to protect the stampede from trampling her and by doing so created further panic by blockading those doors. At this point, a patron in the balcony level decided it was time to hit the fire alarm, based on nothing more than panic.

In this time of so many incidents of gun violence tragedy, it took so little to create sheer panic with 2500 people in a room. It was a hard lesson to learn. The lack of control was immense, both FOH and backstage. Clearly, we were ill prepared for such an event, and it brought many things to light about where we needed to step up our game in terms of security and communication.

1. Our company scheduled an Active Shooter Training for the company and the entire theatre staff. The training is difficult to process because we are used to having "rules" and protocols for so many emergencies. But Active Shooter events have a whole different set of guidelines that leave the decisions to the individual, with fight or flight, and gut survival instincts. It is counter intuitive to most of our training. That was hard to internalize for everyone, and maybe especially for managers who are put to the task of the safety and well-being of the company.
2. We stepped up our communication plan for where each team member should be positioned during a crisis, with each major pathway/doorway being covered and each person having access to handheld radios.
3. We worked with the house to ensure that a system was in place for mass communication even during the alarm system being engaged.
4. We mapped out the best locations for lockable/safe spaces where people could shelter-in-place should they become trapped inside the theatre with an active shooter.
5. We installed a camera on our set that is trained on the house, so that we may see activity quickly during the performance.
6. We created a text group, through a third-party app, where we managers can always reach out to the entire company to check in, give important (emergency) information, and have everybody respond that they are safe in a scenario where we become separated.

In retrospect, a couple of these response actions would have been useful for any emergency situation. But it took that Friday night to bring us to a whole new level of awareness of our vulnerabilities and how we might better prepare. It also brings the knowledge that to some extent, you can't always be fully prepared. You have to learn as you go.

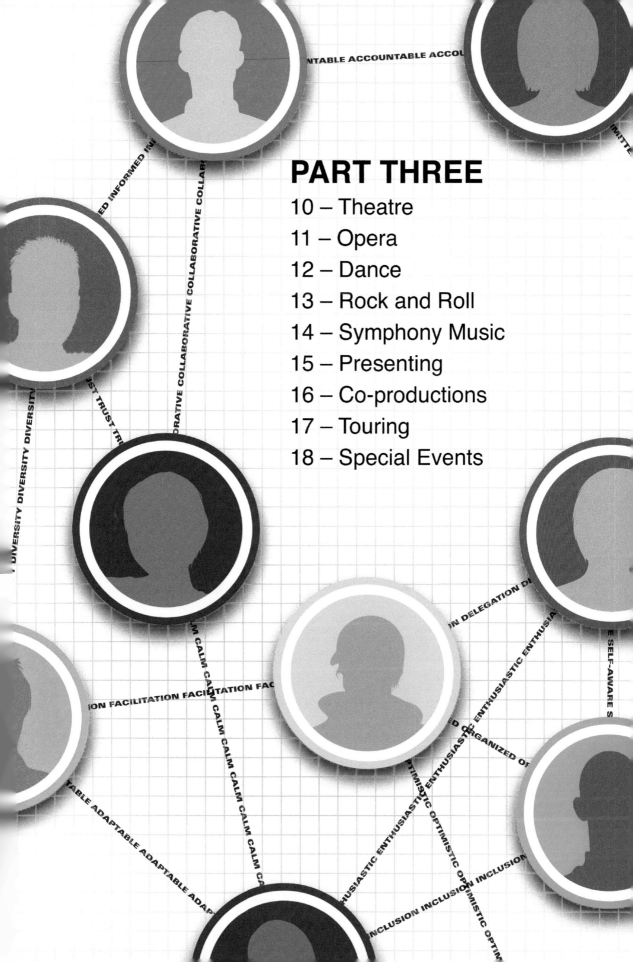

PART THREE

10 – Theatre

11 – Opera

12 – Dance

13 – Rock and Roll

14 – Symphony Music

15 – Presenting

16 – Co-productions

17 – Touring

18 – Special Events

CHAPTER 10

Theatre

There are a large variety of theatrical producing organizations in the United States. For the purposes of this chapter, we will focus specifically on regional theatre, Broadway, and summer stock. There a quite a few differences between these three types of theatres, but the goals of the production manager are the same – produce the show on time, on budget, safely and, in the end, make sure everyone is still speaking to each other. Production managers are also integral to supporting and carrying out the mission of the organization and are valuable parts of the theatrical community.

REGIONAL THEATRES

The largest amount of theatre in the United States is produced by regional theatre companies. These companies are often producing year-round or three-quarters of the year and mount multiple shows in one season. They usually own a theatre space or multiple spaces, and they employ production staff for their own shops. For regional theatre, the production manager is typically a full-time employee and a member of the senior staff. The production manager contributes toward the overall direction and future of the company. If the production manager has a good working relationship with the artistic director, the production manager might be a part of the season selection process and might have a larger say in choosing the creative team.

Regional theatres typically have various departments with which the production manager will need to collaborate. All your professional relationships are important and especially your fellow department heads. Some of these collaborators we previously mentioned in this text, but let us take another look:

Marketing/public relations: This department is responsible for ensuring the general public is aware of the theatre's offerings and of its mission. Marketing staff work with the local press to promote shows/events and to promote the organization through special interest stories. This department is responsible for attracting audiences, selling tickets, and filling seats. Often, this department will need help from the production department for a photo shoot of an upcoming show (with actors, costumes, and props) or perhaps coordinating an interview with a guest

DOI: 10.4324/9780367808174-14

Figure 10.1   Props Artisans Racheal Erichsen and Andrew Morgan put the finishing touches on the Apothecary's Cabinet for the Baltimore Center Stage production of *King of the Yees*
Credit: Photo by Bill Geenen

artist. No matter the request, it is important to be responsive to marketing requests and to work positively with marketing staff. A supportive relationship between the marketing and production departments benefits the entire organization.

Development: This department houses the organization's money-finders. As explained in the Money and Budget chapter, it takes more than ticket sales to keep a theatre going. Contributed income from grants and donations keeps the organization financially successful.

Figure 10.2   "This is a Hilarious Photo of me Taken While I Worked at Steppenwolf. It was at Their Big "Season Kickoff" Event Where We Lead Tours All Around the Theatre – I was in the Wardrobe Room Giving a Demonstration on how We have Actors Change in and Out of False Pregnancy Bellies!" – Dixie Uffleman, Director of Production at the McCarter Theatre Center
Credit: Photo by Mark Campbell

Education: Most regional theatres value education and learning. By training the next generation of theatre professionals and educating current and future audiences, the education department can further the mission of the theatre. The production manager will need to work closely with the education department to schedule events such as student matinees and post-show discussions and may also provide needed information and/or personnel for workshops, camps, and study guides. If your organization values education, it will likely have an internship or apprenticeship program. The production department will need to work closely with this program, as technical and management interns/apprentices will often be supervised jointly by production staff and education staff.

"The single biggest communication success I had when I was at the Denver Center Theatre Company was repairing the relationship between production and marketing. Marketing was seen by the production department as annoying because they would constantly call asking for stuff. The big breakthrough was on a production of *Dracula*. Marketing had set up a relationship with a local newscaster who wanted to dress up like the traditional Bela Lugosi Dracula character for a local broadcast. Our costume shop manager and the crafts supervisor (who was also the designer of the show) were asked to help with the costume. They both got really annoyed, since that was not the costume, we were using nor the type of show we were producing. I told them that the point of this was to show off what we do, not the specifics of what they asked us to do. What are we doing that would be interesting for them? A light bulb went off for the

> craftsperson and he said, 'I'm doing a fang fitting with some of the actors on Tuesday; why don't we have the newscaster come in, and I'll fit him for some fangs?' In the end, the newscaster got a much better story than he had asked for, and the costume shop got to show off their actual, very interesting work."
>
> - Rick Noble, Director of Production at the
> Perelman Performing Arts Center

BROADWAY

A regional theatre and a Broadway theatre can produce the same play, but the process will be quite different. Unlike regional theatre, Broadway shows are produced one at a time and not as part of a season. The scale of the show is usually much larger than regional theatre, and budgets can often exceed several million dollars for a "basic" Broadway show. Broadway theatres are also very large, often holding upwards of 3,000 audience members. As you will learn in the chapter on presenting theatres, "four wall rental houses" are theatres used by producers and presenters and are available in most major U.S. cities. Broadway shows are oftentimes produced in a "four wall" theatre (meaning it comes with nothing but the architecture of the theatre), and the productions are brought in and designed especially for that particular theatre. There are generally no production managers on staff for a theatre. The staff will usually consist of a facilities manager and a house manager.

A group of producers will come together to put a play or musical on Broadway. Producers might develop, organize, and produce the play on their own, or they may use a general management company to assist them. General management companies are brought on to manage the budget, find and negotiate with the theatre where the show will be produced and hire the staff and artists. The producer or general management company will hire a production company to provide production management services. The selection of the production company is usually based on a bidding system, but the contract doesn't always go to the lowest bidder. As is the case in every other facet of production management, relationships can play a big part in the selection process, as general managers tend to hire the same production companies if they can get the work done on time, on budget, and in a friendly environment.

Production managers are among the few people on Broadway who have full-time employment. Directors, designers, stage managers, crew, etc., are brought on for a per-show contract. Production managers are employed by management companies that usually have multiple production managers, assistant production managers, and interns on staff. There are a few freelance production managers on Broadway, but they are rare. A production manager might be hired anytime from one year to one month before a production opens. For a larger musical, it is likely the production manager will be hired at least a year from opening, because the larger the show, the more complicated the production process can be. If the show will transfer from another theatre, London's West End, for example, the production manager may not be brought on until a month before opening.

The production manager on Broadway also serves as the technical director. They are in charge of collaborating with the designers, shop crews, and theatre facility staff to achieve the artistic goals of the show. They must supervise the builds, sign off on design drawings, and oversee the production loading in and loading out. Unlike regional theatre, there are no in-house shops or equipment, so everything must be outsourced. Outside shops need to be contracted by the production manager to build scenery, props, and costumes. Equipment such as lights, sound, video, and automation will need to be bought or rented. Broadway theatres come empty, and each show supplies what they need. When the show closes, everything is removed, and the process starts again for the next show.

The production manager is onsite at the theatre facility from the first day of load-in through opening night. After opening, they remain with the show on a peripheral basis, troubleshooting, and managing issues when they arise. Throughout the process, the production manager communicates regularly with the theatre's facilities manager and house manager to ensure that things run smoothly. When the show closes, the production manager will return to oversee the load-out. Most production managers will begin working on another show once the previous one opens.

One large part of a Broadway production manager's job is working with the International Alliance of Theatrical Stage Employees (IATSE). The theatre where the play or musical will be produced will have its own house crew consisting of a head carpenter, head props master, and head electrician. This crew all belong to the New York IATSE local union, known as "Local 1." The rest of the crew needed to run the show will be hired by the production manager on what is known in New York as the "pink contract." This contract allows people who are not "Local 1" to work. They must be IATSE members, but they can belong to another local, out of town, perhaps. The show crew is employed by the show, while the house crew is employed by the theatre. Everyone will need to work together, and it is the production manager's job to facilitate this relationship.

"A Broadway production manager (also known as the technical supervisor) forms different relationships with lead production staff than you would in a regional theatre setting. For example, you don't start the process with a technical director, so you are responsible early on for overseeing the scenic technical process more so than in a theatre company with permanent staff. And the physical Broadway theatre has its own technical staff so there is facilitation between the show's technical team and the theatre's house heads that you don't normally find. Even in non-profit theatres producing on Broadway you will find some similarities. It really pushes a Broadway production manager to approach the show from a different mindset."

- Celeste Lagrotteria, Production Manager at the
Manhattan Theatre Club

SUMMER STOCK

A summer stock theatre will produce a full season of shows over the summer months. Shows within this short season will overlap with one show in performance while the next show is rehearsing. Builds and changeovers are likely to be only a few days, so there is little time to correct mistakes and make changes. Even more complicating is that many summer stock theatres are outdoor theatres, with challenges such as wisely using daylight, unfortunate weather, and summer heat. As you can guess, most production staff for summer stock theatres are not year-round employees, which means that they will likely not come on board until right before the season begins.

The key to success for summer stock is careful preparation. Most companies employ a full-time production manager who will spend the off-months (September–April) preparing for the upcoming season. During this time, they locate and hire all seasonal artists and staff, designs are conceived, discussed, and solidified, and schedules are set. Rehearsals tend to be quick – one to two weeks, including tech – so there is little time for discovery. Exact details of who is playing what role, how scene changes will occur, and other specifics must be figured out ahead of time. Once the season begins, it is full steam ahead. There is little time for discussion or to think things over. You have to make decisions as quickly as problems arise or "on the fly."

> "Theatre is about compromise; we try to consider all requests. I don't make a decision in a vacuum. I'm surrounded by amazing people, and they all contribute. It's a collaboration. The more ideas in the pool, the better chance we can solve it the right way. I frequently tell people that I am not asking for perfection. We can't achieve perfect here at The Muny; there will always be flaws. What we can do is try our collective best and be proud of the results. If you are not striving for perfection, you can take a few calculated risks and try some new things, and that is exciting."
>
> - Tracy Utzmyers, Production Manager for The Muny

Theatre organizations come in a variety of shapes and sizes, but, ultimately, the responsibilities of the production manager are the same – to support the vision of the creative team and make it a reality. The following case studies are great examples of when production managers were doing just that!

CASE STUDY – *TO KILL A MOCKINGBIRD*

CONTRIBUTOR – LIZA LUXENBERG, PRODUCTION MANAGER AT AURORA PRODUCTIONS

We are there to realize the director and creative team's dream – from paper to reality while being mindful of the production budget, just as it is in regional theatres across the country. How we get to their vision is perpetually evolving once we get into the theatre. The production side of Broadway is truly a family community. As we move from show to show post-opening, while still continuing maintenance during the run of a show, quite often we find ourselves working with a fusion of the talented designers and crew members with whom we have worked on other shows over the years.

A great example of this has been during the run of *To Kill a Mockingbird* at the Shubert Theatre. Just as long-running shows have their maintenance needs, they may choose to have special event performances. In February 2020, *To Kill a Mockingbird* did just that. It was decided that the show would perform at Madison Square Garden for 18,000 New York City Public School students. The performance would be in the round for the first time with about 17x the size of a regular Broadway audience. This would bring on a whole new set of challenges when it came to bringing the show to life.

Several production meetings took place in order to flesh out the design for this one-time-only performance as well as a production schedule that would create a successful show at Madison Square Garden while maintaining the needs of the show that was running at the Shubert the rest of the week. It was decided to take advantage of the arena atmosphere, which meant getting rid of many set changes and creating more staged playing areas where the porch, courtroom, and other scenes would take place, since we had more playing space to work with as well as a limitation on load in time that would make automated scenery less desirable for this performance.

Figure 10.3   Liza Luxenberg on the stage of *To Kill a Mockingbird* at Madison Square Garden

Credit: Photo by Matthew Matulewicz

The set included a full steel deck stage, new props, and scenery units to be constructed and props and costumes to be brought over from the Shubert Theatre. It was my job to help maintain the integrity of the production along with the designers and also arrange for scheduling and trucking for any items needed from the Broadway Production to be coordinated with the Madison Square Garden staff under their work rules, while also allowing for the appropriate turnaround times to get it all back to the Shubert under the most fiscally responsible way.

Meetings took place with company management and hair and wardrobe specifically, because their turnaround times were trickiest when it came to prepping costumes and setting wigs. This had to be coordinated both for the departure of the costumes and wigs to Madison Square Garden but also when they would return to be prepped for the next show at the Shubert. In the end, it was decided to change the performance schedule that week for the sake of both the cast and crew. I spent time with our set design team and prop supervisor on the layout of the ground plan and then bidding out the new elements to shops for approval from the producers and general managers. I coordinated for our crew to be on-site as needed for both the load-in and the performance to help guide the Madison Square Garden crew through the show. A lighting and sound design were created with our design team and the live events company hired to interface with Madison Square Garden and it was loaded in and rung out to accommodate the space.

The cast would rehearse this version of the show during the day and perform the Shubert version of the show at night for several weeks. I spent time with stage management to make sure they were clear about the goals and answer any questions they had about the layout of the space. As this was an event that had never been done before, the scale of the production was quite important while keeping the intimacy of the show alive. The creative and producing and general management team treated this presentation with great care to make sure our production was protected once plopped into an arena environment. We were very pleasantly surprised to see that the students were glued to their seats and completely engaged throughout the entire event.

CASE STUDY – *SHE KILLS MONSTERS*

CONTRIBUTOR – JENNIFER SCHWARTZ, PRODUCTION MANAGER AT THE UNIVERSITY OF MARYLAND, COLLEGE PARK

As a production manager, one thing I have always known is that the ability to remain flexible, improvise, and creatively problem solve in the long term, as well as in the moment, is key. Curveballs are constantly thrown our way at all points of the process, though traditionally most often during tech. In March 2020, the world was thrown the ultimate curveball, and theatres across the nation faced a difficult choice. A pandemic hit the globe, causing everything to shut down. On March 13th, one week before rehearsals for our production of *She Kills Monsters* was supposed to begin, the University of MD informed students,

Figure 10.4   Screenshot from *She Kills Monsters*

Credit: Photo provided by David Andrews/University of Maryland

faculty, and staff that the campus would be closing indefinitely. At the time we were focused on our students, at the chaos and uncertainty they were facing, and felt a need to create some sense of normalcy and joy, if at all possible. For us, that meant continuing to make art, and to provide a safe outlet for them through the rehearsal process we were set to begin. What we didn't anticipate would happen is that our production would become one of the first to take this route of digital performance within the pandemic and would ultimately provide us a unique research opportunity.

CHALLENGE #1: COMMUNICATION AND COLLABORATION

Once it was decided to continue the production using Zoom, wo immediately began to redesign the show, which involved rethinking what everyone's roles would be in this production. That was the first test of my production management skills in the form of communication and management. When you aren't producing inside a physical venue, all of the designs painstakingly created and planned for become a moot point. Our scenic designer was no longer having a structure built on a stage that would create the world of the play. Our costume designer couldn't have students in a room with her for fittings, nor could the shop be on site to build what was designed. The projection designer has to work within a very different and structured platform, Zoom, not created for theatre. The sound designer was the one role that was able to stay in a familiar role. To address all the changes, we chose to embrace collaboration, and rather than trying to rewrite a job description for each designer, the group identified what needed to be done and assigned the work to be shared among the team. The scenic designer worked on storyboards and Zoom box layouts. The costume designer designed and illustrated masks that were converted into digital content to be "worn" by the actors. The projection designer created digital backgrounds and snap camera filters.

The lighting designer consulted with actors on where to place their lamps in their dorm rooms or bedrooms to look their best. Because there was no norm to fall back on, communication was more critical than ever. There could be no assumptions. When an idea came up, the follow up question was always "great, who's taking that on?" I could not be prouder of the design team on this show. They embraced the challenge of creating something new, threw out designs they had become attached to, and created a brand-new version of the show in weeks, alongside the actors.

CHALLENGE #2: COMMUNITY BUILDING

I came to realize very quickly that there was an unforeseen challenge: it was critical to establish a new way to build a community through a virtual platform. We didn't have the luxury of being in a room together and finding moments to connect through small talk on a break, or a shared look across a room. Instead, our company had their voices literally turned off while others were working, and sometimes even their faces. The energy in a Zoom rehearsal is very different from being in a rehearsal room. Reading the room isn't the same, it's difficult to share a laugh and connect. No one walks to the parking garage together. All the moments of bonding that happen naturally when we're in a room together weren't there. Slowly we found ways to use the chat feature to connect and respond to what was happening in a scene, offering laughs or praise to replace the absent applause or chuckles. Our directors also found ways to begin and end rehearsal that allowed time for the company of actors to engage in something outside of the play, but I never felt that we achieved the same level of community we'd find during an in-person rehearsal and performance process.

CHALLENGE #3: PROBLEM SOLVING IN A WORLD WITH THE CORONAVIRUS

And of course, the curveball of the Coronavirus itself became a massive challenge. COVID-19 instantly made this a time more than ever where humanity must take the forefront, and we all must care about one another, be flexible and understanding with one another, and put each other first. Getting the work done became secondary and taking care of one another became a priority. Balancing these two things became a very real challenge. Trying to realize every consideration of what impact a production choice had on people was hard. There was no history to look back on to guide these conversations. When the costume designer wanted to know how to ship costumes to performers, it wasn't as straight forward as providing an address and a FedEx account number. We had to take a step back and realize that what seems to be a simple task under normal conditions could now put people's health at risk. At the time of our production, there was a concern about potentially spreading the virus through surface contact, so sending a package could ultimately put someone at risk. And even beyond that, who did the performers live with? Even if the performers felt comfortable receiving something in the mail, we had to realize that there were many other people involved who potentially didn't have a voice in this decision but were also being put at risk. People like the mother, grandfather, or baby brother also living in the home. We always led our decisions with safety first. Let's not put anyone at risk, or even in a position to decide if they're comfortable with the risk and work only out of what's available in their closets. We didn't want to add stress to make this production happen, we wanted to find the joy in what we do and offer a release from all the stress.

Going through this process was the most rewarding, and most challenging experience of my career as a production manager. It tested many of the skills we talk about in our field every day: communication, collaboration, community, and problem-solving, in a unique way. In the new platform of digital performance, I learned to value flexibility, even more, trust that I can establish new ways of supporting a community in production, and facilitate essential collaboration, becoming a better production manager for having gone through it.

CHAPTER 11

Opera

The major thing that differentiates opera from other disciplines is its scale. With opera, the production manager needs to manage a larger-than-average amount of people, things, and sometimes, even places. A large opera can have over 100 performers onstage, 80 musicians in the orchestra, and 60 technicians behind the scenes. Though one can equate the day-to-day duties of an opera production manager to a theatre production manager, the jobs differentiate when one factors in the scale of the productions.

> "Opera is a large, expensive art form involving many people. Our production budget alone is larger than the entire operating budget of many small and medium-sized theatres, and there are regularly more than 100 people working as part of the production department to put on even a medium-sized show."
>
> - Lee Milliken, Production Manager at The Metropolitan Opera

The position of the production manager in opera grew from the technical director position, just as it has in other disciplines. Historically, the technical director was in charge of the opera production department, as it is in the European model, which still functions without a production manager in many cases. Opera in the United States closely follows a theatre model, so many companies have chosen to put a production manager in place in order to simplify communication and clarify who has the final word. Most opera production management positions were put in place in the mid-1990s but there are still American companies without a production manager position today. As with the European model, if there is no production manager, the technical director, and/or the production stage manager take responsibility for the production management duties described in this text.

DOI: 10.4324/9780367808174-15

"My whole family has worked here at Glimmerglass. I can't remember a time when I did not know what a production manager did. I began as a technical director, and a lot of people started coming to me to get help solving challenges in other areas, and I decide that is what interested me the most."

- Abby Rodd, Director of Production
at Glimmerglass Opera Company

The planning process for opera must occur very far in advance of the performances. There are some opera companies that select their seasons as early as five years out. The reasons for this length of planning are mostly based on the performers. Firstly, principal singers who are in demand are often hired early. In response to this, companies must rush to have seasons determined early enough to be able to contract the best performers. Secondly, it takes a long time for singers to learn the music and work with their vocal coaches prior to showing up for rehearsals. Unlike theatre, all opera performers are expected to arrive at the first rehearsals already knowing all the material. There are great benefits in having a long time to plan, such as having more time to construct a budget and resolve any special challenges before the work begins.

Most opera companies produce only one new opera a season. The remainder of the season will be dedicated to remounting previously performed operas that remain in the company's repertoire or renting operas from other companies. Co-productions are very common in opera. Often, two or more companies will produce a new opera together and then take turns presenting this new work at each of their venues. (See Chapter 16, Co-productions.) It is common for opera companies to have large storage units filled with sets and costumes of productions that will be remounted or loaned out. Cutting down on costs is a necessity when taking into consideration the funds necessary to hire the multitude of personnel that opera demands.

"Perhaps this is a universal part of production planning, but I like to look at it as identifying what all the boundaries are – financial, time, union rules, etc. – then figuring out how to push them in order to achieve the artistic vision. For me this relies on doing the detailed research and planning well in advance, so I know as much as possible about the opera, and then once we're actively in the production process being able to respond effectively to what's happening, even if it means letting go of some of those well-laid plans."

- Molly Dill, Chief Operating Officer at Houston Grand Opera

Unlike theatre, the creative guidance of the production does not fall solely on the shoulders of the director. In opera, you will have two artistic leads – a staging director and a musical director (or maestro/maestra) who will also conduct the orchestra in

Figure 11.1 The College-Conservatory of Music at the University of Cincinnati.
Credit: Photo by Adam Zeek, www.zeekcreative.com

performance. You will often see the musical director taking charge, as it is primarily a musical art form, with the staging director working under them. It is also possible to see them work side by side and share the responsibility of leading the production. There is also an assistant director who plays a large role in the staging of the chorus plus preparing understudies and covers to go on if needed.

Much of the opera planning is done by or in conjunction with the artistic and music departments rather than by the production manager. Orchestra, singer, and chorus schedules are managed by these departments, these are typically the starting point for creating rehearsal and tech schedules. With opera, technical rehearsals are accomplished at a somewhat quicker pace than in a theatre. Because the timing of the show is based on the timing of the music, not the performers, elements such as lighting can be cued without the cast. Often, a tech day will begin with a long lighting session and then end with a run of the show with the full cast where cues are integrated but holds do not occur. Lighting fixes are done before the next run. This quick pace is necessary for the performers. Opera singers cannot be asked to rehearse for an eight- or ten-hour tech day; this could damage their voices.

TIP – You must be sensitive to the needs of your artists – an opera singer's body is their instrument, so be mindful of the conditions of the rehearsal studio, dressing rooms, and theatre. A clean Hudson sprayer dedicated to humidifying the air on stage would be a useful thing to have on hand, for example.

Most opera companies will begin singing with an orchestra only a few rehearsals prior to opening. This helps keep musician costs manageable. The integration of the orchestra usually occurs in the following way:

- Sitzprobe: A rehearsal with all singers and the full orchestra where the focus is on the music. The goal of this rehearsal is to integrate the singers with the orchestra by working through the entire score. It is essential that there is this time for all the performers to get used to each other. This rehearsal is run by the musical director.

- Wandleprobe (pronounced with the W sounding like a V): Similar to a sitzprobe, but the singers are asked to do their blocking while continuing to integrate with the orchestra. Sometimes, the wandleprobe is utilized instead of a sitzprobe because there is limited time, or the performers need the opportunity to review blocking. It's also a useful opportunity to ensure the singers can see the conductor and vice versa.

Opera has a handful of unique technical needs that need to be considered in the theatre as part of the load-in and tech process. A "Maestro Cam" (a video image of the conductor) must be sent to several video screens in the front of the house as well as backstage so that the singers can always see the conductor and must be set up to reduce as much lag time as possible. As many operas are not performed in English, supertitles must be displayed or projected so that the audiences can follow what is being sung.

All opera participants (performers, musicians, and technicians) are usually union members. The exception is the chorus and non-singing roles called supernumeraries. Having so many union members all working at the same time brings up the cost, hence the need to work with certain people only when necessary. The most expensive rehearsals are the ones where everyone is there – cast, musicians, and crew. Consider how even a few minutes of overtime can be impactful in this case. Proper scheduling and communication are vital.

> "Typically, you need to renegotiate with the unions every three to five years. I always advocate for a contract that is as long as possible. The unions respect that it is a drain on the whole company. The more time you spend on negotiations, the less time to have to do your work, and then more problems arise that are going to cause you to want to renegotiate. If you are well organized, good to your people and provide a safe work environment, then the union workers won't have a lot to bring to the table. We have labour meetings pretty regularly where we let everyone speak their mind. This way, they know they are being listened to and they can understand where you are coming from too."
>
> - Vinnie Feraudo, Former Director of Production at Seattle Opera

Opera remains a dominant art form throughout most of the world. As it began in Europe, it is not surprising that some of the most prestigious opera companies are

Figure 11.2   Stage manager Clare Burovac and Director of Production Vinnie Feraudo working at the production table during Seattle Opera's RING rehearsals
Credit: Photo by Bill Mohn

European. It is not uncommon for American opera companies to work with individuals or companies from European countries, as well as companies throughout the rest of the world. Also, many operas are in languages other than English. As stressed repeatedly in this text, the ability to communicate clearly is of chief concern for the production manager. It is hard enough to be a communicator in one language, so one can imagine the extra challenge posed by multi-national and multi-lingual production teams. If production managing for opera is where you are heading, a willingness to understand various cultures and languages plus proficient non-verbal communication skills (body language and intonation) will be a valuable part of your production manager's toolkit.

"We work with a lot of people from France. Their command of English might not be the best, but neither is my French, per se. It's not so much the language but the intonation and limited vocabulary that can confuse and maybe upset an American staff. I once heard a French director tell a staff member something looked like shit. He did not understand what that phrase meant and did not realize it was an insult. He had just heard it used a lot, and if you add that to his tone of voice, it made it sound really bad, when all he was trying to say was that he did not like it."

- Paul Hordepdahl, Former Director of Production
at the Santa Fe Opera

OPERA America (operaamerica.org) leads and serves the entire opera community, supporting the creation, presentation, and enjoyment of opera. The organization is committed to:

- Delivering professional development to artists, administrators, and trustees.
- Increasing appreciation of opera through educational and audience development resources.
- Offering technical support and informational services that foster the creation and presentation of new works.
- Fostering equity, diversity, and inclusion across all aspects of the opera industry.
- Undertaking national research and representing the field to policymakers and the media.
- Managing the National Opera Center, a custom-built facility that provides a centralized space for collaboration, rehearsal, and performance.

Founded in 1970, OPERA America fulfills its mission through public programs, an annual conference, regional workshops, consultations, granting programs, publications, and online resources. It is the only organization serving all constituents of opera: artists, administrators, trustees, educators, and audiences. Membership includes 170 professional opera companies; 450 associate, business, and education members; and 2,800 individuals. OPERA America extends its reach to 80,000 annual visitors to its National Opera Center and over 70,000 subscribers and followers on digital and social media. Representing over 90 percent of eligible professional companies, OPERA America is empowered to lead field-wide change.

The Technical/Production Forum shares successful practices about the demands of mounting new and existing productions, developing co-productions, and carrying out other activities required by the art form.

Opera is a beautiful, complex art form and needs the same quality of production management merited by any other performing art. An understanding, compassionate and educated production manager will immensely benefit an opera company and their artists. Let us hear from two opera production managers who has mastered those skills.

CASE STUDY – *THE (R)EVOLUTION OF STEVE JOBS*

CONTRIBUTOR – PAUL HORPEDAHL, FORMER DIRECTOR OF PRODUCTION AT SANTA FE OPERA

There are a lot of technical skills associated with the role of production manager/ production director and people come into this from a variety of paths. My path began as carpenter/stagehand to assistant tech director, tech director, and then production manager. This path gave me a strong understanding of the technical aspects and meshing them with design as well as insight into operations. Armed with that, I feel very strongly that my role is one of facilitator, bringing the design team and the production staff together.

The production planning timeline for opera is generally three to four years, including about two years from design concept to opening. A commission process can be two–three years of writing the work. One of the most recent operas that Santa Fe commissioned was *The (r)Evolution of Steve Jobs* which premiered in 2017. The commissioning of this work began in 2014. Because the commissioning costs and producing costs can be so high it is not uncommon to have partners for either commissioning or producing or both. In this instance, Santa Fe had co-commissioning partners in Seattle Opera and San Francisco Opera, and they were joined by Indiana University's Jacobs School of Music and co-producers.

As a facilitator, my first role is to be a good listener. As they came to the table with a preliminary design, it would be easy to start critiquing from the point of view of scope, scale, and budget. Instead, I feel it is very important to listen to the entire presentation and really absorb what they are describing. As they present, my notes include phrases or moments that the team is particularly passionate about or elements that are much more defined versus those that are a little vague. I also make notation of ideas and parts that may raise a red flag for me, especially due to the impact on load-in time and changeovers since we are a rep house. Making these notes helps me return to them mentally during the presentation and also flags them for discussion later.

With this production there were several items that clearly were important to the story telling and rapid move from one scene to the next but still required conversation. Additionally, there were clear issues with scale and scope regarding both the budget and the amount of scenery that would need to be installed. The design as conceived involved a series of tall smartphone-like panels that needed to move effortlessly from scene to scene, a grid-like ceiling, and side walls that covered the architectural walls of the stage.

Discussing the moving panels was clearly the highest priority as they were essentially another character in the show. The team expressed interest in having them completely remote-driven. The concerns of the Opera staff included expense, load-in time with time to calibrate, impact of wind and rain, and the potential for power outages. All that said, we had an alternative idea. Since we have no front curtain, we are very used to carefully choreographing the movement of props and scenery. By tracking these panels into a grid in a deck, the crew could consistently move the panels in all directions very smoothly from behind and out of sight. The track system would also keep the panels from being blown off-track in the wind or entirely blown over. Finally, this meant that the panels would work regardless of a power outage or a lightning strike!

The careful discussion of all the requirements and potential solutions and making sure everyone had full understanding of the hurdles and the options available, helped to come to a solution at the end of the meeting. The project could then move forward in a positive direction knowing that there was a package to work on and possible solutions to work on the final design and ultimate construction continued. This process helped to build a trusting relationship with all parties, realizing that everyone would play an active part in supporting the goals and working creatively together toward those goals.

This new opera was one of three productions in this season with extensive projections. Each of the three video designers had their circumstances to deal with

Figure 11.3   Video editing screens on the tech table of the Santa Fe Opera Premier of *The (r)Evolution of Steve Jobs*
Credit: Photo by Paul Horpedahl

and problems to solve but this one was by far the most complicated. Our schedule, coupled with a focus time in the broad daylight, makes relocating projectors for each production fairly impossible. After many discussions with each designer, it was possible to begin to narrow down the locations of the six projectors and which location would have which level of output.

This culminated in a face-to-face meeting with all three designers and the lighting department. Through this careful deliberation and helping everyone understand the more global issues at hand, as well as an understanding and respect for what the other shows were doing, everyone was able to come to a projector layout that could be accommodating to all three productions and be sensitive to the tight scheduling and focus needs.

Opera is such a complex art form to put together with so many technical aspects to guide and assemble. There are many technical skills, from crafting and construction to spreadsheets and scheduling programs that will be great tools to make it manageable. The patience and discipline to listen, translate and negotiate, in my opinion, are the key soft skills that really separate a good manager from a great one.

CASE STUDY – *GÖTTERDÄMMERUNG*

CONTRIBUTOR – AUTUMN COPPAWAY, DIRECTOR OF PRODUCTION – EDMONTON OPERA

In Anishinaabe culture, we learn lessons of responsibility through our teachings, stories, and history; so that we may use this wisdom to invest in kindness for our future. My mother's translation has been, "Leave a person, place, or thing better than you found it." These nurturing morals helped foster my successful career in artistic management. As production managers, we are responsible for our people, our companies, and of course, our productions. Whether the company is producing a new opera, remounting a previous production, or just documenting a workshop, the job is communication, learning from our mistakes, and creative problem-solving.

Although the Canadian Opera Company had mounted pieces of Wagner's *Ring Cycle* in the past, the complete series had never been done by any national company until 2005. *Die Walküre*, *Siegfried* and *Götterdämmerung* were originally designed for Toronto's Hummingbird Centre, but the Canadian Opera Company produced the full Ring Cycle to open their new opera house, the Four Seasons Centre for the Performing Arts. Beginning in 2014, the company remounted one Ring Cycle production per year; and the decade of undocumented knowledge, degradation, and hard lessons were exposed to not just the elements.

It is essential to start remounts at the beginning – and the end. Usually, only 40% of production paperwork is digitized, and often information is stored in decentralized areas due to interdepartmental complexities. Productions will change once transferred to the performance space. Institutional knowledge is important, but spike marks, documentation, labels, creative liberties, and crew members' memories may all contradict each other.

When referencing decentralization as a problem for collecting documentation, I also include music departments. Music cuts can heavily affect future budgeting, with a few bars of variation potentially costing an extra $10,000+ in crew alone. Depending on the maestro, an "as played" pit plot can be useful as well. In addition, ground plans with microphone placements, foldback speakers, and maestro camera placements can also affect repertoire plans.

Unfortunately, *Götterdämmerung* had an outdated, unfiltered plot; different versions and much of the set had to be re-built. This combination created additional challenges, and our initial rep plan was completely inapplicable due to all these factors. After building a few custom plugs and shifting some positions, we achieved the changeovers within the needed time constraints. A change in repertory productions can greatly affect time and physical capabilities. Creative problem-solving and a few compromises can be great tools, especially when bartering for extra time and money to spend on damage control.

The large pieces of the show had been stored in the company's rural aircraft hangars, but smaller elements were undocumented and scattered across our buildings in Toronto. We extracted bits from our scenic shop, two trailer yards, the Four Seasons Centre, both aircraft hangars, and several "time-capsuled" storage spaces within the office buildings. Most items had been hastily stored, exposed to the elements, and broken. Units degrade when not properly stored or maintained periodically. Many of *Götterdämmerung*'s flown units, including the 70' florescent-fixture curtain, had been dismantled and left uncovered. The large overhead "wires" had been rolled into a single tarp and left sitting on muddy cement for 10 years. Inside the mess of cables, we discovered six rodent nests, complete with rodent bodies. Decay, mold, fecal matter, and a raccoon carcass were found among the rake's wooden canvas risers. We rented deep carpet cleaners and power washers, and I even hired an exterior company to clean the elements which felt too dangerous to bring into the building.

Figure 11.4   Canadian Opera Company's *Gotterdamerung*, 2017
Credit: Photo by Gary Beechey, BDS Studios

The safest and most effective solution for the wires was a complete re-build. The original 70' tension cables were crafted with 6' sections of open-cell foam that had the be flame-treated, painted, and individually attached to aircraft wire. In the remount, we were able to find a company that could create long extrusions of recycled black IFR etho-foam, however, there was a catch. The custom widths meant the required order volume far exceeded our needs. I often strive to source out modern recycled material as a replacement and have found this type of thinking can actually minimize production and capital spending in a variety of ways, especially with amortization over years of repertoire. Although the extra tubing has been handy for shipping and other production needs, I am quite certain the next scenic carpenter will find several boxes of this etho-foam in time-capsule storage areas.

Our rebuild budget expanded by 15% to accommodate for additional personnel, material, and PPE needed to prepare the production for the stage. Once onstage, budgetary problems were just as troublesome. We quickly realized crew estimates did not reflect the cost of living increases or decades of contract changes. In order to accommodate the numerous union agreements and production needs, breaks were scheduled in staggered groups to ensure all 350 performers, musicians, and crew were fed within the 3.5-hour rotation. Complete production was 27% over-budget, but in the end, our job is to achieve the vision (or re-vision) and our responsibility to our team.

This industry was built – and continues to be built – on human collaboration and exploration. In live performance, we thrive on challenges and learning new ways of problem-solving for our career, company, and community. My mother taught me the responsibility for these people, places, and things. Our teachers will come from a variety of backgrounds and relationships. Leadership, heads of departments, stage management, elders, present, and future generations can assist us on our collaborative journey. My culture teaches us our places and our things are not inherited from our elders but borrowed from our children. Plan to teach the next generation your story, so that in its remount, they can also have new creative challenges instead of just recreations of the past.

Dance

To understand the duties of the production manager in dance, we need to understand the discipline, the reasoning for the work, and how it all comes together. The unique part of this art form is that its driving force lies within the movement. The story, the themes or even, sometimes, the music take a secondary role to the movement of bodies in space. "Dance" is an all-encompassing art that contains many styles, but for the purposes of this chapter, we will focus on two types of dance – ballet and contemporary.

BALLET

> "At the second performance of *The Daughter of the Snows*, this change turned into a complete fiasco. The wings, as well as the set at the back, cracked, toppled over, and broke in pieces. The machinist at that time was Legat, a relative of the Legat family of ballet dancers. The disastrous incident of the scenery so affected him, that he lost his reason right there on the stage."[1]
>
> - From the memories of Marius Petipa, Choreographer (1818–1900)

The quote above leads us to understand that there was a technical supervisor as part of ballet even as far back as the 19th century. This machinist is no doubt the technical director as we now know it. As technology progressed and electricity became a part of the ballet, the technical director began to take on the role of lighting, as well. And as productions became more and more complicated to achieve, the stage manager joined the team. The position of production manager in ballet grew out of the need for one person to wrangle the various technical elements, budget, and schedule. The job of the production manager in dance is very similar to other performing art forms. The difference lies in handling the unique nature of the discipline.

DOI: 10.4324/9780367808174-16

Figure 12.1   The College-Conservatory of Music at the University of Cincinnati
Credit: Photo by Adam Zeek, www.zeekcreative.com

The origins of ballet date back to the 15th century, when European nobility was entertained by and often participated in dances as part of large celebrations such as weddings and coronations. In the 1600s, ballet existed mostly as a component of opera until the 19th century, when it emerged as an independent entertainment. Most of the classic ballets that we know today began in this period—*Coppélia*, *Swan Lake*, *Giselle*. This is also where the dancers first began dancing on pointe shoes and tutus first made an appearance.

The modern ballet world exists as part of what some term the elite arts – a highly specialized and honored form of dance that people often pay a great ticket price to attend. The lavish production elements and skilled dancers, whose training often begins as children, make it a challenging and often costly performance to mount.

Ballet companies are similar to other large producing entities in that they have departments such as marketing/public relations, development, business, and production. Dissimilarly, they have departments and personnel unique to this art form.

- Ballet master/mistress: This person (or persons, in some larger companies) oversees the upkeep of the company of dancers by leading a daily conditioning class during rehearsals and performances. They are also tasked with leading rehearsals to reinforce the choreographer's work. They may also be able to re-stage or "set" classical works on the company in lieu of the choreographer.

- Music administration: Almost as important as the movement in many ballet companies is the music. Most ballets are performed with live orchestras, so the synthesis of the music and the orchestra is important to a successful production. The head of the music department is the conductor or maestro/maestra. This person selects and rehearses the musicians and then conducts the orchestra during the performance. The conductor often will have support staff, including a librarian and a music manager. The librarian is tasked with making sure the correct sheet music is distributed and archived for later productions, and the manager schedules and contracts the musicians. There is often a full-time rehearsal pianist as well who plays for all of the rehearsals and company classes.

- Health and wellness: Ballet is hard on the body. Most dancers have only a few years in their prime before the art form begins to take its toll. Injuries are very common, so the need for a physical therapist, masseuse and other health and wellness professionals is common. Many large companies have these positions on staff or have on-call relationships with local health care professionals.

- Education and training: Many ballet companies incorporate a school with the goal of training the next generation of ballet dancers. Often, the head of the school and the teachers are former or current dancers in the company. Students in the school might serve as extras in large ballet – very common in productions of *The Nutcracker*.

The season of a ballet company is likely to include a few different types of performances. A *narrative/story ballet* is a two or three act long ballet with a plot and characters, such as *Sleeping Beauty* or *Romeo and Juliet*. These ballets might be presented with the choreography of the original creator or they might be reimaged by a new choreographer. A *repertory program* is an evening made up of more than one ballet, sometimes as many as five or six, that are short in length, usually based on a theme or idea, and often do not include a plot or characters. The program might be connected by the works of one choreographer, composer, or a common theme. Many ballet companies also include local, national, or even international tours as part of their season. (See Chapter 17, Touring.)

Some productions, such as the story ballets, might include a variety of production elements – scenery depicting multiple locations, costume changes for each scene, etc. Some, however, might be very simple, with only one costume per dancer and no scenery other than black side masking and a blue scrim backdrop, commonly referred to as a "black and blue." Most repertory programs require simple production needs, so you can easily transition between works without having to take a long break or intermission for changing scenery. Many ballet companies do not own a theatre, so they must find roadhouses that will allow them to present their productions. Most companies choose to perform only a few shows over one or two weekends. There are many factors that go into determining the number of shows such as the market, ticket prices, house size, venue staff salaries, venue rental costs, and other programming. The exception to that is *The Nutcracker*. This popular show, with its holiday theme, attracts large audiences and is a sure money-maker for a company. For this reason, it is usually performed multiple times over weeks or sometimes months.

Some ballet companies have productions in their "repertoire," meaning that they have someone on staff who can stage the choreography and they have the production elements in storage, with set pieces and costumes that can easily be reused. Not having to start from scratch results in major cost savings. Companies who hold onto these production elements for their repertoire can generate revenue by allowing these production packages to be rented by other ballet companies. The production manager of the company that owns the production will work closely with the production manager of the company renting the package to negotiate the fees, shipping, and return.

Some companies choose to create new work, or "premieres." Creating new work follows a similar timeline to other new performing arts productions. With premieres, the production manager facilitates the choreographer and designers through conceptual and design processes, similar to theatre productions. The process will result in executing production elements. Rehearsals are necessary for all ballets, but the rehearsal process will most likely be much longer than if existing choreography was used. It generally takes about one year from conception to performance for a new ballet.

Ballet companies produce new work less often; therefore, the need for full-time production artisans is unlikely. The exceptions are that most ballet companies employ a full-time lighting person, and it is also common for there to be a small costume staff. One of the most important production elements of any ballet is lighting. In some cases, it may be the only design element. For that reason, many companies choose to hire a full-time resident designer. Some companies may choose to have a lighting director who might serve as both a designer and head electrician. The small costume staff of at least one or two workers fits and maintains costume inventories and facilitates the process of renting costumes to other companies. When it is necessary to build scenery and props, the production managers for ballet companies often contract with independent shops or hire individuals for show-by-show needs.

Perry Silvey, former Director of Production for the New York City Ballet, sums up the work of the ballet production manager best: "There is not much that is

Figure 12.2 Tiffanie Carson and Ellie van Bever in *De-Generate* (2012) choreographed by Christopher K. Morgan
Credit: Photo by Brianne Bland

absolutely necessary for ballet. A dancer can dance on a beach on the sand if they wish, but as soon as you come into the theatre, you have to prioritize for them. They have to have the floor, it's the first thing. Then you go from there and add every layer that is appropriate – music, masking, lighting, etc."

CONTEMPORARY DANCE

Contemporary dance came about mid-20th century and accepts inspiration from all forms of dance, creating new performance experiences. Contemporary dance also closely aligns with the Performance Art movement which emerged at the same time. This form of dance can be challenging to understand and watch, as it does not often lend itself to a clear story or idea. Choreographer Christopher K. Morgan explains that "there is no mysterious language that only dancers and choreographers speak. Each viewer's own experiences and knowledge that they bring to viewing the dance are all that are needed. Trust that. And know that your viewing of these dances is a valuable part of the choreographic process."

Production managing for contemporary dance requires an open mind. The ideas that emerge from the choreographer will be plentiful and many might be so unique that it will take you time to wrap your head around them. Find ways to say yes and share in the excitement with the choreographer for the ideas presented. Together you will create something brilliant and memorable.

> "The type of folks who get into lighting design also have the brain and the mindset that a production manager needs, so the leap is not that far. Most dance groups don't have a production manager, so the lighting designer is often pulled into making other technical things happen."
>
> - Jon Harper, Lighting Designer and Production Manager

Contemporary dance can be performed and experienced in a variety of venues ranging from traditional theatres to non-theatrical settings (also termed a site-specific work). Contemporary dance might be performed as a solo program, a shared program, or in a festival. Let's look at each iteration:

WORKING IN A THEATRE

There are dance-specific theatres throughout the country or flexible-use theatres that can present dance among other art forms such as theatre or opera. Similar to ballet, the type of floor is very important. Many dancers prefer a vinyl floor (often called a Marley floor, named for a company that used to produce them), while others prefer a bare wooden floor. Regardless of the surface, the floor needs to be a "sprung floor," which means that the top wooden layer should have space directly under it to allow the floor give. Dancing on floors that are not sprung (concrete, linoleum, etc.) can be very harmful to dancers, resulting in injuries. As production manager, you will also have to plan for many of the same technical elements as you would for a theatrical presentation, such as masking, lighting, sound, costumes, and sometimes scenery and projections. The production manager of the company presenting the work will need to work closely with the production manager at the venue to ensure clear communication and accommodation. (See Chapter 15, Presenting.)

Figure 12.3   *Visible Seams* created by Erin Crawley Woods in the Clarice Smith Performing Arts Center
Credit: Photo by Zachary Z. Handler

SITE-SPECIFIC WORK

An increasingly popular choice for contemporary dance is to move the performance beyond the walls of a traditional theatre and create choreography using a non-traditional space. Site-specific work is so named as it uses the location as the inspiration for the movement, patterns, and emotional qualities of the dance. The site-specific movement grew out of visual art installations that similarly used space as inspiration. The site can be anywhere – the lobby of a theatre, a stairwell, a city street. Not utilizing a theatre space can provide logistical challenges for the production manager, especially when planning how to incorporate, acquire, and utilize elements such as lights and sound. Also, one must carefully consider many factors that we take for granted within theatre spaces, such as permits to use the space, creating a "backstage" and, if performing outside, the weather. There is also the question of the audience experience – are they seated, and, if so, where, or are they encouraged to move among the performers. In general, audiences are expected to sit and watch, so if something else is required of them, it's best to prepare them ahead of time and/or use performers to help them know where to go and what to do.

SOLO CONCERT VERSUS SHARED PROGRAM

Many choreographers aspire to produce or be presented in a solo show, meaning they are the only choreographer on the program. If this is the case, then complete control of all elements resides with the choreographer. The light plot, masking, projector placement, and so on are as the choreographer and their design team desire. However, if it is a shared program with one or more choreographers, then compromise is necessary. Shared programs are common in contemporary dance. Often, dance works are short in length, which lends to a concert with multiple components. Shared concerts can also be more economical, especially if the choreographers are required to find and rent their own venue.

DANCE FESTIVALS

Dance festivals occur throughout the United States, bringing together multiple choreographers to present work. Presenting in the festival format often means collaborating on a predetermined physical setup of the stage and light plot. Because there are many works being brought together in one theatre space, there is usually a strict time limit for technical preparation and for striking after the performance. There may also be a time limit for each dance performance. Most dance festivals will employ a production manager to oversee the entire festival and make sure things run efficiently. The creation of the tech and performance schedule is a complicated task for the production manager, as these festivals may have 10 choreographers or more within a short period of time.

Unlike ballet, there are fewer contemporary dance *companies*. There are some successful companies, such as Doug Varone and Dancers, Susan Marshall and Company, and Camille A. Brown and Dancers. As you can tell from their names, they are based around a founding choreographer. Rarely, if ever, do these companies perform the works of different choreographers, though many collaborate with their company dancers to create the themes and movement of their performances. Most choreographers do not have the financial resources to assemble a company of dancers and support a full season. It is more likely that choreographers assemble a group of dancers for a single performance opportunity. In these instances, the dancers might not be paid or are paid a percentage of the box office receipts. For these less-funded single performances, the choreographer might have to take on the production management functions as well.

Production managing for dance can be a challenging yet rewarding undertaking. If you love to dance and are inspired by the creative process, you will certainly enjoy this work. And if you have a desire or aptitude toward lighting and production management – dance could be the perfect place for you! It's important to know that dance artists have rarely had training in technical theatre and production management aspects of the performing arts. Unlike most undergraduate theatre programs, dance programs rarely require their students to take technical/production courses. Some choreographers, who are accustomed to producing their own concerts, might find it difficult giving over responsibility to a production manager. Others might be grateful to finally allow someone else to handle the logistics so they can simply create!

CASE STUDY – *ANNA KARENINA*

CONTRIBUTOR: CODY CHEN, GENERAL MANAGER (FORMER PRODUCTION MANAGER) OF THE JOFFREY BALLET

In my very first season with The Joffrey Ballet, the company premiered *Anna Karenina*, a brand-new full-length story ballet co-produced with The Australian Ballet. The production process had started long before I joined the company. When I arrived, my position had been vacant for months and the company was also looking for a new general manager. I began by scouting for information about this ballet from paper trails, my predecessor's emails, and conversations with colleagues, yet even after a great effort, I was not able to get the full picture. Thankfully, the company retained a project manager for this production during the interim. I reached out to the project manager, and we sat down and had a proper onboarding. The meeting not only brought me up to speed but also clarified some puzzles from my research. When the new general manager joined the team, we divided up tasks and shared progress with each other. Delegation allowed the team to streamline processes and communication ensuring information was not lost and deadlines were met.

The creative team consisted of a group of prolific artists who lived in different parts of the world and had multiple projects in progress. Having a production meeting with everyone in a room was challenging. We tried teleconferencing, but the process was inefficient, and the outcome was not satisfying. Small decision-making quickly became urgent. Through the new general manager, we learned that the same creative team would be dry-teching another premiere for his previous company in early fall. This was an opportunity not to be missed. With some arrangements, we secured an hour during the creative team's busy schedule and flew a group of staff there and back on the same day to meet with them in person. It was not the cheapest design meeting, but progress was made that we would otherwise not be able to make. All things considered, it was a wise investment.

Figure 12.4   Joffrey Company Artists Anais Bueno and Alberto Velazquez in Yuri Possokhov's *Anna Karenina*

Credit: Photo by Cheryl Mann

The scenery was built in a European shop and the international freight, in this case, required extra effort. After the sea containers carrying the scenery took off in mid-December, they endured an unexpectedly long voyage across the Atlantic due to severe weather conditions. When the ship finally docked in New Jersey, a winter snowstorm raged across the northeast USA and created a huge backlog at the port and affected rail operations. I was on the phone with the shipper daily to guarantee our shipment remained on his priority list. When the containers reached Chicago, a polar vortex was in the forecast. We were two weeks away from the load-in and could not afford further delay. I spoke with our carpentry team, and everyone was eager to put their hands on the scenery as soon as possible. We unloaded the containers on the day when Chicago's windchill dipped to minus 50 degrees.

Prior to the load-in, we met with the design team to discuss the lineset schedule. The lineset schedule was complicated because after the show premiered in Chicago, it was scheduled to tour to a theatre whose stage is 20 feet shallower than at home. We consulted the designers on the hang, especially on the reduction necessary for the tour. The designers elected to focus on the premiere and decide on adjustments after the show was made. In hindsight, my preference would have been to develop a plan while the design team was in residency. After opening, the company's artistic and production departments collaborated and solved the problem by eliminating the less-used scenic items to free up overhead real estate and scaling down the deck units. The ballet looked different at the second venue, but we were able to set up the production on schedule and still maintain the design integrity.

After a 50-hour work week in the theatre, I received a request from the choreographer to change the floor on Saturday after lunch. The black linoleum, originally selected, made the ballet look too dark and artistic was hoping that a gray floor would lighten up the show. The change involved hours of work. Adding a Sunday call was impractical as an eight-hour minimum crew call on a double time rate would put a dent in the already stretched budget. Moreover, the crew would need a day of rest before the technical rehearsals and opening. To decline this request was not something that felt right to do, so I needed to devise a solution that balanced artistic pursuit and fiscal responsibility. I had a discussion with the project manager and our props master/union steward. After examining various scenarios with the union rules, we decided to move the dinner break earlier and add a three-hour call afterward. During dinner, the project manager rented a truck and two stagehands met him at our warehouse to load the floor. I organized dinner for the team. By the end of the day, we managed to change the floor with the least amount of expenses and minimum impact on the schedule. It was a team effort and the change later proved to be the right call.

Anna Karenina premiered to critical acclaim and box office success. After the curtain came down on the opening night, everyone felt a sense of pride and relief. The production was a huge undertaking and we rose to the occasion. As one of my mentors always says to me: it takes a village.

CASE STUDY – *SISTER'S FOLLIES*

CONTRIBUTOR: JON HARPER, CURRENT MANAGING DIRECTOR (FORMER PRODUCTION MANAGER/TECHNICAL DIRECTOR) AT ABRONS ARTS CENTER

When I got hired in 2013 to work at Abrons Arts Center on Manhattan's lower east side as the new production manager/technical director, I was very excited because all three theatres were beautiful each in their own unique way and most of the work being presented was contemporary dance. In our world, we call this "downtown dance" to contrast with "uptown dance" which includes ballet, larger companies like Alvin Ailey, and anyone that you might see at City Center. Contemporary dance as a genre here comprises a huge range of movement-based practices, performance art, and things created by the dance community that doesn't even involve humans moving through space. A lot of times the technical requirements are as complicated, if not even MORE complicated than the average theatre show. An open, creative, and excited mind is necessary for production managers to have in order to participate in a healthy way in this space. It is our job to make sure that things are getting done safely and within budget without crushing everyone's dreams (too much).

For instance, we put on a show called *Sister's Follies* for our centennial celebration in 2015 that celebrated 100 years of dance and performance history in our main theatre. It was our largest commission ever for a show. Basil Twist, the master puppeteer, created the show with us and focused on the first era of the theatre from 1915 to 1928. It starred Joey Arias and Julie Atlas Muz as the ghosts

Figure 12.5 *Sister's Follies* at the Abrons Arts Center
Credit: Photo by Richard Termine

of the two sisters who founded the theatre (Alice and Irene Lewisohn). The sisters narrated as we went through, sometimes reminiscing and sometimes fighting as siblings are known to do. In order to make them more supernatural, the creative team decided that they wanted to fly both actors over the stage so that they could, well, be ghosts! They flew back and forth, up and around each other, their emotions driving their actions, even at one point getting into a battle! To make this happen we had to build a large truss over the stage which would be both the structure for two flying rigs to fly our two "ghosts" of the founding sisters above the stage and as a platform for puppets manipulated from overhead. Figuring out how to do this safely took a lot of outside-the-box thinking and a lot of saying "yes, IF" and "no, BUT" instead of shutting outrageous ideas down from the start with a "hard no." We made sure to have a good team of aerial dance riggers on board and got to work figuring it out.

This was definitely a show with "10 pounds of stuff in a 5 pound box" as the saying goes. Every inch of the onstage, overhead, and backstage space was taken up with puppets, scenery, trick lines, and all manner of other things. Historically, the sisters had created many avant-garde performances during this period, and we were able to research a lot of what they had done and attempt to recreate it with a humorous twist. It was delightfully low-tech stuff that fits well with the theatre architecture and the fun take on the history of it. For instance, there was a dramatic flood in one scene that drowns everyone and was the end of the play we were recreating. We used the same method they had all those many years ago, using a blue scrim pulled up from hiding on the floor in front of actors, scenery, and everything, slowly and shakily rising until everyone is "underwater" and the play ends.

Throughout this process, both the show's technical director and the primary puppet builder under Basil would come to me at different times with this look of "OK, so I have to ask you this thing, and I'm pretty sure you're going to tell me there is no way in heck that we are going to able to do this." Each time, I would always respond with enthusiasm and support. Sometimes I did have to say no to their requests either because of safety or budget concerns but would then set to figuring out how to make the same thing happen but in a different way. A year or so later, I asked the technical director for a recommendation for another position that I was applying for. He wrote the following:

> Jon allowed me and my company to come in and take over his newly refurbished scene shop to turn it into a wild frolly of puppet building, and a large-scale rigging project to occur onstage simultaneously with calm, patient, and watchful eyes. When we were low on manpower, Jon would be suddenly present to help us set up truss for a flying performer rig, or to troubleshoot any issues we had on stage…I expected to hear a lot more "No's" in regard to the amount of unconventional requests I had for Basil's wild and relatively unconventional show of which, I should add, I had many! But instead, I found a curious and creative colleague in Jon, and together we were able to think outside the box and find clever solutions to our rigging and other technical quandaries which Sister's Follies presented. Had he not been at Abrons for the four months of our time there, our show might have been a disaster.

I feel like the spirit of this commentary is the spirit with which we should always approach production management. It is certainly not always easy, and certainly not always possible depending on the behavior of our collaborators. However, when we can, it means that whether we are saying "yes" or "no," everyone recognizes that we are all part of the same team, all working together to make the best show we possibly can.

NOTE

1   Petipa, Marius. *Russian Ballet Master, the Memoirs of Marius Petipa.* London: A. & C. Black, 1958.

Rock and Roll

> "An organized show is not hard to achieve as long as you are on top of the details. Pay attention and do what needs to be done ahead of time, and then your show day should be seamless and organized. Remember that Proper Prior Planning Prevents Poor Performance"
>
> - Michael Richter, Production Manager for REO Speedwagon/Richter Entertainment Group

The glamorous world of rock and roll and the touring music business is another artistic genre that requires a reliable and competent production manager at the helm. Whether on the road and touring or having a staff job as a venue's production manager, the job of the production manager is fast-paced and has many moving parts that need careful management on a regular basis. Much like production managers in other artistic disciplines, flexibility and patience are the top attributes of a production manager in the music business. John Sanders, a top production touring professional whose recent credits include Sting, Paul Simon, KISS, Def Leppard, and The Eagles, agrees and says:

On a typical show day, a production manager could have any number of people coming at them in a very short amount of time. For instance, the first thing prior to load-in, venue personnel will want to see stage placement and dressing room assignments, the truck drivers will want to know parking and order of trucks unloading, and the bus drivers will want to know where to park. While all of this is happening, crew members will want to know about the location of catering and laundry, riggers will want to see a tickets-sold map for an audio hang, and the list goes on ... and all of this within the first ten minutes of walking into a venue. It can be overwhelming and having a great deal of patience and flexibility are strong qualities of a good production manager. These attributes will get you through event days while maintaining a cordial and professional demeanor. All of this takes discipline. If you cannot discipline yourself, you won't be a good production manager.

DOI: 10.4324/9780367808174-17

Figure 13.1   Sunrise load in, San Diego
Credit: Photo By Jay Sheehan

Being flexible refers to dealing both with people and with situations. Dealing with
the physical needs of the production requires quick and flexible thinking on the part
of the production managers, as each venue has its own quirks, both good and bad. As
Sanders notes, some venues have truck docks, some don't; some venues have plenty
of dressing rooms, some never have enough; some venues have great local crews, some
have poor labor crews; some venues can get a show up in four or five hours; some
venues may take eight hours for the same shows; some venues can hang your entire
show; some venues can hang 50% of your show.

As you can see, production managers need to be flexible and work together to seek out solutions to the challenges they face to make a concert happen.

TOURING NEEDS VS VENUE CAPABILITIES

What are the similarities and differences between the TOURING production manager and the VENUE production manager? Both have goals that they need to attain, with the main goal being to safely load a show into and out of a venue in the most efficient manner using the resources available.

When it comes to the differences between the two jobs, Sanders says:

> *A venue production manager and a touring production manager are different in what they are experts of. A venue production manager is (or should be) an expert as it relates to the capabilities of their venue and should be able to communicate those capabilities to the touring production manager. They do not need to be an expert in the details of a show but only how their venue capabilities can provide for the show's needs. A touring production manager is (or should be) an expert as it relates to the needs of the performance and should be able to communicate those needs to the venue production manager. If both the venue and touring production managers maintain the same course of action to achieve their goals as noted above, then they will be successful in safely loading the show in and out in the shortest amount of time, in the most efficient manner and with minimal or no issues.*

Figure 13.2   Load in for "Feeding America Concert"

Figure 13.3   Setting out the truss line

Figure 13.4   Adding the shade roof

Figure 13.5 Posts are in

Figure 13.6 Ready for sound check

Figure 13.7   "Feeding America Concert" featuring Chicago
Credit: Photos by Jay Sheehan

With regard to touring, one may think that it's an easy life on the road since they get to do the same show each night but there are some challenges. The production manager in the touring aspect has a few more hurdles to jump over compared to the venue production manager. The first and most obvious is the fact that 80% of the world's tours will travel on tour buses. This will include the band and band's staff, including the production manager. Learning to live with up to 10 other crew members in a single bus can be a challenge. Sleeping quarters are approximately 8 feet × 3 feet, generally, there are no showers on the bus, groceries are often shared (or fought over!) and the main living quarters on the bus are shared with your fellow travelers. Getting along is essential to a happy tour!

Living on the road has its other issues, as well, such as eating healthy meals, getting enough rest, and keeping proper hygiene. Schedules for crew oftentimes find them eating at abnormal hours or late at night. Exercise is challenging while on tour, and special attention needs to be paid to personal well-being. All of this adds up to some real stresses for people on tour, and the production manager must always be at ready to deal with these added challenges.

That's not to say that the production manager that has a venue job doesn't have some of the same challenges. Early load-ins, bad catering, and cranky stagehands can certainly be found in non-touring applications as well. Either way, the rock and roll production manager must be flexible and adapt to the ever-changing environments for themselves and their staff.

VENUE PRODUCTION MANAGEMENT

Large venues will usually have a staff venue production manager to represent the venue. They will handle the "advance of a show" (more on that later) and communicate the needs of the touring show to the venue's staff and vendors. This is the primary job of the venue production manager, and like in the other artistic disciplines, this information needs to be collected and disseminated. When representing the venue, the production manager must always have the best interest of the venue in mind. This can, at times, cause some distress between the venue and touring production managers, but the art of compromise and negotiation are essential components of the production manager's toolkit. Each entity is working for their own agenda, their own set of bosses, and their own budgets needing to be met. Venue production managers may be trying to find ways to save money for the venue or local promoter while the touring production manager is asking for more labor to help his touring crew get the show in. It is a constant negotiation between the two parties, each trying to get the most out of their resources.

> "A good thorough 'advance' is important so the day goes seamlessly. In my opinion, there is no reason everything can't be in order from the start of the day to the end of the day if both the touring production manager and the venue production manager pay attention to all the details given during the advance."
>
> - Michel Richter, Production Manager for
> REO Speedwagon/Richter Entertainment Group

ADVANCING A SHOW

The first step when planning a large music event for the venue is the dissemination of information from the band's contract and rider. Usually, this document contains everything that the venue production manager will need to know to get the show "advanced" with the touring production manager. "Advancing the show" will be a very common term you will hear when working as a production manager in the music business. Advancing means getting and disseminating as much detailed information as possible to all parties in advance of the show's arrival.

THE CONTRACT AND TECHNICAL RIDER

The contract not only contains the artist's salary, or band fee, but it will also contain all the technical needs that the tour will either be bringing with them or will need locally sourced from the venue production manager. Technical needs, labor needs,

Figure 13.8   Rock and Roll stage, Cancun
Credit: Photo by Jay Sheehan

hospitality and catering needs (those items put in the band's dressing rooms), and security calls, are all part of this sometimes cumbersome and detailed document. Once the venue production manager receives the rider from the touring production manager or agent, the actual "advance" can begin. As you begin to read contracts and riders in your career, you will start to understand what items will affect you the most. Usually, there are many pages at the beginning that are the mandatory legal jargon (such as cancellation policies, insurance needs, etc.), and, while this is important information to have and to understand, the integral parts of the rider that affects the production manager are the technical needs and hospitality.

It is prudent to ask the touring personnel if you are working from the most current rider. It is not uncommon to see outdated riders while working as a production manager, and you must stay on top of making sure you have the most current rider.

TECHNICAL NEEDS

Bands that are "carrying production" mean that the tour or artist is providing the show with the equipment and is traveling with it on the trucks. Lighting, audio, video, automation, and special effects are all items of the touring production gear list. On many tours, an entire truck can be dedicated to a wardrobe or other items that make the artist feel at home. (The Rolling Stones used to carry two trucks filled with video arcade games for the band and their backstage guests to play while waiting for the show to start!)

The tech rider will let you know if the band is carrying production or partial production or if you will need to rent out or provide "local sound," "local lights," and "local video," as some of the smaller or newer touring bands may not have the capacity or resources to carry their own production. The rider will indicate what you will need to acquire. It is not uncommon to see specific requests for audio gear, such as a certain brand of speaker or make and model of the front-of-house audio console. Specialized lighting is often asked for, with several various brands and models of moving lights and lighting consoles. Special effects are often discussed in this section of the rider as well; requests for CO_2 tanks for confetti cannons or pyrotechnics are not uncommon.

With regard to audio, as mentioned above, some artists may ask for a particular brand or make of audio speakers for the main PA (PA is still a term used in rock and roll and stands for public address). The monitor board may also be a specific brand request. Some artists and audio engineers are very particular (and SENSITIVE) about specific brands of gear, so be sure you read and understand their requests.

Another important portion of the technical rider is called the audio input list. This is especially important for your sound crew to have, as it contains all of the instrumentation and audio channel assignments going into the main audio console. Additionally, this list will contain microphone types used and even what type of microphone stand is used.

The last important piece of the rider puzzle is the stage plot. The stage plot is the equivalent of the ground plan and will be a valuable source of information for the production manager. This document will (or should!) have the placement of all equipment that goes on stage. Audio monitors, drum risers, microphone placement, keyboard placement, and space for the technicians to work in are all part of the stage plot. Having the plot ahead of time will help expedite the load-in. If you don't see one, ask the production manager. Much like keeping and maintaining a prompt script in theatre, the technical rider is a document you want close to you at all times, so keep it handy either in your binder or on a tablet so that you are prepared to answer (and ask!) as many questions as possible when it comes to advancing the show.

TIP – As in many of the performing arts, most music tours today will have a light plot indicating what is being used or what needs to be outsourced locally. If you don't see it in the rider, make sure you ask for one from the touring production manager. The light plot is especially important if you need to acquire lighting from your local lighting equipment provider, as they will use this document to prepare the light rig in the shop and send it to the venue.

Figure 13.9

LABOR NEEDS

The massive amount of equipment in the trucks requires a great number of people to unload and set up. Typically, tours will carry department heads, such as a stage manager, lighting director, audio engineers, automation, video technicians, etc., but will need local crew to supplement the rider in order to get the equipment set up in a timely manner. It is not unheard of for bands like U2, Lady Gaga, or Madonna to call up to 100 local crew members to get their shows loaded in. A previous Lady Gaga tour incorporated close to forty 53-foot trucks and needed an army of crew to get the job done. It is the venue's production manager who must secure the labor needs as presented in the rider. The good news is that most major cities with large concert venues also have a local stagehand staffing office, and the in-house production manager simply calls the labor office to ask for the amount of crew needed. It is imperative that the local production manager has a good working relationship with the local stagehand labor provider. The local production manager will always expect top-notch labor and having a close relationship with the labor company helps to ensure that the touring stagehands are appropriately supported.

Labor numbers are clearly indicated in the rider, and it will usually look something like this:

- Load in: 9 am
- Four truck loaders
- Four lighting crew

- Four audio crew
- Four video crew
- Two backline crew
- One up rigger
- One down rigger
- One electrician

****

- Show Call: 6 pm
- Four stagehands
- Two follow spot operators
- One wardrobe

****

- Load-out: 11 pm
- Four truck loaders
- Six lighting crew
- Six audio crew
- Four video crew
- Two backline crew
- One up rigger
- One down rigger
- One electrician

It is not uncommon to see crew numbers get increased for load-out, as the touring production manager has one goal in mind at the end of the night, and that is to get all the equipment taken down in a safe and efficient manner, as the next stop may be several hours away. Having a good local crew helps get this accomplished and gets the band and crew headed toward their next stop.

HOSPITALITY

Touring personnel usually have two goals in mind when first getting off the bus in the morning: a hot shower and a good breakfast! This is where the artist catering and hospitality rider will come into play. Made famous by Van Halen's 1982 contractual demand that brown M&Ms be plucked from the group's candy bowl, the catering and hospitality rider often reflects the delightful or difficult nature of the individual artists. (More about the brown M&Ms later.)

The venue production manager should take careful note of the hospitality rider and start to make arrangements with the local caterer to procure the items needed for the day. Like with the labor company, most if not all of the major cities around the globe have a local catering company that will handle this for you. It is not the production manager's job to go and shop for food. Your local caterer will take care of that. It is the production manager's job to make sure that the rider is fulfilled. This hospitality rider will not only include a guide for breakfast, lunch, and dinner but will also contain the food requests for after the show, dressing rooms, stage coolers, the production office, bus stock, and towels for showers. It is not unusual for the artist to request a specific type of meal on Monday, Wednesday, Friday, etc. This assures some variance to meals and guarantees that the touring personnel won't be eating hotdogs and burgers seven nights a week!

The hospitality rider is a living, breathing document, ever-changing, as artist needs can change on a daily basis. Make sure that you have the most recent hospitality rider prior to advancing your show. You can get the most updated rider by contacting the band's production or tour manager or the band's agency. You may also get a copy of the contract from the producer if you are working with these bands in a "corporate special event." There is no one person to ask for the rider; ask all your contacts until you find it. Having an up-to-date rider will make your day go by much better if the correct rider requirements are fulfilled. A well-fed artist and crew mean a happy artist and crew. (Most times!)

Touring riders will often times have items requested that may seem strange or difficult to get. Don't get discouraged or caught up in the idea of why the artists need these items; just do your best to get them and make it happen for the touring personnel. It is not unusual to be asked to cover dressing room walls with drape, have special lighting (not fluorescent!) in the dressing rooms or provide any other creature comforts of home. Again, always remember that the artist and crew are living on the road and not in their own homes. It is the job of the venue production manager to make the tour members feel at home. If you or your venue gets this reputation of taking care of the artist and crew, generally speaking, the good word will get out to the other tours traveling around the country. Like theatre, the touring world of the music business is a small one and touring personnel talk to each other. Being on the good side of the tours will always be a bonus for the local production manager and for the venue. No one wants to be known as the venue that doesn't do their job or, worse yet, doesn't care about the touring group.

So what exactly do they ask for in their dressing rooms? As you read the following, try to read with a sense of humor and not a sense of "are you kidding me?"

The rider of a popular artist (who will go unnamed!) required the performer's dressing room (which has to be draped in cream or soft pink) to be outfitted with two cream-colored egg chairs, one of which should have a footstool. A coffee table needs to be "Perspex modern style." A pair of floor lamps should be in "French ornate style," and the singer's refrigerator must come with a glass door. As for the dressing room's flower arrangement, they want "white and purple hydrangeas, pink & white roses and peonies." If those flowers are not available, they will settle for a "selection of seasonal white flowers to include white orchids." However, promoters are advised, "ABSOLUTELY NO CARNATIONS." That warning is, of course, underlined.

When it comes to hotel provisions, this artist requires a "1-bedroom presidential suite" in a "5-star property." And free internet service and a complimentary breakfast must be provided to the performer and their touring party. Chauffeurs, the rider notes, are not allowed to "start a conversation with the client." They also are directed not to stare at the backseat through the rear-view mirror. Drivers should also not "ask for autographs or pictures, and especially not while driving!" Finally, their ride should be outfitted with "four water bottles."

A second example comes from another popular performer. On this tour rider, the singer required promoters to stock their backstage roost with "Cristal champagne," which they consumed via "bendy straws." Next, they asked for a $200 bottle of cabernet sauvignon and her dressing room "outfitted with two dozen white roses and vanilla aromatherapy candles." As for the furniture in her "living room space," they want "no busy patterns; black, dark grey, cream, dark pink are all fine." The room "should be about 75 degrees," and a "lamp or clip light" should be provided so that "harsh lighting may be turned off" in their backstage bathroom.

When another artist headlined at a local university, they banked a $750,000 payday for their performance. But this chart-topping performer did not get every perk requested in their concert rider, since the school does not provide artists with alcohol, tobacco, or $400,000 luxury vehicles. This artist demanded that promoters provide them with ground transportation while they were in town performing. Specifically, this star requires a late-model black Maybach (either the '57 or '62 model) with tinted windows. The dressing room (72 degrees, please) must be stocked with Sapporo beer, vodka, tequila, and two bottles of $300 champagne. This performer also needs two bottles (at $200 apiece) of 2004 Sassicaia, which their rider helpfully describes as a "Red, Italian Wine from Bolgheri Region." Additionally, they require "good quality" peanut butter and jelly, one martini shaker, 12 shot glasses, and a pack of Marlboro Lights.

It can often seem like a chore to get all of those items for the dressing rooms or stage, and sometimes the requests can be a little challenging. But all of these items are put in the rider for a reason, and that is to assure a happy and top-notch performance by the talent. While we may think some of these dressing rooms or technical equipment requests to be strange or petty, it is important to remember that the touring artists and crew don't have the luxury of waking up in their own homes every day. They live in a bus, live out of a suitcase, and generally don't have the comforts of home. The rider requests help to close that gap a bit and to help create a feeling of home for those who work on the road. You shouldn't look at the rider as anything more than that – a document that will help the day go by smoother and could help everyone get along a little better.

All this being said, dressing room riders can be funny or frustrating for the venue production manager. Take it in stride and do your best to get it fulfilled. Once you get the hospitality rider, it is always fair game for the local production manager to ask the touring production manager if they can make any cuts to the rider in order to not waste product or labor, or money. Most times the answer is "No – get me what's on the rider." That is the easy way out, and some touring production managers don't want to deal with changes or don't want to deal with an upset artist if the "bendy straws" aren't there to sip the champagne. Fair enough. On the flip side, there are artists and production managers who do not want to see wasted food or beverages and will make cuts to the rider based on what is actually needed that day. Perhaps the artist won't want that "cheese platter for six" or "deli tray for ten." It is worth asking the band's production manager, at the very least.

And about those brown M&Ms in Van Halen's dressing rooms? This famous story comes from the fact that David Lee Roth, the famous frontman of the band, always demanded brown M&Ms be removed from the candy bowl in his dressing room. He did this not because he hated the brown M&Ms but because he wanted to see if the venue production manager and catering company actually read the rider. If the brown M&Ms were in the bowl, legend has it that the management would get an earful from Mr. Roth!

> **TIP** – Make sure that when you ask about making cuts to the rider, you ask with a tone of "trying to save wasted product" and not about trying to save the promoter or producer money.

SECURITY

As a venue production manager, you will be asked to provide backstage security for the various positions around the artist and their entourage. The rider should clearly indicate the various positions needed, but it is up to the venue production manager to communicate those needs to the security company or operations manager of the venue.

A typical security call in the rider may look something like this:

- Two (2) persons to be available at all times from the time the crew arrives to ensure the security of equipment, crew members, their vehicles, and personal property throughout the day.
- A minimum of two (2) additional persons (dependent on the integrity of the backstage area) to be available from 2:30 pm to ensure the safety and security of the band upon their arrival at the facility, until their departure from the facility.
- From thirty (30) minutes prior to doors opening to the public, until all the public has left after the performance:
- One (1) person at each access point to the backstage area.
- Two (2) persons for the dressing room area.
- Four (4) persons (two on each side of the stage) at the base of the stage access stairs or access points, whichever is applicable.
- Eight (8) persons to be positioned in front of the stage, behind the barricade.
- Two (2) persons to be placed to secure the front-of-house mix position.

The security meeting, usually held about an hour before the doors to the venue open, is one of the most important meetings of the day. During that meeting, the tour manager or tour security director will go over the day's "pass sheet." The pass sheet is a visual look at all of the backstage and tour passes issued for that day's event. Usually, color-coded and dated by city, the pass sheet clearly indicates what areas are accessible to those pass holders on that given day. It is not uncommon to have five to six different colored passes, all indicating a different level of security access.

> While backstage passes are cool to have and to give out, remember that the backstage area is a workplace and that guests should not be permitted to wander around without an escort. Historically speaking, the backstage party was indeed that, but in these modern times, the backstage area is becoming more of a place of business and less of a party hangout.

VENUE TECHNICAL PACKET AND ADVANCE CHECKLISTS

While the rider should contain everything you need to know to produce the show, unfortunately, there are those riders or touring production managers that miss the mark, and you, as the venue production manager, will need to seek out additional information. Having a "venue technical packet" and an "advance checklist" are important tools for you to use during your advance with the touring production manager and should be used every time you advance a show.

VENUE TECHNICAL PACKET

If you find yourself in the role of the venue production manager, you should have a venue technical packet ready to send to the touring production manager. The technical packet should contain all relevant information about the venue's physical and technical layout. This is information that the touring production manager will need in order to do his or her job efficiently.

Here are some examples of what should go into the venue's technical specifications packet:

- Venue address
- Shipping address
- Venue capacity
- Curfew times, if applicable
- Decibel limits, if applicable
- Contact information on important people at the venue, i.e., production manager's cell, operations managers, general manager, box office, production office phones, transportation company, audio head, lighting head, etc.
- Contact number for the person responsible for ticketing and production holds
- Contact number for whoever is paying the band at the end of the night (also known as settling)

- Stage dimensions
- Size of rigging grid
- Front of house mix position dimensions
- Distance from the front of house position to the stage (important for audio and lighting crew to determine cable lengths needed)
- Power available for lighting, audio, video, buses, etc.
- Load-in information/loading dock info
- Dressing room layouts

You will note that many of these questions are going to be asked of you during your advance call or when you are required to fill out the production questionnaire. While you have done your due diligence in creating and disseminating the venue technical packet, don't assume that the touring production manager will always read it. Many times, the touring production manager will be seeing your technical packet for the first time when they first contact you.

> **TIP** – Don't get discouraged or ask yourself "didn't they read my technical packet? All the information is in there!" Just answer the questions that the touring production manager presents to you.

ADVANCE CHECKLIST

The advance checklist is the document that the venue production manager should keep ready when preparing to talk to the touring production manager. This list will assist you in ensuring all questions are answered prior to the band's arrival on show day.

Here are some examples of items that you will need to know and should have on your advance checklist.

- Get contact information of everyone important on the tour. This will include the tour manager, production manager, lighting designer, audio head of department, artist agency and catering, and merchandise seller contacts.
- What are the labor calls?
- Is a production "runner" needed? (A production runner is someone locally who has a car and can go out and get items needed at the last minute. This is usually an entry-level position for those trying to break into the business.)
- What are the lighting and sound needs?
- What are the power requirements needed for the show?
- Is there open flame or other special effects?
- What are the catering and hospitality requirements?
- How many buses and trucks are you traveling in?
- What are the dressing room layouts?
- How many towels are needed for showers for the crew?

- Will the band need local ground transportation, such as vans or limousines?
- Does the artist need stair access from stage to house?
- Will merchandise such as tee shirts, hats, etc., be sold during the event?
- How many backstage passes will be used?
- Will we or can we release any ticket production holds? (More on that later)

The above list of questions should be answered during the advance of the show. As mentioned earlier in this chapter, the advance of the show will be your main responsibility during the pre-planning stages. A proper advance will save you a lot of time on show day if you know everything that's going to happen. Of course, the unplanned will always happen, but having your show advanced well may help prevent many other additional challenges come show day.

TOURING ADVANCE CHECKLIST

While the above points are important information and questions to ask the touring production manager, there are even more questions the touring production manager will have for you about your venue and its operations. These questions will often be delivered in the form of the "venue advance checklist." This checklist should be filled out by the venue production manager and sent back to the tour as soon as possible. This information will then be used by the touring production manager to create the itinerary documents for the touring personnel.

Here are just a few examples of some questions that may be asked of you during the advance:

- Stage size/wing space size of your venue
- Dimensions of riggable grid area above the stage
- Dimensions of riggable grid area downstage of the proscenium
- Number of trucks that can park at the loading dock
- Number of buses that can park backstage
- Is shore power available for buses? (Shore power is the power that buses connect to so they do not have to run their generators. Using shore power saves generator gas along with eliminating gas fumes and excessive noise. When an option, always use shore power.)
- Is a forklift on site?
- Do you have in-house follow spots? If so, what type, amount, and location?
- What power is available onstage or backstage for lighting and sound equipment? (Remember that lighting and audio should always use separate power services. When needed, video can often share with others if separate video power is not available.)

As you can see, a sizeable amount of information needs to be exchanged between the touring production manager and the venue's production manager. Having proper checklists and venue technical packets helps to ensure that the correct information is being conveyed to the necessary staff on the tour.

Figure 13.10   Getting ready for sound check
Credit: Photo by Jay Sheehan

PUTTING ON THE SHOW

Once the show has been advanced by phone between the two production managers, you will have an opportunity to start preparing your venue and vendors for the band's arrival. Security, lighting, audio, video, and stagehand providers can all be contacted now. Most likely, you will be contacting your local stagehand company to secure the additional stage crew needed to get the show loaded in. The next vendor you will contact will be your catering and dressing room hospitality company. At this point, you should have made any cuts or changes to the rider and can confidently pass on that information. Make sure you have accurate counts for the meals for the band, crew, and guests.

> **TIP** – When discussing meal counts for the day, the venue production manager must not forget to add the venue's staff meals to the order Oftentimes, key staff members will need to be included in the meal count numbers, as they don't get a chance to get away for a meal.

Lastly, get in contact with your lighting, audio, and video company (if using local gear). Prepare them for the show by relaying information provided for you or have them contact the tour's department heads directly. Oftentimes, the touring audio head will want to have a direct conversation with the venue's audio head. This ensures effective communication about the audio needs of the show.

TICKET HOLDS/PRODUCTION KILLS

One area you will want to pay attention to when working in a venue will be to inquire about any production holds or "kills" needed to support the production. It is not unusual to kill or hold seats for front of house mix position or the "mix shadow" (the mix shadow is the area directly behind the front-of-house mix position, usually having obstructed views of the stage.) Other production holds could be for cameras, camera platforms, follow spots, follow spot platforms, or any other piece of equipment that may take up seating. Having this information early and getting it to the box office manager is a critical step in getting the show to run properly. There really isn't anything worse for ticket holders than to show up only to find their seat has been taken up by a camera and riser. Having the proper box office advance helps to save the patron from having to deal with this type of situation and potentially ruining a great night. Make sure you ask about any production holds and get that information to your box office manager during the advance. Also, make sure you have a copy of the venue seating map with the production holds, as you may have the ability to release some tickets back to the box office after loading in.

> **TIP** – Temporary stairs leading from the stage to the house can also create a need for production holds. Make sure you confirm this during your advance!

Not every seating diagram will be perfect, and not every production manager will have the exact seating kills held correctly. During load-in, make sure that you check the seats affected by the production and keep the box office informed of any changes or additional seats that need to be held. In some instances, the seats may have already been sold, but the production still needs the seats for equipment. This will result in the relocating of the ticketed guest. "Re-Lo's" are another term you may hear when dealing with box office in the music industry. Having a minimal number of guests affected by the production is one of your main goals, so stay on top of this very important area.

LOCAL GROUND TRANSPORTATION

In some instances, band members may fly into the local city and avoid the tour bus. When this happens the venue production manager will be asked to provide local "ground transportation" for the artists to get to the venue (or hotel) and then back to the airport. On some shows, the ground transportation crew stays very busy shuttling the band and crew between hotels and venues between sound checks and show time. In cases like these it is essential that the production manager has a great relationship with a local ground transportation company as getting the artists to the venue safely and on time is the number one priority. As is for so many production manager scenarios, constant communication, and good advance is the key to success. This is especially true when it comes to ground transportation. Late or canceled flights are always a possibility and can throw off the day's schedule. Making sure you communicate with the drivers about these potential delays is vital.

> "One of the things I learned early in my career was to forge relationships based on trust between me and the production managers. I also learned to think like a production manager. After a few shows together, I could anticipate what the production manager needed based on our experiences together. It's all about having a good advance conversation with them and having accurate and up to date flight information. I always communicate about any flight delays so the production manager can adjust the schedule if needed. You must be adaptable in this business when it comes to the constant changes to the band's travel plans. Our goal in the end is to get the band to the venue safely and on time."
>
> - Duane Lester, Owner - Avalon Transportation and Livery

When it comes to providing ground transportation, having responsible drivers is of the utmost importance. The drivers are really ambassadors in the customer service business and should remember that they are representing you or the promoter. Drivers must know that texting or talking on the phone while driving is prohibited. The drivers must also defer from talking to the artists while in the car. While it's true that the drivers may be carrying rock stars that they idolize, good drivers are taught from the beginning that they should not ask for autographs or talk to anyone that they are driving, unless they are asked a question first. Artists can be temperamental and a driver that doesn't stop talking could interfere with their preparation while they are in the car and set their mood off in a negative direction.

"As a driver, I know that I am in the customer service business, and I am representing the promoter. If I do a good job, then it's a positive reflection on the promoter as well. Getting the artist to the venue safely and on time is always my goal. Also, it's all about the little details. I offer them FIJI water, (the preferred water amongst rock stars) and set the air flow controls to their desired temperature. I also have just about every type of cell phone charging cable there is. All those small details are appreciated by the artists, and they respond favorably when drivers go the extra distance to make sure they are comfortable."

- Michael Walsh, Professional Driver to the Stars

As is the case for all communication, it is vital that the production manager has the names and phone numbers of the drivers and the drivers should always have the name and number of the production manager. Constant communication is essential, and the production manager should stay in close contact with the limo or SUV drivers so that they can accurately prepare for the artist arrival. By keeping in touch with the drivers, the venue production manager will be ready to meet the artists upon arrival and will make sure that the dressing rooms are prepared and that the stage is ready for the sound check.

TIP – A good production manager will have a flight tracker app on their phone so that they may check on any early or late arriving flights. If a flight is delayed and the artists can't make it to sound check, the rest of the day's schedule will be in jeopardy and the production manager must be ready to adjust.

While the venue production manager often takes responsibility for the ground transportation, they will rarely get involved in the arrangements of the actual flights or hotel accommodations, as that is usually in the hands of the band's tour manager. While it seems that "picking up someone at the airport" is just a simple task, it really is one of the most vital parts of the concert operation and careful attention must be paid to ensure that the artists and crew arrive safely and without incident.

Once all of these other duties have been completed, you sit and wait for the show trucks and buses to arrive. Show day is an exciting day for both the touring and local production managers. Because you are usually the first to greet each other, this is an opportunity for you to make a good first impression. Give the touring production manager a tour of the backstage areas. Catering, dressing rooms, production offices, and any other backstage amenities should be pointed out. You don't get a second chance to make a first impression, so make sure your venue is in good shape for your guests. Next, the stage manager will want to know about power locations and stagehands. Point out where everything is located and introduce the stage manager to the local crew chief or venue stage manager. Unlike the theatre stage manager, who calls cues, the rock and roll stage manager is more of a stage manager of people and equipment. Your last order of business first thing in the morning should be to attend the "chalk out" session with the touring production manager and rigger. Much like taping out the ground plan in theatre, the chalk-out session is simply marking on the stage the various "rigging points" needed to get the show flown off the grid. Accurate chalk-out session ensures that the production will hang safely and properly.

During the advance, you may be asked to provide a production runner who knows the area and can get the touring personnel items needed at the last minute to get the show on. Introduce this runner as soon as possible in the morning and get the day started.

> **TIP** – Good production runners are essential to the overall success of the event. Having someone that knows the local area and can get items on the fly or last minute can be a valuable asset to both the production and you, the venue production manager. This is also a great entry-level position for those interested in being a part of the concert event excitement.

If you have done a proper and complete advance, then the rest of your day should be about making sure tasks are handled on an as-needed basis. Putting out theoretical fires and attending to the needs of the touring production personnel become part of your task list. While the tours are fairly self-sufficient, attention must be paid to the details to make sure that the tasks are being completed in a timely manner.

> **TIP** – Many times, the touring act CANNOT accommodate the opening act, and a second front-of house-board must be brought it. If this is the case, make sure you have ample room and power at the front–of-house mix position. If you don't, you might have to kill some seats to accommodate the second front-of-house board.

After sound check, and as mentioned earlier, there will most likely be a security meeting that takes place in the production office. This will be the chance for the tour's security director to go over the pass sheet, general rules about photography, and eviction policies of the venue, should fans get out of hand. The production manager, along with the venue's operations manager, should attend this meeting to ensure all security policies are understood and adhered to.

After the security meeting, the next step is to open the doors to the venue. You should check with the house manager or operations manager to assure that they are ready. Security and ushers should be properly placed. The touring production manager will want to know that security and ushers are ready and that the stage barricade (if used) is staffed properly with the correct amount of security guards. Once you have clear indications that the staffing is correct and ready, ask the touring production manager if they are ready to open the doors to the venue. Once you have the green light, let the house manager know that you have the all-clear from the stage to open the house.

As you get closer to show time, there is less for you to do as the venue production manager, as the touring production manager really runs the show at this point. The touring production manager will get the artist ready and communicate with the tour manager, touring stage manager, and crew about the start of the show.

> **TIP** – Don't expect concerts to always start on time. Many factors will contribute to the late start, such as traffic or parking problems, issues at the box office or, at times, because the artist isn't ready. Perhaps there aren't enough people in the seats yet for the artist's ego to start. (Yes, this happens.) The reasons run the gamut, but make sure, as best as you can, that you and your front-of-house staff knows when the show will start.

The show will then tend to run its course. The opening act will go on, usually followed by a 15-minute change-over and intermission. Once the headliner is set and onstage, "settlement" (paying the band) and the load-out planning can begin. The touring stage manager will usually get with the venue production manager and start discussing crew strategies for an effective load-out. Meanwhile, you may also be planning an after-show meal or bus shopping trip with your runner. The end of the show brings with it another load-out and packing of the trucks for the next stop.

CASE STUDY – WEATHER

CONTRIBUTOR – JOHN SANDERS

I took one look at my weather app, and I knew my phone and radio would blow up at any moment. It was coming our way and evacuation was inevitable.

The outdoor concert season brings its own set of challenges, and the response is different from one city to the next, and from one country to the next. Most outdoor venues subscribe to a number of services available where meteorologists keep a 24-hour watch for potentially dangerous weather headed their way. Several of them are based in Norman, Oklahoma, otherwise known as "Tornado Alley." They really know their weather. And many of those services provide worldwide coverage.

I was overseeing one of the biggest stadium tours this one year, with most shows happening in open-air stadiums. We started in the UK and Europe and finished with a run of shows all over North America. Out of about 45 venues we played, about 40 of them were open-air. The tour ran from June to October, a time of the year where you can experience all types of extreme weather.

Naturally, I subscribed to the weather watch service. We had a very vested interest in the tour and wanted all the help we could get. The first thing I did prior to the tour starting was to send them a list of cities that the show was playing in. I also sent them the starting date for the stage build in each city. Additionally, I sent them my cell number as the first point of contact they must call if they see some adverse weather coming toward the venue. At that point, the weather service starts monitoring each city when they come up on the calendar. It's also normal for the weather service to provide you with an app for your phone and to allow access to their system via a computer.

The satellite and Doppler radar information provided is nearly real-time … about a 5 to 7-minute delay. Plenty for what we need in our business. And of most importance, they are very good at forecasting whether adverse weather will pass over your open-air venue. If you are staying informed and check the weather each day, you will be able to anticipate the phone call. When I see the number from Norman, OK pop up on my caller ID, I should already know why they are calling. For outdoor concerts, the ticket almost always cautions "Rain or Shine" – meaning the show must go on.

However, when adverse weather is headed to your outdoor venue, the show may not go on if too much danger is present in the storm. The weather I'm referring to is that which includes thunderstorms. Convective activity is the most extreme weather form and can result in lighting, intense hail, intense rain, and very high winds, potentially leading to the most extreme weather, tornadoes. Any one of these may delay the start of, or worse yet, be show-stoppers.

Having an advanced conversation about the weather can only better prepare you for when you have the situation arise on a show day. The best preparation one can do is to do talk about different scenarios and resulting plans of action in advance and review it again come show day. The law of primacy … last done is best remembered.

Each venue has its own policies and procedures about what they do in the event of adverse weather. Some of the newer outdoor venues have enough space to respond with what is termed "Shelter-In-Place." By architectural design, this is where they have enough space to evacuate all persons in the seating area, including floor/field seating, to shelter under cover of the venue outside of the seating areas. This space includes the concourses, restaurants, tunnels, concessions areas, restrooms, etc. Coverage protection from weather provides safety.

Older venues may not have enough concourse space to shelter everyone, so they may respond with a shelter in personal vehicles. This would require allowing any patron to leave the secure venue and shelter in their own vehicle, hopefully, parked in a nearby parking lot. Those who may not have a vehicle, they will likely stay inside under the remaining cover the venue provides. The challenging part about this is you must conduct another search of all persons prior to re-entering the venue as they have left the secured perimeter. This takes time and delays the start of the show even more.

When the decision is made to evacuate the seating area, one of two decisions will likely be made: first is to delay the start of the show, wait for the weather to pass, and then allow guests back to their seats and start the show; the second option is to cancel the show and send everyone home.

The second option is made when the weather is just too extreme and/or is expected to last for too long of time.

It was load-in day in New York, the day before show day, and we conducted a strategic incident response meeting with all related tour and venue staff, police, fire, medical, traffic, emergency management, port authority, and transportation. We discussed and determined a plan of action for a weather evacuation.

We determined the location of the incident command center; we set up a means of communication for all decision-makers with backup modes of communication; we determined a time to meet before the show; we determined the parameters required for executing a show delay and a show-stop; we determined who would provide the public address system to make any announcements, we ensured the venue staff would back up the public address system with the use of message boards all throughout the stadium; we determined who would make those announcements, and we determined who had ultimate authority to cancel the show.

Those with the decision-making authority an evacuation would be asked to convene a meeting at the incident command center 30 minutes prior to the decision being made. We went back to our duties. I was constantly checking the weather. The one thing you can always count on when doing outdoor shows, weather changes. I was anticipating some adverse weather to be in the area come show day.

Come show day, everything was going very well, but the weather was still the ultimate variable. You never know what it's going to do until it does it. Weather was looking good, so we opened doors as we normally did, at 5:30 pm. Show was scheduled to start at 7:30 pm. The headliner would take the stage at 8:30 pm. Fortunately, there was no strict curfew from the venue, but the NY/NJ transportation authority did limit how late the subway trains ran from our event location. This presented a factor to consider how long a delay could be if folks could not get home if the show ran very late.

This was our Doppler radar at 6:00 pm show day:

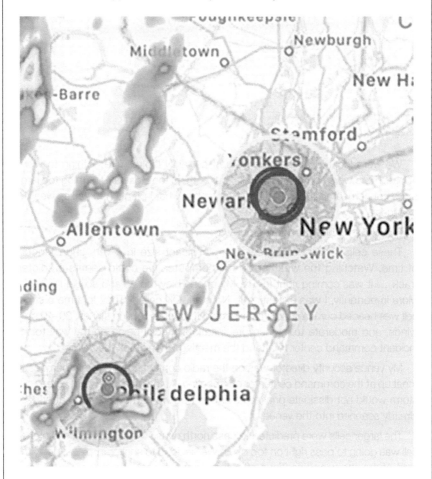

Figure 13.11   Severe weather approaches the venue
Credit: Image provided by John Sanders

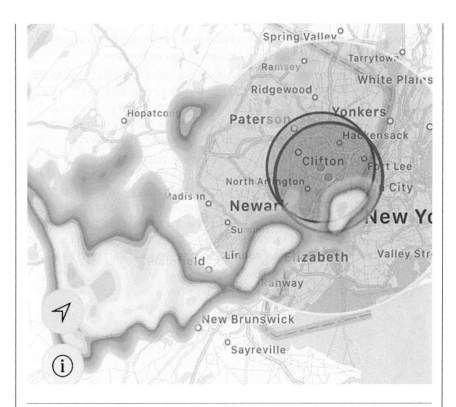

Figure 13.12   The storm arrives at the venue

Credit: Image provided by John Sanders

We were located at the blue dots. It certainly looked like nothing to worry about. There were some smaller cells, but nothing too close and nothing too large to be concerned about at the time. Remember what I mentioned earlier, weather changes!

By 8:00 pm, this was coming our way:

These cells formed and grew to a significant size in a very short amount of time. Watching the weather on my computer, we could see its predicted track ... it was coming right for us. My phone blew up ... and so did my radio. More importantly, I was expecting it. Norman, OK called. They told me a storm cell was headed our way and was expected to contain lighting strikes, 30–40 mph winds, and moderate to intense precipitation. I recall being on my way to the incident command center to attend the meeting when I took the call.

My venue security director was on the radio contacting all relevant persons to meet up at the command center for our meeting. At the meeting, we all agreed the storm would not dissipate prior to its arrival. And we had over 75% of attendees already scanned into the venue.

The larger cells were predicted to pass north of us. The smaller, but still intense cell was going to pass right on top of us. We decided to shelter-in-place, delay the start of the show, and continue after the storm passed. The tour sound system was turned on, and the chosen public address announcer took to the stage to announce the shelter-in-place order. Messages were sent to all message boards.

Figure 13.13 Stadium signage informs patrons to shelter in place
Credit: Image provided by John Sanders

The public address announcer guided fans to areas of shelter in a very timely manner. I would estimate we had the seating area cleared in about 20–25 minutes. We put people under shelter everywhere we could … had to. We had 50,000 people at the show.

The storm hit us head-on about 20 minutes after the seats were clear. Lighting strikes were well within a couple of miles of the venue, the rain was moderate to intense, and the winds were strong. It was a good decision to delay the show. The storm lasted about 45 minutes. As soon as it passed over us, the rain stopped, and the winds died down to a light breeze. When the last lighting strikes hit greater than 5 miles beyond our location, we initiated the all-clear and allowed fans back to their seats. Another 30 minutes passed, and we were ready to start the show.

With the show delay, we had to deal with the transportation element. We had to ensure the fans would be able to get home. The New York/New Jersey Transportation Authority made sure of that by running the trains much later than normal.

All told we delayed the show for approximately 2 hours. Not too bad under the circumstances. Had the larger cell hit us, or if there were a long line of storms that followed, it may have been a showstopper. We started the show a little after 10:30 pm.

It was all made possible by pre-planning, advance discussion, creating a plan of action, and proper execution. This involved the creation of an incident response plan, with the proper decision-makers, with an open discussion of what plan of action to take under any run of scenarios. We previously discussed this same scenario we encountered on show day. And although the execution of the plan was not without some minor flaws, it was all but flawless to those in attendance. This positive outcome was made possible by a room full of event management and production professionals who put the safety of the guests at a higher priority than all else. And the show still went on.

FOLLOWING THE CONCERT, TRAIN SERVICE TO NYC WILL RUN VIA HOBOKEN/PATH. BUSES TO NYC PORT AUTHORITY WILL ALSO RUN REGULARLY AFTER THE SHOW.

Figure 13.14 Stadium signage regarding after show transportation
Credit: Image provided by John Sanders

Symphony Music

> "Blend and balance: it's all you need to know when working with a symphony orchestra. I find this way of thinking easier to manage than a group of individuals acting independently."
>
> - Paige Satter, Director of Facility Administration at the San Diego Symphony

When it comes to events that involve music and musicians, the production manager must be able to adapt to working with many different genres of music. As we have seen in previous chapters, the production manager plays an integral role in the various processes, and the same tools and training are required for the production manager in classical music. Most major national and international cities have a large symphony orchestra with multi-million-dollar budgets. These orchestras, depending on the season, can perform up to 50 weeks a year, at times, presenting several different programs in a week. The Los Angeles Philharmonic, the San Diego Symphony, and the Boston Symphony Orchestra are just a few orchestras that employ full-time production managers and have very busy production teams.

> "Many of the following tips can also apply to working with orchestras as part of a musical. Broadway orchestras require just as much, if not more, planning to make sure they have the resources they need within the often-confining spaces of the orchestra pits."

> "The production manager is one of the most important jobs at symphonic events and concert festivals. They are liaisons, coordinators, facilitators, leaders, and voices of reason. They are a vital link to a successful rehearsal and concert."
>
> - Katie McBride-Muzquiz, Director of Operations for Mainly Mozart, Inc.

DOI: 10.4324/9780367808174-18

When we think of production management for an orchestra, you may think "how much is there to do? Don't the musicians stay in one place and play music?" The answer may surprise you. The production manager (typically part of orchestra operations) is an invaluable and indispensable asset to the team and must be heavily relied on throughout the production process. Like in the other genres of art forms, to be successful, and effective, production managers must rely heavily on the tools in their toolkit. Organization and communication skills are once again at the forefront of the work. Communication in the orchestra world is no different than that found in other forms of live entertainment. Production managers must communicate clearly, effectively, and efficiently.

> "Planning and communication are key for what I do. In a typical season, we can produce over 100 different concerts and events. To do this successfully, I need to stay one step ahead of everyone and ensure that my colleagues are aware of what's going on. This includes many departments. Everyone at the Symphony plays a part in producing concerts and therefore, they need to have the latest information to do their jobs effectively."
>
> - Paige Satter, Director of Facility Administration
> at the San Diego Symphony

When working with symphony orchestras, it's incredibly helpful to have experience either as a musician or have worked with musicians in the past. Orchestras are made up of 70–100 musicians with individual concerns and needs. Therefore, being sensitive to what a musician is going through is important. The production manager must ensure that the environment is safe for not only the individual but also their instruments. They must ensure that the lights on the stage are not in musician's eyes while making sure there is enough light so they can read their music. They must also set the correct kind of chair, so the musicians are comfortable while performing. Being aware of airflow and temperature so that the safety of the instrument must also be considered by the production manager. These are just a few examples of the care needed to work with orchestras, large or small.

> "Because an orchestra is so different than theatre or rock and roll, you really have to think globally and be more sensitive to the orchestra musicians. Instruments (age and value!) tunings, concert programming, lighting, audio, air-conditioning/heating issues (it can't be too hot or too cold in the venue – this can cause great harm to instruments), and union regulations are all a big part of the daily life of a production manager."
>
> - Jennifer Ringle, Former Production Manager
> for the San Diego Symphony

Figure 14.1   Dekelboum Concert Hall in the Clarice Smith Performing Arts Center
Credit: Photo by Ryan Knapp

RELATIONSHIPS IN ORCHESTRA OPERATIONS

Like the various art genres we work in, building and maintaining relationships with those involved with the project will become the key in getting your goals and tasks completed. When working with orchestras, one of the production manager's primary relationships will be with the conductor. This person may also be referred to as maestro/maestra (Italian meaning "master" or "teacher") or music director.

Also, like other artistic directors, the maestro is a person that sets the vision for the concert season through programming (determining which music is performed at each concert), inviting guest artists, and having the long-term artistic vision for the organization. They are also very involved with how the orchestra is set up and the design of the stage plot (a diagram that shows which musician and which instrument sits where).

> "Being a conductor has many similarities to being the quarterback of a football team. The maestro is going to receive a large share of the credit (or blame), and to be sure, the podium is the focal point through which much of the energy in a concert flows. But as with a quarterback, a conductor relies on many right-hand people for success, and one such key person is the production manager. A great production manager makes all the stage elements flow seamlessly, freeing the conductor from worry about those concerns and allowing them to concentrate on the ultimate task at hand – the music."
>
> - David Chan, Concertmaster of the Metropolitan Opera Orchestra

The production manager should always meet with the conductor or guest conductor prior to rehearsals starting. This first meeting will help you to understand their vision and to begin to help facilitate bringing that vision to fruition. In this meeting, the maestro should explain how that week's program should work and flow.

Every set up of the stage will be different and every musical piece may have a requirement to move musicians, chairs, music stand, stand lights, and microphones. Smooth transitions are the key to a successful concert so getting your game plan in order is a vital outcome of this meeting. In this meeting, the production manager must be clear and realistic with the maestro about how long the transitions may take, as they may decide to talk to the audience to cover the time of the changeovers. This would also be a good time to ask the conductor if they plan to speak to the audience at the top of the show, or if they will go right into playing the first piece. Once you know this, communicate with your sound team so that they are aware of the microphone needs for the conductor.

> "It is crucial to understand that the best way for a production manager to surmount any challenge is to use their skills in communication, respect, and trust to their advantage. The goal for the symphony production manager is to have a smooth transition from first rehearsal to strike. This puts them in a unique visionary role, where they seek to maintain order through the chaos,

Figure 14.2 At the music store

Credit: Photo by Jay Sheehan

and to obtain the objective – to have a successful concert and to ensure that the musicians, guest artists, and the maestro/maestra have everything they need to perform their work."

- Katie McBride-Muzquiz, Director of Operations for Mainly Mozart, Inc.

IT'S MORE THAN JUST MUSIC

Like theatre and special events, production values are becoming an important element in the orchestra world and technical demands are being put on the production staff more and more. The use of video and specialized lighting is becoming a regular component at classical music concerts. Orchestras are now performing live soundtracks to major Hollywood films and the use of IMAG (Image Magnification) is being used more and more often, especially with popular guest artists. With increased artistic elements comes a need for increased organization. While the tasks of the production manager may vary from organization to organization, you can assume that the production manager is involved from the beginning to the end of the creative process.

Season planning may be one of the tasks that the production manager gets involved in as well. Now more than ever, organizations are planning two and three years out to create various financial scenarios and make more informed financial decisions. Season planning is an essential part of the organization: it establishes the artistic vision through programming, it is used to create the budget, and it creates a platform to publicize the season to its subscribers and single-ticket buyers. It also can lead to the development of new projects and identifying the need to fund those projects through grants and donations.

Once the season is established, the production manager takes on the task of building the budget. This is one of the most important responsibilities the production manager has each year. The budget considers the number of musicians required, venue rental fees, piano rental and tuning costs, guest artist fees, and musician travel expenses. These are just some of the figures you will need to get your season budget in order.

Another important role of the production manager is to determine the rehearsal and performance schedule. The production manager must be fully aware of the number of "services" (rehearsal or performance block of time) allowed each week so that the schedule follows union regulations. The musician's collective bargaining agreement for many orchestras dictates the number of hours per day and per week the musicians can work. This is done to avoid musician fatigue and to avoid overworking their bodies. At some organizations, the production manager is involved with hiring guest artists and arranging housing and transportation for them. Additionally, the production manager may be asked to secure additional venues for rehearsal and performances if the concert takes place in an offsite location.

SETTING THE STAGE

Another task that the production manager is responsible for is ordering any stage equipment that will be needed for the concert. How many risers are required and in what configuration will they be needed? How many chairs and music stands are needed for this program? Music stand lights? Wind clips for holding down music to the music stand when playing outdoors? What about stage heaters for the musicians if it's an outdoor venue? Determining the number of chairs required for each "section" of the orchestra is also the job of the conductor and the production manager.

(A section is a grouping of musical instruments: first violins, second violins, violas, cellos, double basses, woodwinds, brass, harp, keyboards, and percussion are typical. Section sizes vary depending on the number of musicians required for the piece of music or concert). While it is the conductor that makes the final determination on the size of each section, it is the production manager's job to make the stage plot a reality.

> **TIP** – It is always helpful for the production manager to create a ground plan for each setup and transition to help visually explain to the crew what will be needed for the musical number. It is important for a production manager to have familiarity and be able to do some basic navigation in a couple of different drafting programs (AutoCAD, Vectorworks, Sketchup, etc.).

The orchestra stage plot typically looks like this: (Note that the woodwinds and brass are made up of different instruments within that section family.)

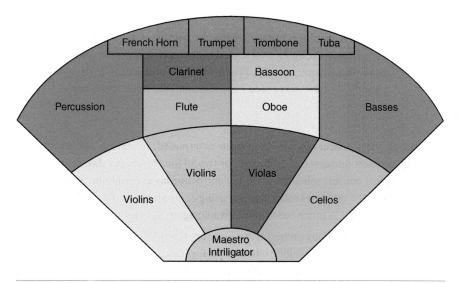

Figure 14.3 Typical orchestra seating layout in America
Credit: Image by Joseph Garcia

After the sections are established and chairs and music stands are put in place, the orchestra librarian places the sheet music on the music stands. Like a theatre script with blocking notation, all the sheet music has been "bowed" and marked up for each section and for each chair. (Bowing ensures that all string instrument bows are going in the same direction: up or down.)

The amount of work preparing music for a symphony orchestra should not be underestimated. The job of a librarian requires specific training, organization, attention to detail, and concentration.

> **TIP** – These days many orchestra musicians prefer to use an electronic device, such as an iPad that contains their music. The production manager should be aware which musicians are choosing this method as the musicians may not need a stand light when using an iPad. Additionally with the increased use of iPads comes an increased need to set up a charging station for those musicians with low battery levels.

At this point, the production manager has determined stage shifts and piano moves (if any), guest artist entrances, and any other technical needs for the concert and gives that information to the stage manager, who can now begin to get their book in order. Providing this information to the crew is vital at this point. Audio needs, video playback, and stage moves involving chairs, risers, pianos, etc. all need to be communicated as soon as possible. Musicians need rehearsal, so do the stage crew to ensure all stage moves are performed smoothly.

> **TIP** – At outdoor venues where the orchestra is being amplified by microphones, the audio crew should be told specifically if there are any stage moves that involve musicians changing chair positions in their sections, as microphone cables may need to be disconnected prior to the move.

Once all these concert factors have been determined, rehearsals can now begin. Typically, a union orchestra will rehearse for two to four hours per day, four days per week. A typical concert schedule is Friday and Saturday evening and Sunday afternoon. Many of the orchestras also have a touring component, so the production manager can be involved in much more than just managing a performance!

Working for a symphony orchestra can be a very rewarding experience for a production manager. Producing a major orchestral performance is a challenge and requires a large collaborative effort. The production manager in orchestra management is a vital part of that senior producing team.

CASE STUDY – *THE ARTIST IS ALWAYS RIGHT*

CONTRIBUTOR – DREW CADY, PRODUCTION MANAGER FOR THE PHILHARMONIC SOCIETY OF ORANGE COUNTY

In my earliest days as a symphony orchestra production stage manager, I was working with a very strong-willed guest artist who had already demonstrated their need to be "in control" about all decisions on the stage and was now insisting that we give them more rehearsal time than had been agreed upon, and that the orchestra were able to provide within the confines of their American Federation of Musicians contract limits. Knowing the tight budget that the orchestra kept on Pops programming (vs. classical programs), particularly given the high fees that many "pops" guest artists command, there was seemingly no easy solution. I approached the guest artist and as calmly as possible explained that we had reached the limit of what we could ask the orchestra to do in rehearsal hours for that week, and would it be possible that we could find another solution rather than force an expensive overtime increment for the entire gathered ensemble of 80+ musicians. [**NOTE**: Union contracts can be precarious when trying to keep a tight budget with guest artists. The visiting artist does not typically understand that even a half-hour overtime increment can cost thousands of dollars when you multiply it by 80 musicians. That is why the terms of a guest artist's contract must be closely monitored, to assure that there is a defined limit to the amount of rehearsal that will be required, and clearly agreed to by orchestra management.]

"Another solution," as it turned out, **was** the solution, as it quickly became clear that the guest artist was not feeling ready, given the amount of rehearsal time that was defined and simply wanted to see what power they might have to control the stage plan and schedule of the show day. Through a short, calm, and friendly exchange, we were able to compromise, and give the artist more time on the stage with their small ensemble of players who were touring with them, thus eliminating the need for expensive overtime for the orchestra. Within this conversation, I made sure to let the artist know that we really wanted to find a comfortable outcome for them and that we had their best interests at heart and were willing to hear them and give them some creative alternatives to the original demand. Sometimes the stress of touring can overcome an artists' professionalism and to offer a calm, sensitive ear to them, is what is needed most. In concerts such as these, the artist is the main event, and your job is to find a way to resolve any concerns or issues that they may encounter while doing their job as the headline performer. Just remember that "the artist is always right,"

This is, perhaps, one of the single most important mantras of my career as a symphony production manager. This is not to say that you won't find artists along the way who simply do not make sense or are making demands that are unreasonable.

You will in fact find all these circumstances. Your quest is to find a solution within the context of these unhappy moments. Always remember that it is the guest artist who is going out on that stage to expose their soul to a room full of audience, and that your job is to assure them that they have a calm setting in which to accomplish this. No amount of technical skills can overcome this shortfall – this is often a personality issue, and you have the ability to make things smooth regardless of what the artist is telling you. Stay focused on the end game, which is a seamless, fabulous concert performance. Recognize that every guest artist has their individual needs and the more you can accommodate these, the better chance you will have, to witness this successful outcome. Most importantly,

Figure 14.4   Mainly Mozart Stage
Credit: Photo by Ken Jacques

don't become judgmental about what the artist is doing or saying, and don't take any criticism personally. Think of creative ways to help them find their sense of calm before they go out on stage and perform. If it means accepting responsibility about some overlooked detail of their rider, or simply tuning in and really being present and listening to their concern, you are the one who can control what happens, by being empathic and professional.

One of the greatest lessons learned in these tough situations, is that the solution may be much simpler than what is being demanded by the guest artist. Seeking that unique answer, which not only assures the artist that you do have their best interests in mind, but also avoids an economically damaging outcome for your organization, and that is the ultimate goal here. Take the time to examine all alternatives before jumping to any conclusions. Seek out others who can advise the options that you have and look for allies within the artists' management (their music director, tour manager, publicist, etc), who might have knowledge about what could ease the tension and resolve the issue. It won't always work the way you initially perceive, but if you keep your cool, and remain positive, you will almost certainly have a mutually satisfactory outcome.

Presenting

> "The only thing you have to sell is service."
> - Carolyn Satter, Former Production Manager and President of USITT

It may be difficult to imagine that production managers may actually have to "sell" something. Mostly, we are expensing and spending money on things such as materials, supplies, venue rentals, etc., and we aren't really in the business of "selling" anything. But that is different for the production manager in a presenting theatre. Unlike the production manager in a producing theatre, where we have to answer to directors, designers, and upper management, the production manager in presenting theatre has to answer to "clients" who are renting the theatre to produce their own event. Being a presenting theatre production manager has a mixed and varied set of job duties and functions; this chapter will help you determine the similarities and differences of this exciting world.

Carolyn Satter, Former Production and Facilities Manager for the San Diego Theatres, explains that "the theatre that creates a product and develops a set, costumes, lights, etc., is a producing theatre. A presenting theatre means we, the theatre managers, and owners, present a wide span of entertainment or other types of presentational options for a paying audience. We may have a dance recital one day, a two-day university graduation the next day and then the national tour of *Wicked* loading in for a three-week run."

The presenting theatre can be known as a four-wall rental because when you rent the theatre, it comes basically with "four walls" and little else. Some four-wall theatres come equipped with some basic lighting and sound gear or they can have no equipment at all. One analogy may be to consider the producing theatre as a film studio, complete with writing staff and directors to produce and make the movie. On the flip side, the presenting theatre may be seen as a movie theatre, simply a place to present the movie. Either way you look at it, production managers in presenting theatres not only have the traditional duties of the production manager, but they also have an extra level of customer service they will need to master in order to be effective in their jobs.

DOI: 10.4324/9780367808174-19

Figure 15.1   Concert Hall at the John F. Kennedy Center for the performing arts
Credit: Photo by Jay Sheehan

So just what is customer service all about, and how do you define service? What extra steps does the production manager have to take? Satter goes on to say that "customer service means that you have to hear what the client is saying, what they are trying to say and understand what they would like the event to look like in the end. We need to talk about the concept; we must offer suggestions and help them produce their event. That's our job. We have an embracing attitude in our venues. That's what customer service is all about."

For Eric Fliss, Managing Director of the South Miami-Dade Cultural Arts Center, customer service is all about response time to the client: "The client is expecting me to be able to turn around a cost estimate quickly. That is customer service. In order to do that, I need my team to evaluate the technical rider. By evaluating the rider carefully, it tells the client that 'we care' about your event. The rider will help the production manager figure out what equipment we have and what we need to get and to submit estimated expenses to me. That also has to be done in a timely manner. And THAT is how a production manager provides customer service."

"A great skill for a presenting production manager to have is amnesia: forgetting entirely what you did last time. By having amnesia, it makes the producer be obliged to look at it with new eyes and tell you exactly what is coming in the door in the current show. If anyone ever says to me, 'it is like last year,' I immediately tell them, "I have no recollection of what you did, so let's start at the beginning."

- Bill Foster, Former Production Manager at the
John F. Kennedy Center for the Performing Arts

Production managers in presenting theatres are in a unique situation where they must answer to clients renting or producing in their theatres. While there are riders to adhere to and contracts in place to help guide us, oftentimes the group renting the theatre may be new at producing or in the city for the first time, and the production manager is instrumental in helping to get the show up and running. The skill sets for being a production manager in a presenting theatre model are the same as in the other artistic disciplines: understanding the communication process and how to get things done efficiently. This is extremely important when it comes to dealing with clients and listening to what they need. Satter continues and says that "Our core skill sets are the same, with an additional skill added, what I call insight skill. That's the ability to stand back and watch a series of events unfold while being aware of any red flags that may be coming down the line. That takes time and experience. You can't really teach insight, but if you've had enough errors on your production management judgment, your toolbox gets filled with ways to solve problems. That's what I mean by insight."

Figure 15.2 Backstage view of the Kay Theatre at the Clarice Smith Performing Arts Center at the University of Maryland
Credit: Photo by Ryan Knapp

As you begin to gain experience, you will begin to gain the insight that Satter discusses, and you, too, will be able to apply that to a situation where you can help the client save some money or time.

> "The production manager is oftentimes the person that has the most contact with the client or artist. It is essential that they understand the vision and are sympathetic to that vision and to the artists. You should instill confidence that you are working toward that shared vision by demonstrating that you are balancing costs and cost controls along with maintaining a high level of service."
>
> - Eric Fliss, Managing Director for South Miami-Dade
> Cultural Arts Center

ADVANCING THE SHOW

To "advance" is to "get ahead in position or time." To "advance a show" means to get out in front of the show as early as possible and start getting the production details worked out. Many production details will need to be advanced, and clear, concise information should be at the forefront of your work. Additionally, understanding the technical contract rider is of great importance for the production manager in presenting theatre. Much like the music business, the presenting theatre production manager must be adept at reading and interpreting the rider. The presenting production manager doesn't need to be an expert on the show that's coming in; rather, they need to be an expert in understanding the physical limitations of their own venue.

What are other core duties that the presenting production manager deals with? Some smaller shows that come in may not have a production manager, and the presenting production manager may have to act as the client's production manager. Here are a few things you will need to know in order to be an effective production manager in presenting theatre.

GET THE SHOW INFORMATION/READ THE RIDER

Once the booking department of the presenting theatre has signed the contracts for the show, they should send you the technical rider to peruse. This rider will look similar to the riders found in the music business and will contain information such as labor calls, ticketing needs (or production holds), and technical equipment requirements, such as line set schedules, light plots, and audio plots. If there is no technical rider, then the fun for the production manager really begins, as you will have to do your best to track down as much information as possible from anyone who will help you. Rely on your lighting staff, audio staff, and other key

Figure 15.3   Thank You notes to the audience - Live Art in Richmond, VA
Credit: Photo by Jay Sheehan

personnel to help you come up with a basic lighting plot and audio input list based on what you know.

> **TIP** – Try tracking down where the act or talent has played before. You may be able to contact the production manager at that venue and ask what details you may need to know.

LABOR CALLS AND MANAGEMENT

Labor calls, labor budget estimates, and labor management will be one of your larger tasks that will need to be completed, and it is your job to try and have a good working relationship with the crew. Know your crew and help them understand what you are working toward. Fliss agrees and says that "every venue or facility has a mission, and it is essential for everyone working in that venue to know and understand that mission. It is the production manager's job to convey the mission and to establish expectations that are aligned to the mission."

With regard to the rider, it should clearly indicate how much labor is needed for the load-in, run-of-show, and load-out. In the case of the event that doesn't have a rider, you, as the production manager, will need to determine the labor calls based on your past experiences or previous show files. Additionally, you will be the labor liaison between the client and the crew chief to ensure that breaks are taken and that no overtime is being anticipated. No one likes surprises, especially the client and especially when it comes to money. Once you assess the event labor needs, you will need to create a budget for the client. Make sure the client knows all of the anticipated expenses ahead of time. You should prepare a written estimate and have the client sign the estimate.

> Most of the larger "roadhouses" will have an IATSE contract or "yellow card" in place, so you should be sure you understand all of the working conditions with regard to breaks, meals, hours worked, etc. On many IATSE calls, there will be a crew chief, also known as a steward. This steward will work with you to ensure that proper breaks are taken and that crews are properly released at the end of the day.

The labor budget should be built around the worst-case scenario, considering the various rules that you might be under. Some production managers will do a "contingency" line item on the labor budget that covers unforeseen issues, including a longer load-in or technical challenges with equipment. This contingency can be anywhere between 5% and 10%. Some production managers prefer to not use a contingency. (For more on contingencies see Chapter 7, Money and Budget.) The labor call will include the number of load-in crew needed, number of run crew needed for the performance, and number of crew needed for load-out. As mentioned earlier, supervising the labor crew will be your focus for the run of the event, as the production manager must be sure that the load-in and event are happening on schedule. Keeping a careful watch on the situation and assessing the labor needs of the production happen regularly. This is where it's helpful to have that "insight" that Satter discussed earlier. Being able to quickly assess and ascertain the labor needs if things aren't going as planned is a true skill of the production manager. It is your job to keep labor on track and on budget.

> **TIP** – If you start to see that things aren't going as planned and that the load-in schedule may be affected, make sure you talk to your client as soon as possible about the possible overages regarding the labor budget.
>
> Try to do so without an alarmist approach but rather with a focused conversation on where we are at and what needs to be done to stay on target both schedule-wise and financially. This would also be a good time for you to present options for saving money or offer a different solution to a problem that could result in cost savings. Schedule a regular check-in/update chat with the client during load-in (like at the lunch break) to offer a progress/status/changes report. This way, they know to expect it and know that you're looking to keep on top of potential overages.

TICKETING NEEDS OR PRODUCTION HOLDS

One of the first things you should do as the presenting production manager is to scan the rider for any production holds for ticketing or seating. A production hold means that some technical equipment may either take up the existing seat or obstruct the view of the audience member, thus making the seat unsellable. Once you review the rider, get with your box office manager to secure the production holds prior to tickets going on sale. Share this information with your client. This is a very important step and shouldn't be overlooked, as the consequences on show night are not fun for the house manager. Having to relocate patrons who can't see around a speaker stack or other obstruction is an unnecessary and avoidable step for the front-of-house staff if the production manager does their job with regard to production holds. Don't forget that part of your job as production manager is to release the production holds once the show loads in and you can check if the originally planned obstructions are still an issue. If not, you will then be able to release the tickets back to the box office for sale to the general public. As in rock and roll and other artistic disciplines, you shouldn't forget this very important part of your job and your day.

TECHNICAL EQUIPMENT NEEDS

Much like the riders in the other artistic disciplines, the rider for a show in the presenting production manager's world will contain information on either the equipment that is being provided by the production or what equipment needs to be sourced locally. Make sure you read this thoroughly and do as much as possible to acquire the elements needed for the production. If the show doesn't have a rider, then it will be up to you to discuss the needs of the event with the client. This is where your customer service skills will come into play a great deal. Satter says:

> as we speak to a prospective client at our theatres, the first thing I ask is "What is it that you're doing, and how do you want to do it?", and we then offer suggestions regarding the technical and labor elements. Some clients we will become far more involved with, and some we may not get involved with at all from a technical standpoint.

Figure 15.4 Ironstone Amphitheatre in California – Richter Entertainment Group
Credit: Photo by Jay Sheehan

DRESSING ROOMS

Regarding dressing rooms, the presenting production manager may get involved with the touring stage manager or the local producer to assign dressing rooms for the show. Careful note should be taken when reading the dressing room rider, as it may contain language that allows certain performers to be on stage level or have a restroom in their dressing room. Sometimes minor hospitality requests will need to be addressed. Proper signage should be put up indicating directions to dressing rooms as well as dressing room assignment postings on the dressing room doors.

> "Budget, budget, budget … because many things are contingent on an accurate estimate, such as artist fees and ticket pricing, a good advance is essential in establishing accurate costs to avoid surprises."
>
> - Eric Fliss, Managing Director for the
> South Miami-Dade Cultural Arts Center

MANAGING THE EVENT BUDGET/SHOW SETTLEMENT

Another one of the main duties of the presenting production manager will be to monitor costs associated with getting the show presented, primarily in the area of equipment and labor. Monitoring labor calls involves keeping track of regular and overtime hours worked, meal breaks, meal penalty pay, etc. Keeping your client informed of the status of the labor budget should also be one of your top priorities throughout the day. All of these costs are then sent to the theatre manager, who will do a night-of-show "settlement" and pay the client the profits from the evening after deducting costs of venue rent, crew costs, and equipment costs.

> "We have to be transparent in order to be successful. You must understand that every decision you make has a financial impact on the people who rent your venue. The last thing I need to do is surprise someone at the end of the night when I present the invoice to the client who has rented the theatre."
>
> - Carolyn Satter, Former Production Manager
> and President of USITT

Being a presenting production manager can have its challenges. It can also have great rewards, as you will get to work with a large group of very diverse projects and people. You get to be the one who is in on many of the decisions, both financial and operational or creative. You get to be the one that understands how the pieces fit together and how the collaborative relationships between front of the house, ticketing, security, etc., all work together. You have to know what successful collaboration looks like, and that simply comes with experience and time. Satter closes with this wisdom:

During the event, you must be the cheerleader of the team you're working for. You've got to be the one ... whether it's the client, a stagehand, a security guard or a member of housekeeping, if they come to you with a situation, you've got to be the one that says let me take care of it.

And THAT is selling service!

CASE STUDY – SUZY EDDIE IZZARD

CONTRIBUTOR – HERMAN MONTERO, FORMER PRODUCTION MANAGER AT THE ARSHT CENTER FOR THE PERFORMANCE ARTS

The natural tendency of a presenting house is to pack the calendar as much as possible. By doing this you offer your audience many more options. It wouldn't be odd to say that in a one-week period you can see seven different shows and sometimes more, if you are in a multi-venue performing arts center. In such an organization, booking confirmations and calendar holds start years in advance. Careful consideration is given to the time of year, specific date, and where it lands in relation to the other shows both on the calendar and in the community. While considering the latter, an additional detail considered is the financial burden that a show potentially creates by booking it too close to other shows.

At the Arsht Center, every two years, the development department produces the family gala called the Imagination Ball. Sometimes the theme of the evening is driven by the headliner of the event, which for this particular year was iLuminate – "an immersive mix of dance, music, light, & laughter." Using that as our concept, the room was filled with UV paint, black lights, glow sticks, glow bracelets, glow necklaces, etc.

Figure 15.5 Entrance to the Imagination Ball
Credit: Photo provided by Herman Montero

This is also one of those events where everyone is on stage. To provide a little bit of context, the event took place on the main stage that hosted seating for 500 at 50–72 inch round tables that were under a "canopy" of 400 upside down, white umbrellas. Stage left we had our "food truck" buffet; consisting of custom-made facades that the catering team served out of. Then in the rear stage was iLuminate's stage with a dance floor in front of it for the kids. When it came to the schedule, we started the production process six-months in advance. The load-in week itself happened in a six-day period; load-in-Tuesday/Wednesday, focus-Thursday, program Friday, rehearse-Saturday, show-Sunday, followed by load-out. Now comes an unexpected element.

About a month prior to the Imagination Ball, our programming team gets wind that English comic Suzy Eddie Izzard is doing a book tour and her agents are looking for routing options through South Florida. Naturally, this prompted lots of excitement from our Programming team. The catch though was that the only week Suzy Eddie Izzard could perform in South Florida was, you guessed it, the week of Imagination Ball. Furthermore, it had to be a Friday or Saturday night show for the numbers to work for all involved. No one wanted to pass on this opportunity without looking into all the possibilities first. So, the next internal stop was for programming and development to sit down together and discuss their options. After a very quick conversation, I ended up being the next one in their line of sight. As the production manager for the Imagination Ball and for the venue, I became the determining factor on whether or not we could make an offer and what the parameters of that offer would be… no pressure.

I sat down with Eddie's tech rider, the gala's schedule, and considered the main purpose of each event. What was the primary message that each department wanted to convey to their audience? What was that one element of each production that could not be sacrificed at all? Knowing that adjustments would have to be made to each event – what assurances could I provide demonstrating that the original aesthetic, the heart and soul of each event, would stay true to its original intent?

After deliberating the answers to all those questions and so much more, my next step was to sit down with the two departments and sum up my mental journey. I first provided them with some context and, in broad strokes, educated them on the domino effect that was going to be caused once we decided to insert Suzy Eddie Izzard into the middle of the Imagination Ball schedule. We talked about the changes in finances, scheduling, and equipment. I also made sure to make it clear to everyone (Suzy Eddie Izzard's team included) that everyone had to give up a little to make this happen. Development had to give up a day, programming had to take on some additional expenses, and Suzy Eddie Izzard's team had to agree to a reduced version of their show. Ultimately, all of the above was agreed to, and a formal offer was made for that Friday. It was now time to turn my attention to the other half of the picture – the crew.

I updated everyone and made sure we were all on the same page and together we began to steer both shows onto the new path. Despite having had five-months of planning under our belt, we now had to create a whole new timeline/plan to accommodate this new insertion. Since I already knew what the Imagination Ball needed, I started off by focusing on Eddie's needs. I also knew it was going to be easier to have the bigger event absorb the small show, as opposed to the other way around.

In brief, Suzy Eddie Izzard was set to play proscenium with a full stage black drop, projector/screen, two overhead electrics, one FOH electric, up lighting, three microphones, and a table. All within a 12' deep x 32' wide footprint. Knowing this, with the Imagination Ball designers, we began to adjust the Imagination Ball's load-in plans. At the same time, I started to advance with Eddie's team to gauge what kind of flexibility they had.

For the Imagination Ball, we only had to adjust the downstage portion to make it all work. We added a full-stage black drop and a projection screen to the line set schedule and hung it on Tuesday. The lighting designer helped us open some space on the first electric/FOH and we set aside some PAR lights for the floor. We then removed the seating from the pit and brought that to the stage level. Finally, our catering team adjusted their schedule, which allowed us to not put down the first two rows of tables. When it was all set and done, Eddie's changes were minimal. The rear projection became front, two overheads became one, and the footprint became 9' deep x 50' wide.

Once Friday came, it almost felt like a day off in comparison to what we had been doing the days prior. Suzy Eddie Izzard showed up late afternoon for a sound check, joked about the tables, and put on a great show. FYI – I'm a big fan, so I'm biased. The settlement was all done during the show and since the lines of communication were open and transparent from the beginning – there were no surprises, and nothing was questioned. The whole team was very accommodating, and I was out the door by 10:30 pm that evening.

The next day we came in around 11 am, finished setting up the downstage portion and went straight into rehearsals. The day was over by 5 pm and we were set for a great Imagination Ball the next day. It was then followed by a very smooth load-out and yet another surprise-less settlement. Everything had come under budget; everyone made a profit and because collaboration and communication were at their best – everyone walked away with a smile.

CASE STUDY – CALIFORNIA STATE UNIVERSITY SUMMER ARTS

CONTRIBUTOR – SHANNON PRINGLE, SENIOR MANAGER, PRODUCTION

Communication and transparency are of utmost importance for effective production management in a presenting organization. One of the best tools for communication between the production team and the visiting artist for a special event is the technical rider.

The presenting series at California State University Summer Arts represents an amalgamation of several types of theatrical production, including special events. We work with emerging and established visiting artists from all genres of artistic expression including theatre, music, dance, visual art, writing, and media. Our season features a different guest artist public event nearly every day, as well as a repertory-style presentation of student work.

Typically, the exchange of technical information for the event includes the submission of a technical rider from the artist(s) to the production team in advance of the event. A technical rider (also known as a tech rider or rider) is a document that lists the technical needs and requirements of the artist to present their event. Sometimes the rider is extremely detailed, down to the acceptable temperature range for the dressing room and specific brands of microphones to be used. The rider may also include information about the artist's merchandise to be sold, the type of food and beverages the artist requests backstage, and the amount of time the artist requires between rehearsals and performances. Sometimes the submitted rider is a boilerplate document that is vague as it may apply to the basic needs of the artist rather than the requirements for a specific show. And then, there are some artists who may not have a rider to provide to you, at all.

In many cases we are able to accurately predict what the artist may need based on their genre; however, we want our guests to have a personalized and professional experience with our program, which means not making general assumptions or leaving things to chance. To help mitigate the lack of technical information on the vague and non-existent riders, and to augment and better personalize the information provided in the more thorough riders, I created the Summer Arts Technical Request Form (Tech Form) to serve both our artists and our production team. The purpose of this Tech Form is to provide artist- and event-specific technical information that is valuable for the production team to prepare for the artists' arrival. It wasn't necessary for the Tech Form to present itself as another overly formal, legal-looking document. The Tech Form needed to feel approachable. When creating your own document, use your own experiences and consult with your production team to determine what information you need from the artists to help the team to do their jobs well. The form also needs to be a living document with properties that are updated each season to best address the needs of both the artists and the production team.

Upon receipt of this information from the artist, whether via the Tech Form, artist rider, or both, I synthesize all content, including information about the performance venue, our production team, and technical services provided while

Figure 15.6   Setting the light cues
Credit: Photo by Shannon Pringle

the artist is in residence. The personalized information is then returned to the artist and/or artist management for acceptance and approval. This is to ensure that all parties are in agreement regarding the technical details for the upcoming event.

The clearer these details are between the production team and the artists, the more congenial and productive the professional relationship is going to be. One of the most favorable compliments received regarding the Tech Form, as well as a reflection of the artists' working relationship with the production team, has been when the artists ask us to either forward our technical information to their next performance venue or ask us to create a more comprehensive standard technical rider for them based on the information collected for our presentation. One specific example – we presented a dance company that expressed their production needs via language that conveyed mood and emotion more than specific production terms. They lamented that each tech at a new theatre felt like starting from scratch because they felt more comfortable conveying information in person rather than in advance, which resulted in a longer technical rehearsal process. We took their visual and emotional language and "translated" it for production purposes to provide them with a rider that encompassed the artistic qualities they desired and the technical information that a production team needs to be prepared.

The exchange of thorough information between the artist and the production team in advance of the event is ideal, however, what do you do if you don't hear back from the artist or for some reason that the artist is reluctant to provide the breadth and depth of information that you need to best support their event? It is incumbent upon the production manager to find out the reason behind the hesitancy so that you know what steps you need to take to secure this important information. I caution you not to rush to judgment as to why you have not received the information. Be open, patient, and forgiving. In the end, you as the production manager, are doing everything you can to support the artist, and you are also doing everything you can to provide your team with the information and tools they need to work efficiently, effectively, and safely.

How the Technical Request Form helps to support production leadership:

> The questions I ask help me to build the schedule for the season, hire the appropriate staff we need for each performance, and budget for all production expenses. Through the information I gather, I also learn more about craft and creativity, which in turn, helps me to be a more engaged production manager.

How the Technical Request Form helps support the artists:

> Both artists with riders, and those without, have conveyed that the Tech Form has helped them consider more of the details of their own performances, as well as more of what it takes behind the scenes to make their magic happen. My questions encourage the artists to assess their work from a broader perspective and really think about what production support is feasible and reasonable for their vision. Additionally, I've been told that the attention to detail helps the artists feel more a part of the Summer Arts community while in residence, even if in residence for just a day or two. We treat artists as individuals from the very beginning of our professional relationship with them. And when they return to our program, they know they are in good hands.

How the Technical Request Form helps support the production team:

> The Summer Arts production team appreciates having clearer, advanced notification of expectations which has significantly reduced that sense of feeling uninformed and unprepared. I look to eliminate unnecessary scrambling and tension by providing as many tools as possible to encourage and support the success and professional growth of my team.

Everyone wins!

Now this is not to say that we don't still have our fair share of surprises, malfunctions, or miscommunications. During reflection and assessment of the previous season, I fine-tune our processes, including the Technical Request Form. What questions or concepts appeared clear and direct in previous seasons, but didn't quite land with a particular artist this year? I take ownership of how to continue to grow as a strong communicator, advocate, and yes, production manager.

CHAPTER 16

Co-Productions

Popularity is increasing for performing arts organizations to work together to produce a show or event. It's an opportunity for two (or more) organizations to share knowledge, skill, and resources toward a common goal. This growth in cooperative productions (or "co-pros" for short) can be motivated by companies hoping to decrease costs and time constraints, expose their audiences to different work from across the country or internationally, or merely a desire to work together on the same show. One organization will originate the production, meaning they will likely accommodate the rehearsals, build the physical production, host the first run, and then ship the necessary elements to the next venue. The subsequent organizations will receive the production requiring them to load in the physical production elements from the originating venues and often re-rehearse or re-tech sections of the show before the run commences. A complete explanation and exploration of co-productions could fill an entire book, but here are a few key points to consider if you find yourself producing a show with another organization.

WHAT IS THE GOAL OF THE CO-PRODUCTION?

You should understand why this project was proposed and conceived. Often, the artistic leadership of the partnering organizations initiates the process. Perhaps the organizations have similar artistic goals, and they hope an artistic partnership will allow the organizations to learn from each other. Or the opposite could be true – the partnering organizations are artistically different and want to explore those differences through the co-production process. It is also possible that the artistic leadership of the partnering organizations had a previous relationship and are excited to work together once more. Whatever the reason, understand it, for it will guide your work to come.

DOI: 10.4324/9780367808174-20

> "Not every partnership is a co-production. Imprecise use of language can lead to confusion from the start."
>
> - Co-Production Handbook, Resource from the OPERA America Technical/Production Forum

WORKING WITH ANOTHER PRODUCTION MANAGER

As we have stated before, the role of a production manager can be a lonely one. Working on a co-production is a great way to collaborate with a knowledgeable and kindred colleague. This collaboration allows you the opportunity to learn new techniques and practices. However, this can also be challenging, as there are now two (or more) people making decisions normally made by one. For a co-production, establishing positive working relationships with everyone is important, but the working relationship you establish with your fellow production managers could be vital. Clear communications early on about how you will work together, and regular check-ins will make certain communication is effective and feelings are not being hurt, nor are toes being stepped on.

The role of the production manager in a co-production will vary based on whether you are originating or receiving the production. If you are the originating production manager, it is best to keep the other theatre(s) in mind as you create the production and stay in close communication with your partner production manager. Regular check-ins throughout the process are very helpful. It's also great to include your partner in the design process and early meetings with the creative team so that both theatres are being equally considered as the project comes together. One of the worst things you can do as an originating production manager is to create a project which cannot successfully transfer to the next theatre.

> If by chance you find yourself co-producing with an organization that does not have a production manager, you must ask for clarity on how to move forward. It may all end up falling to you. You will not only want to be aware of that but able to negotiate the terms of the increased work.

BUDGET

As mentioned before, co-productions might be a way to use funds more economically. More can be achieved with funds from two or more partnering organizations, or savings can be achieved with each organization spending less. Clearly communicating the budget and cost-sharing expectations should be done at the beginning of the co-production process so there is never any confusion. Create an itemized list of expected shared and non-shared expenses and which organization is going to pay for what. The importance of careful budgeting and clearly identifying financial obligations is paramount. The bane of many co-pros has been ambiguous communication on financial matters. Not only should you clearly identify and communicate budget responsibilities but make certain to discuss what occurs if production expenses exceed projected budgets. Are there emergency funds to cover unforeseen expenses? Make sure that budget conversations happen continually. Managing a co-production can be a complicated endeavor. Foreseeing every budget concern or possibility will better prepare you for the entire process.

> **TIP** – Production managers should share their typical budget templates, discuss why those templates work for each of their organizations, then create a shared template that tries to achieve the aims of each. Review this with the general manager, managing director, and/or head of finance at each venue to make sure it works for them too.

SCHEDULE

Scheduling is not as simple as placing two different production schedules next to each other and calling it done. Scheduling a co-production can be incredibly challenging, as you now must consider at least double the number of items, personnel, and scenarios. Begin with deciding who will open the show first and when, then work backward from this date to schedule the rest of the originating production and work forward from the same date to schedule the subsequent productions.

Important things to consider:

- How does each organization structure their tech process? Should they match for ease of the co-pro?
- How much time will it take to strike, move, and load into another theatre?
- Will brush-up rehearsals be needed prior to the second tech?
- How many crew will it take to successfully run the production? The number should match for each leg, so the running of the show does not suffer.
- When will designers get contracted? Which organization will initiate that process?

> "It is ideal to involve the partner company production managers from the design process through the build, to ensure that the production will fit and play well in each venue. Ideally the partner companies will have similar venues, but if you can include in the build the flexibility for a range of venues this can also increase the potential for future rentals."
>
> - Molly Dill, Chief Operating Officer for Houston Grand Opera

Figure 16.1   The College-Conservatory of Music at the University of Cincinnati
Credit: Photo by Adam Zeek, www.zeekcreative.com

PHYSICAL PRODUCTION

It is unlikely that the partnering organizations will have identical performance venues. Every theatre is unique. Even two proscenium theatres can be different from each other in many ways. It will be important for your designers to have venue drawings for the spaces early in the process so that they can design effectively for the uniqueness of each space. For example, if one of the spaces is smaller, it might make sense to select the dimensions of the smaller stage to use as the footprint for the set. You will then be assured that the set will fit in every space. The creation of a consolidated ground plan is very helpful – either by the scenic designer or the technical directors of the venues.

Another important determination to be made is whether all elements of the physical production will be shared by both organizations. If one venue is significantly larger than another there might be more scenic elements required for one that won't transfer to the other. If there is a shared cast, then costumes will likely be shared. Props (depending on the size) can usually be shared. It might cost more to transport a set to the next venue than it would be to build it a second time; however, this duplication of materials might not appeal to your organization's environmental consciousness. The partnering organizations will have to decide what is the most cost-effective and stays within the organization's guiding principles.

The two theatres might have their own equipment for automation, lights, sound, and video and will likely not share these items. However, designers must take these inventories into account when they conceive the design to make sure it is achievable in both locations. It might be the case that one theatre has more lighting equipment than another. The solution to achieving the design in the theatre with the smaller inventory might mean an equipment rental, but if that is not financially feasible then the designer might be best served to design based on the most restrictive inventory.

TRANSPORTATION

Early in the process you should work out how the physical production elements will get from organization A to organization B. The size of the physical production will help determine the right sort of vehicles that will be needed. In an extreme case, you might need to rent a truck or engage the services of the trucking company to transport the items. Some trucking companies will allow you to store the items in the truck for a period of time if you pay extra. This can help if the show is not moving directly to the next theatre.

If the transfer is happening internationally then transportation gets exponentially trickier as now you must consider freight moving from country to country. The costs can vary wildly between transporting items by air versus by boat, and of course, the time you have to get things from one place to another will have to factor in. The other big consideration is customs and how you will get clearance for these items to enter another country.

Attention should also be given to what happens to items after the production closes at the final location. If prop or costume elements were used from organization A's stock, then likely they will want them back and transportation of these items will need to be considered as well. If the items are small perhaps they can be shipped back. However, if they are large you might need to consider using a vehicle to make the returns. In most cases, all these transportation costs would be shared between the partners.

> "Working on an international co-production in China was the largest learning curve I have ever experienced. Not only did we all need to understand the culture differences, but their way of producing theatre is completely different than ours. They did not have a production manager nor understand what that position was for. I had my work cut out for me and, in the end, won them over to the necessity of our profession!"
>
> - Cary Gillett

STAFFING

In most situations, permanent staff of the partnering organizations will participate in the co-production (i.e., technical directors, master electricians, costumers), but what about those who need to be hired in – performers, designers, stage managers, run crew, etc.? Hiring the same performers and design team for each presentation of the project is

Figure 16.2 *A Midsummer Night's Dream* – a co-production between the University of Maryland, College Park and the National Academy of Chinese Theatre Arts in Beijing
Credit: Photo by Stan Barouh

important to establish continuity. There is nothing stopping you from changing the stage management team or run crew if necessary; however, if it can be avoided, it will certainly help the productions run smoother. If the partnering organizations are in the same city, these hiring decisions will be much easier. If the performance spaces are a great distance apart, the logistics (i.e., travel, housing, per diem) for sharing stage managers and/or running crew will become more complicated, no more complicated, however, than the sharing of performers. One way to overcome this challenge is to hire people who are native to each location. For example – half the cast and crew live by location A and the other cast by location B. This way, for each section of the production, only half of the people need to be housed. This could work similarly with the design team.

> **TIP** – In many instances, the technical director of the originating venue (or someone from the scenery department) will have to go to the next venue to help with load-in. Make sure to plan for this as you consider the schedule.

AFTER CLOSING

Before the co-production process begins, you should have a discussion with the partnering organization(s) about what happens after the production has concluded. If one organization paid for the costumes, then it seems likely they would keep the costumes, but if the costs were shared, then who gets them? Perhaps they stay as a shared resource, and one organization agrees to store them. Or perhaps both organizations cover the cost of a shared rental facility.

The future of the production is always something to keep in mind. Is it possible for one of the two organizations to remount the show on their own? If so, how would that work in terms of billing, income, etc.? If another organization wants to rent part of the physical production, who will receive the rental income? These are important questions to consider before they come up.

> **TIP** – Put it all in writing! Make a contract that both organizations sign with all of the details that have been worked out. Don't risk jeopardizing your relationship with another organization or production manager.

CASE STUDY: COOPERATIVE PRODUCTIONS – "DO YOU THEATRE LIKE I THEATRE?"

CONTRIBUTOR: LAWRENCE "LARRY" BENNETT, DIRECTOR OF PRODUCTION AT THE ALLIANCE THEATRE

There are several things to consider when choosing how to approach a cooperative production or co-pro. Artistic, administration, and production all play a big role in the decision-making process, but the big question I always ask is "do you theatre, like I theatre?" This phrase was born as an inside joke between Cary Gillett and me. As we began our co-pro journey with the production *Twisted Melodies* and started to see all the different ways each theatre created art, it became apparent early just how different those processes and procedures were. Seeing these differences, I jokingly said to Cary, "it's obvious they don't theatre, like we theatre." That became the mantra of this journey, and we'd use it whenever major differences became apparent.

Figure 16.3   Kevin Rolston as Donny Hathaway in *Twisted Melodies*
Credit: Photo by Richard Anderson, used with permission of Baltimore Center Stage

Before I joined the team at Baltimore Center Stage (BCS) as Associate Production Manager, we produced a production titled *Twisted Melodies* in 2017. Melodies is a one-person production based on the final day in the life of Donny Hathaway. Because of its popularity, we decided to remount the production and bring on co-production partners to "tour" and share the cost. All the production elements were preserved, saved for the scenery which needed to be rebuilt. We identified The Apollo and Mosaic Theatre Companies as our partners for this production.

BCS is in the League of Resident Theatres (LORT) with a "B sized" theatre designation, the Apollo is a presenting house, and Mosaic is on a Small Professional Theatre contract. This is important because it means each theatre has a specific and unique way they produce or present the art they make. Specifically, because Apollo is a presenting house, they could not put performers on Actor's Equity Association (AEA) contracts, but BCS could because of our LORT designation. That means we couldn't "tour" with the Apollo in the traditional sense. How we worked around this is that BCS contracted the artists and technically the Apollo presented our production of *Twisted Melodies* in their theatre. Mosaic was able to issue all their own contracts for the production and we could tour in the traditional sense.

Communication is very important with the partners, as well as with the creative team. Because BCS was the originating theatre, a lot of people looked to us to (help) solve a lot of issues and to have the latest information. Looking back, as the originating production manager, I wish I would have taken more of a leadership role to centralize information and calendars, but that is above and beyond expectations. Everyone was asking BCS for guidance, advice, and information, so taking more of a central role, would have streamlined a lot of conversations and decision-making. There is a fine line between being the go-between and centralizing communication and making sure you are not stepping on folks' toes but ensuring everyone has the information needed.

All three partners needed to agree on the size of the project. *Twisted Melodies*, although a one-man production, is (and can be) surprisingly complicated. There is a lot of automation, lighting, and media involved with the show. Because all three partners produce/present differently, each venue had its own set of challenges. This mostly centered around the equipment needed to execute the design. Here are a few things to illustrate how we all produce theatre differently.

PERSONNEL AND SCHEDULE

Other things to keep in mind when determining scale and scope is labor cost (union or not), making sure everyone knows which contract you are producing under and what those expectations are, including load-in, tech, and preview times. The Apollo is a union house, meaning they use IATSE (IA) to install and run their productions. Baltimore and Mosaic do not use IA labor for their productions. This is important especially when it comes to scheduling and number of staff needed to complete the project. IA labor has specific rules, protocols, and pay scales and structure for crew calls. As such, Baltimore not being an IA venue has a full-time staff in each of the following departments: scenic, costumes, props, lights, sound, and media/projections. Consisting of department heads and shop personnel. Conversely, the Apollo (as a presenting IA house) has no need for full-time staff like a producing theatre needs. They do employ full-time staff members who act as their "technical director," a head electrician, and a production supervisor. Since they are IA, they create crew calls with the local union hall to staff their labor needs. Mosaic does not have full-time staff and like Apollo, they only staff a few full-time positions: head electrician, A/V person, and production manager. They hire other crew people as needed on a show-by-show basis.

What I learned is every organization has their own timeline for when they fully engage with the project. If I would have had conversations sooner and compiled documents explaining the timeline for the entire project at all venues, we could have avoided many bumps in the road. As the originating theatre, we needed to get everyone's buy-in before we could move forward with certain aspects of the build and purchasing/rental for the production. Because *Twisted Melodies* wasn't the only production these organizations were producing or presenting, trying to get everyone on the same page at the same time, proved more difficult than we anticipated. This led to BCS taking on a larger role than we expected, and we became the central hub of information for everyone, which was a complicated place to be.

EQUIPMENT

The renting of lighting and media equipment is not cheap, especially when the costs are not split, and the potential rental contract is roughly four months long. Each theatre has different equipment in-house, and it became very apparent, very quickly that we would need a rental package to make sure we maintained consistency at each venue. With rentals come budget restrictions and what is affordable for everyone. I wish I would have had more in-depth and open conversations surrounding lighting and media earlier.

SPACE RESTRICTIONS

This was a unique challenge, but the Apollo and Mosaic each had pre-existing standing projects in the theatres that needed to be worked around. On Wednesdays, the Apollo had tours and amateur night, and Mosaic (don't own their own venue) had church services on Sunday that needed to take place during the run of the show and the scenery and other production areas needed to allow for these services to happen. I quickly learned to ask about how space restrictions would work with the schedule and making sure we planned around them, because moving them was a nonstarter.

TIMELINE OF PROCESS AND NEEDS

Discussing timelines is very important, especially for us as the originating theatre. With any co-pro, generally, the last venue has a lot of time between the beginning of the co-pro process and when the production loads into their space. That some-times can lead to their sense of urgency and immediacy not being the same as the originating theatre, who has much less time to get things in order. One thing I would have done differently would be to create a master schedule for all venues. It could have possibly avoided some issues surrounding housing, travel, and material cost because all the theatres would have agreed to the same producing timeline and expectations sooner.

What we quickly learned as we engaged with the Apollo and Mosaic, is that they do operate differently than we do at BCS. These differences, some of which I would have never thought to ask about, became the biggest places of friction and needing the most attention to figure out. In hindsight, doing more research on the organizations prior to jumping into the process would have helped me know what questions to ask; my first question being: do you theatre, like I theatre?

CO-PRO AGREEMENT

Writing a co-pro document is or can be tricky, especially as you identify and navi-gate all the tricky landscapes with all the organizations involved. These things include but are not limited to pay scale and structure, housing, fee payments (including materials costs), staffing, personnel traveling with the show, billing, etc. There is a lot to consider and the one thing I wish I would have paid more attention to and spelled out more clearly were artist fees, housing, and material cost. All three theatres had different expectations and processes around how fees and payments are paid. In the original agreement, all theatres would contract and pay the creative team separately, which in theory, generally, works well, but because everyone has different timelines and procedures for vetting and processing payments; it became difficult to track who got paid and when. Hindsight, I wished I would have pushed for BCS to pay all the creative artists upfront or and a predetermined schedule and the co-pro partners to reimburse us as part of their money owed to us.

Once (if) you get everything sorted out on paper, the actual production is "the easy part" (he says laughing out loud). There will always be problems along the way, but doing the production is the part everyone knows well and is just a matter of adapting the production elements to travel or whatever is needed for the next stop. Once we were actually doing *Twisted Melodies*, everything fell into place.

My biggest takeaway from *Twisted Melodies* was the timeline around discussing the load-in, tech, previews, and performances. Everyone has a different schedule and works on shows in a way that suits their process and infrastructure. Making sure those processes and adjustments are worked out early and it may save a lot of miscommunication and confusion down the road.

Sending someone to travel with the show is an interesting proposal to consider. Not everyone has the staff and/or time to send someone to oversee or be the liaison. In this very specific example, we did send our TD out with the show to answer questions as the show loaded in. Looking back, I wish I would have insisted on having a representative from each venue come and watch the load-in and tech process. We did bring folks down to see the production and do a backstage tour. This is something to figure out either way early on.

There are a lot of things to consider when doing a co-pro, by laying out the entire process as a whole and layering in the other partners producing processes (and idiosyncrasies), will help the project run smoothly. Asking a few key questions early and often will save everyone down the road. You will never prevent anything that can go wrong, such as the beauty and curse of live theatre, but you can minimize as much as you can. So remember, when considering a co-pro make sure you ask: "do you theatre like I theatre?"

CASE STUDY – WORKING WITH ANOTHER PRODUCTION MANAGER

CONTRIBUTORS – VERONICA BISHOP, FORMER PRODUCTION MANAGER AT CINCINNATI PLAYHOUSE IN THE PARK AND JARED CLARKIN, DIRECTOR OF PRODUCTION AT MILWAUKEE REP.

We have been co-producing partners for over five years and our projects have ranged from straight plays, *Two Trains Running*, to complex musicals*, In the Heights* and *Destiny of Desire*. Fortunately, our working styles are very similar, and we were able to establish trust for each other right off the bat. While mounting a straight play has its challenges mounting a musical that plays in three venues bring about very specific issues that normally need quick resolutions. To coordinate the design, engineering, and execution of these projects you must trust that the person originating the production is not only thinking about how to make it a great production for their organization, but for all the organizations involved. Because of our confidence in each other and the companies we work for, we were able to move projects forward efficiently while keeping the other production manager in the loop. As the receiving production manager there is a lot of "letting go" and faith you must embrace as you rely on your producing partner to make the best decisions for the group which is why developing these relationships before you embark on a project together is extremely helpful.

Prior to assembling the creative team and beginning the design process, most co-productions start out with a conversation between the production managers from each organization to further their understanding of each other's style and priorities as well as outline the available resources and schedule for the project. Our working relationship began as a production manager to technical director before Veronica was promoted to production manager two-thirds of the way throughout the process on *In the Heights*. For us, this involved several phone conversations and emails as we built on the relationship we started to foster when Veronica was a technical director.

It is important to have a system for updating all co-producing partners with design research, drawings, sketches, and schedule information. A back-and-forth method of sharing information (SharePoint, DropBox, Google, etc) needs to be agreed upon from the onset. It is rare that two different organizations will be using the same platform, so having the flexibility to meet the producing theatre on whichever platform they use is helpful. The scale and scope of In the Heights were difficult to manage between three theatres because one theatre was not utilizing the same sharing method as the other two spaces. This meant a lot of back and forth between the two of us to ensure all the information was shared properly.

Ensuring your production teams are on top of the project is the first step of communication before you reach out to your production manager partner. We worked with our stage management teams to include all the department heads for all producing partners for every production. In weekly staff meetings, we would touch base on any concerns or issues about any segment of the project in an attempt to head off any major issues or discover how we could support our partner theatre. While we were working on *Two Trains Running* our prop departments were sourcing different props from both theatres to reduce cost and transportation expenses. Our electricians and technical directors had to coordinate over a dozen hung doors between the two very different spaces. Even through staff turnover at our organizations, the connection between our production departments remains strong. Often, we find that our production area heads are on the phone with one another shortly after our initial conversation working to make sure that each department is aware of the specific needs of the production or the unique architectural challenges in our respective spaces.

When a company is faced with the additional complication of multiple co-producing partners keeping the limitations of every space in mind during the creative process is critical. Unlike a tour, there isn't a "standard" set of guidelines that the originating theatre can rely on or impose on the receiving theatre(s). Any meetings, minutes from meetings, conversations with the creative team, rehearsal, and performance reports were shared throughout the creative process and mounting of the production. This gave us day-to-day insight on the development of the project and allowed us to reach out if we spotted an issue that could become huge for our space well in advance. Looking back, we would have added a standing weekly call among the production managers; a very quick 10-minute phone meeting ensuring that all the balls were staying in the air.

Coordinating the music for *In the Heights* was particularly challenging. Hiring one band to travel with the show was not financially feasible, so we needed to find a way to maintain the integrity of the show while working with local musicians that would have limited rehearsal time with the actors. To do this we combined

Figure 16.4 Set for *In the Heights*
Credit: Photo by John Houtler-McCoy, Technical Director (Milwaukee Rep)

live musicians with tracks that were recorded in the studio. This combination of live and recorded music allowed the music director the flexibility to respond to the changing tempos of the singers each night while also delivering a high-quality full orchestra sound. Milwaukee Rep had employed this process before, but it was new territory for the other co-producing partners. The production managers spent many hours discussing how this process would work and developing backup plans to make sure everyone was comfortable with the process. We employed a Q-lab workspace that could be triggered by either the musical director or the audio engineer to fire the music cues. A click track was employed to be sure the musicians were in synch with each other as well as the recorded instrument parts. Since Milwaukee Rep had experience with this arrangement, they agreed to supply all the audio hardware to make the system work. This allowed us to lay out and label all the equipment, which expedited the load-in process at the other theatres.

Dealing with all the personalities on a co-production in a productive manner can be challenging. When you are originating a show, you don't want to pre-label the creative staff, but at the same time, not warning your counterpart of potential issues doesn't give them the leg up they may need to get ahead of a potentially volatile situation. The production managers should be completely candid in their private correspondence to make sure real barriers to the successful mounting of a show are avoided. As the originating theatre works through the tech process observation of how the creative team interacts with each other, the cast, your staff, and the director is another detail the originating production manager needs to be able to communicate for future productions' success. We make it a habit to have phone conversations after a show has opened to review how the tech process went and to give any warnings about potential issues rising from personality conflicts.

Production managers are the hub of information, and they need to know what information to push down the right pipelines. If we are successful, information should pool in our office so we can ensure that all parties are kept in the loop. It seems most of our time could easily be spent chasing answers down from creative staff members. Radio silence is death to the process whether it is a co-production or not! In this world, the production manager's job is to provide clear, concise, and accurate information sharing, this function increases exponentially for co-productions. Laying the foundation of that communication early on in any co-production process it will put you on the road to a successful collaboration. While we first met working on *In the Heights* our relationship has continued to grow and strengthen by connecting with each other at events like League of Regional Theatres (LORT) conferences and USITT where we have been able to compare notes and bounce ideas off each other when dealing with similar situations that we may be facing in our organizations. Even during COVID-19 we found ways to stay connected with weekly regional meetings with other production managers. This networking has become an excellent way to continue to build upon the strong foundation that we have created while creating new relationships with future production manager collaborators.

C H A P T E R 1 7

Touring

"As a touring production manager, I represent the production, the company, the look, the entire picture and the way everything works together. Know your show and know what's critical and what's ideal. That way you know when to fight, when to compromise and when to really make a stand, and that's diplomacy."

- Perry Silvey, Former Director of Production, New York City Ballet

Broadway tours and other large tours are very different from standard regional theatre productions. Touring is about bringing a great show to the guests. As you learned in the Theatre chapter, the scale of the show is usually much larger than regional theatre, and the tour will always have a technical rider. A tour, which loads in and out, has to go together, come apart, go into and out of trucks every single week, and has to be built to withstand the rigors of touring. The show must also conform to fit into a truck, typically 8 feet × 9 feet × 53 feet. Because of this, truck space and efficiency are paramount on the road. Understanding how this all works with the technical rider is essential for the successful production manager.

As we have learned in previous chapters, production managers must be flexible, adaptable, and diplomatic. As a touring production manager, you will have to rely on these very important traits. On tour, it's about learning other ways of adaptation and being flexible, as every show in every city may call for a different set of answers for different circumstances.

While this chapter is geared toward touring in the United States, it is important to point out that USA production managers are also asked to tour internationally. Adding an international leg of a tour requires more flexibility and many additional skills. For instance, the production manager may be the one that oversees the truckload and creates and signs the Import/Export Carnet document for Customs which includes an inventory and valuation for every single item crossing the border. Many times, smaller tours may have to hire a private trucking company to take their sets

DOI: 10.4324/9780367808174-21

Figure 17.1 Ironstone Ampitheatre
Credit: Photo by Richter Entertainment Group

and costumes across international borders. Not a small amount of work! Transferring overseas via shipping containers comes with its own special headaches too (like the possibility of your container dropping off the side of the boat due to high waves and not knowing about it until it pulls into the next dock weeks later).

In addition to the above challenges, you may have to brush up on several different languages to communicate. Not all international tours travel with a local interpreter, so make sure you have a good language translation app on your phone. It may get you out of a bind if you are having trouble communicating.

Always remember that you are a guest in their house, and you should be expected to respect the local customs and work rules. While we Americans may like to take a 30-minute lunch break and get back to work, or work over the break without eating, in Spain the rules are clear. A 90-minute lunch break is mandatory. Basically, the entire country stops from 1:00 pm to 2:30 pm. These longer lunch breaks are evidence that Spain believes in some type of work/life balance much more than many other countries in the world.

There are other challenges beyond language barriers that you will encounter on the road in Europe. For instance, all time notations are written in the 24-hour clock also known as "military style" (Make sure you know what time 18:00 is before you go!). Also brush up on your metric system learning. Have a metric system convertor app if you are not up to speed on metric notations. Another challenge you may have is money exchange from US dollars to Euros. It might not be a bad idea to get some Euros in the USA before you leave just to have some in your pocket when you land. Also, remember your European electrical plugs. Your standard 120v phone chargers won't plug into European 220v wall outlets. Make sure you don't leave the USA without your new charger. You may just need it at the airport when you land.

There are many, many, other challenges that are involved with international touring. This chapter only scratches the surface, so continue to do your research before you sign that contract!

> "The biggest difference between touring and producing a show in one space is time. On tour, you don't have any. You have to be efficient and fast. You have to know your show inside and out, both artistically and technically and prioritize accordingly. And you have to know how to recreate that with different equipment and limited inventory. You have to be able to translate, not just language, but gear. You also have to have great self-awareness of your own skills and abilities. If one has a handle on those three things, one can tour well."
>
> - Joseph Futral, Director of Program Planning and Operations at Baltimore Center Stage

In the flexible world of touring, some touring companies are able to bring in their own full production, and some travel with partial or no production. Partial production means that you are only bringing a part of your show's requirements to the venue, and the rest of your needs will be supplied locally via the contract rider. Carrying no production at all means that 100% of the tour's needs will be supplied locally via the rider. Once the show's production company or production manager has been selected, they, along with the show's lead carpenter, will put together the show's technical contract rider. The technical rider, one of the most important documents to a production manager, will include such items as the show's lighting plots and lighting equipment needs, as well as audio plots and audio equipment needs. Power and other electrical items and needs are also discussed in detail. Dressing room, quick change booth space, and size of the front-of-house mix positions are all included in the rider that the production company and production manager create and maintain.

The production managers on tour must be ready to make changes on a moment's notice based on the limitations of other resources such as time, the venue's physical limitations, and labor requirements. All will need to be taken into account when making decisions on the road. On tour, questions need to be answered quickly and efficiently so we do not waste our resources.

> "The relationship with the venue starts with your advance. Send good information about your show and your needs. By doing so, you are establishing trust...the foundation for all relationships."
>
> - Matthew F. Lewandowski II, Production Management & Design

The best way to prepare for answering these questions quickly and efficiently is to know your show inside out and understand all of the inner workings of not only the scenic elements but the rigging plot, light plot, focus chart, audio cues, etc.

Figure 17.2   Inn at Rancho, Santa Fe
Credit: Photo by Jay Sheehan

Perry Silvey, former Director of Production for the New York City Ballet, says, "Not every theatre is the same. You know you're going to adapt. You have to quickly decide if that's a compromise I can live with or that's the one I can't. The earlier you make the right decisions, the more time you save and the better your show ends up looking. Knowing when to be flexible and when not to be flexible is also very important. There are times you have to demand for things and times you have to save your fight for the important moments." As you can see, knowing your show is important. So what tools can we use in order to know our show? Start out with getting it all out on paper. Get your load-in and performance schedules done early so others can comment and get back to you.

"To be a successful touring production manager, you must always keep an eye on the full picture. Also, remember that there are other people in the room and that everyone has a need. Try to use empathy in your process as you bring the team together and lead the charge. Also, know that everyone

> on the team may have different priorities, but the production manager's priority should always be to the show, and to keep everyone happy and safe, productive and professional."
>
> - Matthew F. Lewandowski II, Production Management & Design

Starting with a site visit (or site survey) is also always advisable when resources allow. Having a real look at the actual site can answer many of your questions ahead of time. If, for instance, the front-of-house mix position is too small, accommodations must be made to accompany the footprint of the front-of-house mix position. Seats may need to be killed, and that would obviously affect the box office. During your site visit, you may also look at the backstage space, looking for wing space for set carts and quick-change booths. (For more on-site visits, see Chapter 18, Special Events.)

> During the 1990s, many large touring theatres were reconfigured to accommodate the huge production spaces needed for Andrew Lloyd Webber's Phantom of the Opera. That tour really set the standard at the time for theatre renovations, as many theatres had infrastructure changes to accommodate the huge production. Today, it is not uncommon to hear that "If your theatre can fit Phantom of the Opera, it can fit any show!"

You should also get to know the building you are going into. Get the venue's technical specification packet or check their website for technical specifications (or "tech specs"). By understanding the theatre's layout, you will have a much better chance of figuring out if the show will fit into the venue. Compare what is in the theatre with what is required by the rider. By knowing this information, you will have a better communicative process with the venue's production manager, and this will make your advance go much smoother.

> Early in the process, you should establish a relationship with the venue's production manager and get the advance started. Getting this relationship solidified early will help relieve or resolve many of your potential issues. It is always nicer to get off the bus and meet someone you have already established a relationship with.

You should also understand any labor regulations in that city or that particular building you are going into. Find out if the venue uses IATSE labor, and make sure you understand all of the working conditions of the contract beforehand. Is this an IATSE yellow card show? (More on yellow cards later in this chapter.) Knowing when overtime begins or what triggers a "meal penalty" becomes your responsibility.

Are separate truck loaders or separate equipment pushers required on this contract? There will always be new challenges with labor when you get to the venue, so you should be prepared to discuss any such challenges. Maybe the full crew didn't report at the call time, or a rigger forgot a piece of climbing equipment. Things happen, so be flexible and ready to alter your labor plan if needed.

> Many IATSE stage calls may have "non-working" department heads. Don't fear, as that doesn't mean they aren't working. It just means that they are managing people and are not required to be part of the counted crew for load-in, show, and load-out.

You should try to know your local crew's names. This will go a long way with creating a good working relationship and diplomacy while you are visiting another venue. Diplomacy is an important element of touring. Be a calm production manager and give the local crews a good feeling that you know what you want. Crews really appreciate it when the production manager knows the show's needs. If you're calm and have a clear knowledge of your show, your crew will respect that.

> "Most people respond well to striving for high standards, as long as they are treated with respect and directness. It seems to me a way to get the best out of people. We try not to scream and yell or make derogatory jokes, but make the local crew feel like they are an important part of what we are trying to achieve, the same way our ballet masters and dancers and musicians make us feel. We are a team, and we try to give the locals a chance to join the team."
>
> - Perry Silvey, Former Director of Production, New York City Ballet

The production manager on tour also has the cast and touring crew to take care of. The proper nurturing of talent is no different on the road than it is in a home-based venue.

When going into the venue for the first time, you, along with stage management, should make sure the dressing rooms are clean and workable, and appropriately marked. Clear way finding or signage should be put up around the venue, indicating clearly where things are, such as the green room, exits to front of house, or the wardrobe department. Many times when on tour, large "runways" of white gaffer's tape on the floor indicate which direction the talent should go. Either way, make sure you have a clear pathway and proper signage backstage.

> **TIP** – Before you put tape on the floors, check with the local venue manager to make sure tape is allowed on the floors' finishes!

The wardrobe department and technical staff will need their space and their work boxes in the right place. Company management needs their room, as well. As the production manager, you should try to anticipate what everyone will need in the theatre. The musicians also need some care, whether in laying out the orchestra pit or making sure they have changing rooms, as well. The first day in a new theatre is always a bit of a challenge, with people trying to find their way around the theatre and the neighborhood. Production managers should do their best to be ready to answer the plethora of questions that may come their way. "Where can we get coffee?" is always a favorite.

> "When you go into someone else's venue, make sure you don't touch anything before asking. Asking is important and by asking you are showing respect to the venue."
>
> - Matthew F. Lewandowski II, Production Management & Design

Many factors will determine if a show is going to go on the road or not. The most likely of these factors is the ability to make money for the show's producers or investors. If the show is a hit, it is most likely destined to be put on a national and sometimes global tour. In New York City, this is where a production "company" comes into the planning process. The general management of the Broadway tour will hire the production "company" to design, build and production manage the Broadway tour.

Figure 17.3   Brooklyn Academy of Music's Harvey Theatre
Credit: Photo by Ryan Knapp

Aurora Productions in New York City is an example of a production company that produces first-class Broadway productions and tours of shows that have already happened in New York City. (Some tours can run simultaneously with the Broadway show.) Usually brought on early in the process, Aurora, which has the production manager on staff, begins to put the show together. Usually working six months to a year out, scenic plans are sent out to scenic studios for the competitive bidding process. Simultaneously, the production manager is getting bids on lighting packages, audio packages, and video equipment. Labor requirements for loading in, running, and loading out the show are also under the watchful eye of the production manager assigned to that show from the production company.

If a Broadway show decides to tour, the production manager is usually offered the Broadway tour if the same production company produces the tour. This is known as "right of first refusal" in some contracts. (For more on right of first refusal, see Chapter 8, Hiring and Casting.) If that production manager decides that they do not want to continue in the role as the production manager, another production manager will be assigned to the show. The same "right of first refusal" usually holds true for Equity production stage managers and Equity stage managers who have completed the Broadway run. (It should be noted that there are also non-union tours that travel around the US)

> "Road people oftentimes just want to be road people for a long time. You do have an opportunity, although a little harder now, to live off your per diem and put your money away in a bank account. You do that for a few years, you end up with enough to put a down payment on a house, and on tour, you can get a leg up on doing that."
>
> - Ben Heller, President of Aurora Productions

The production company's production manager usually travels to the venue when the show goes into production at its "production city." For the first national tour of *The Book of Mormon*, the production city was Denver. In a process that took about four weeks, Aurora's Production Manager Ben Heller (now President of Aurora) loaded the show in, put the show into tech and dress rehearsals, and made sure the production got into previews safely. Heller then left the Denver company and went to Los Angeles to oversee the first "jump" from Denver to Los Angeles.

Once the shows get into their second city, the production manager usually heads back to their home base, and the production stage manager, along with the head carpenter (also known as the production carpenter) and company manager, takes on the role of the production manager while on tour. At this point, the production manager is back at home base, working on getting another Broadway tour together. Oftentimes "leap frogging" cities, the head carpenter will then take over and fly to each city to do an advance site visit if needed. As mentioned earlier, if the physical limitations of the theatre are in question, such as the front-of-house lighting and sound mix position, the carpenter will work out the spacing details while visiting the venue. Discussion on what lights to cut, what scenery may not be used, or any other issues will be resolved ahead of time. This makes for efficient use of everyone's resources, as knowing as much ahead of time as possible will obviously help you problem-solve. The head carpenter on tour is a major help to the production manager and production stage manager, and attention should be paid to this very important relationship.

> "The biggest, most helpful thing is to be humble and willing to learn. You really are traveling as ambassadors. Behave accordingly."
>
> - Joseph Futral, Director of Program Planning and Operations at Baltimore Center Stage

At some point, the touring crew is also hired by the production company. For *The Book of Mormon*, the show has what is known as a "pink contract" status with the IATSE union. That allows the production company to hire their own technical IATSE staff to travel on the road. Having your own staff, such as carpenters, electricians, audio crew, props, and wardrobe crew gives the shows consistency and gives producers the best chance at success. Local crews are brought in to supplement the load-in and running of the shows in the various cities on what IATSE calls a "yellow card." The yellow card (yes it's actually still yellow!) lays out the local crew numbers in each of the cities the Book of Mormon travels to. Using upwards of 20–30 local crew, it takes a virtual village to get the show loaded in, sometimes in one day. Trained very quickly, the local crews often get less than two hours to prepare for the opening of the show!

> "As a touring production manager, you hold the artistic responsibility in your hands once the design team leaves. That means you have this precious cargo that you are responsible for because no one else is there to check the work. It's up to you to maintain the artistic integrity. You are the representative to make sure the audience receives the piece in the way that it was intended by the director and the design staff…and that is a huge responsibility."
>
> - Heather Rose Basarab, Production Manager at Northwestern University

Production management for tours is very much like production managing for the other various disciplines. Attention to detail, flexibility, ability to multi-task, and excellent personal relating skills are still at the top of the list of tools being used in this discipline of touring. Life on tour is all about flexibility and diplomacy. Remember that you are a guest in someone else's house. Each house may have its own set of rules that need to be followed. Do your best to follow these rules, and you will be welcomed back. At the end of the day, the venue's production manager should say, "That was a good group. We want them back again in our venue" – a good goal for any production manager to have!

CASE STUDY – NEW PICKLE CIRCUS

CONTRIBUTOR – HEATHER ROSE BASARAB

When we arrived at the venue, coffee in hand and ready to go, the loading dock was suspiciously empty: no truck. Inside, we received some shocking news. Our show, sent by barge up the West Coast to the small, southern Alaska town of Valdez, was grounded on a sandbar in the harbor, the victim of an unusually low tide. Nothing would be accessible until a high tide at 4 am the morning after our scheduled performance.

I was a beginning theatre artist, working as the lighting director and assistant production/stage manager under Kathy Rose for the New Pickle Circus, a theatrical, European-style circus in the days before the Cirque was a household name. I felt panicked; the situation seemed overwhelmingly catastrophic. Canceling seemed the obvious move: no stuff, no show. But a call to our managing director confirmed that rescheduling was impossible, and cancelation would be devastating for the presenter. We were instructed to see if we could come up with something.

In retrospect, the experience in Valdez gave me the production management tools that I have relied on ever since. Production management is solving the puzzle of creation with limited resources and plenty of hurdles, all while embracing the idea of Yes. Valdez gave me a step-by-step primer.

Slow down to speed up: A good plan is worth the time it takes to formulate it. Production management is as much about mental state as anything else– staying calm, keeping things in perspective: we tackled the problem in chunks.

Question/assess: Our first step was to confirm the diagnosis; there had to be some way to access our equipment. Our rigger spoke with the harbor master, thinking we could hire a boat. Apparently, the barge was truly inaccessible; another boat would be just as likely to run aground, and transferring equipment from one ship to another would be prohibitively time-consuming at best and potentially disastrous. Listen to the experts; know when to abandon a plan and regroup; don't be afraid to try something different. The theatre is an iterative process based on revision. We gave up on our forlorn container and started from scratch.

Prioritize the artistic needs: practice flexibility: Do you really need what you think you need? I met with the cast and the rehearsal director to brainstorm artistic options with limited resources. By luck, several of them had performed a corporate gig the night before we left and had carried key elements on the plane: balancing chairs, a slack wire, a trapeze, some juggling equipment. All had ideas for what acts could be salvaged and what could be added to cobble together a performance. We sketched out a show order and made a list of the bare minimum equipment we would need. Lists are life!

Invite collaboration, trust the crew: We regrouped with the house staff to share our list and determine what might be possible to acquire and build a new schedule. Their creativity and willingness laid the foundation for our show.

Figure 17.4   New Pickle Circus Poster by René Milot Illustration Inc, Illustrator & Creator

The crew leaped into action reaching out to every corner of the community. The house head literally put out an all-points bulletin over the radio: the circus is in town and this is what they need! He updated the list each hour as hilarious and helpful items rolled in: the high school had audio equipment for the band; another school had tumbling mats; a construction firm offered a very large tarp as a backdrop (very kind, but no thank you). The UPS driver promised to drop by as soon as her route was done to collect large items in her truck.

Delegate, let people do their job: The volunteer fire department was able to provide enough equipment and knowledge to devise an aerial rig. A local blacksmith fabricated custom plates and uprights for the slack wire based on a napkin drawing and a conversation. (He also suggested that I avoid eye contact with the three wolves in the back of his truck.) By late that night, we had traveled every road in Valdez and installed a basic circus of found objects.

Prioritize: Don't get caught up in perfection. Kathy and I put together a schedule for the next day, maximizing time in the space. We truncated focus, cueing, and sound check; lighting and sound worked over the top of training and rehearsal on stage. We focused on giving the performers as much time onstage as possible to work with the improvised equipment and the new show order. Polish was abandoned in favor of the heart.

Remember why we do this: Collaboration extends to the audience too. It seemed like the whole town streamed in when we opened the doors half an hour late. The theatre was packed; announcements were made to put small children on laps, people were sprawled in the aisles.

Our concern for fire regulation was brushed off; the crew pointed out the Fire Marshal in the center section with his kids. The theatre is about connection with the community; touring theatre is about finding community everywhere.

Five o'clock the next morning found us laughing and joking as we met our shipping container at the dock.

Special Events

> "Just ask any musician or live performer and they will tell you that the positive collective spirit of the audience means everything when creating a successful performance. The same is true with special events, and good production managers help to achieve that collective spirit by attending to all the details. It's the small inconspicuous details that ultimately create a positive energy and atmosphere that guests feed off while interacting in the venue space and ultimately with each other. Paying attention to the details helps guests to feel special, appreciated and valued. That positive collective energy level is the unseen detail and the ultimate ideal that production managers should strive to create for an event to be successful & memorable."
>
> - Bettina Hahn Osbourne, Event Designer – Bettina Hahn Events

All special events have a great deal in common with theatre. Both have audiences, lighting, audio, décor, scenery, and performers. Scripts are often used, and sometimes even costumes are a big part of the evening. Special events are very much like theatrical productions, but may not have as much theatrical infrastructure, something that we often take for granted.

There is no doubt that corporate and special events contain elements of theatre, and a good production manager is essential to the overall success of the event.

There are many types of special events, including not-for-profit fundraisers, awards ceremonies, corporate theatre (meetings and conferences), and exhibitions. In all the various types, it is the production manager's main responsibility to take the designer's or client's concepts and bring them to a physical realization. Acquiring lighting, video and sound vendors, managing labor, working with computer assisted drafting (CAD) drawings, and dealing with ongoing problem-solving are all a part of the day's work for the production manager

DOI: 10.4324/9780367808174-22

Having an accurate, scaled drawing of the venue will help identify any potential challenges of fitting the physical elements of the production into the venue. So the importance of having a consolidated ground plan, section plan, and schedule cannot be emphasized enough. Without these documents, you will have a very difficult if not impossible chance of having a successful event. Early in your planning process, it is vital that you determine who will be responsible for taking the lead on creating and updating both the drawings and the schedule. These updates need to be done daily and, in some cases, instantly and onsite. Who will do these needs to be negotiated as it can be one of several team members that do this? Often it is the events producing office, sometimes it's the events production manager or technical director and sometimes it's the venue's production department. Because changes happen fast and last minute in these types of productions, it is critical to have a dedicated person to update drawings and schedules as they occur.

One thing is a constant for the production manager, whether it be the performing arts or special events: Nurturing and maintaining relationships is crucial for success. Oftentimes, the client is the first relationship you will need to establish. The client will usually provide you with the overall concept of the event as well as the extent of the production and design elements expected. It is the production manager's responsibility to set, maintain, and manage the client's expectations. Many times, certain aspects of the production may not be able to be realized due to limited resources, such as time, money, or space. Learning how to have an alternative option or how to say "no" to the client properly and in a timely manner is another important tool in the production manager's toolkit.

Figure 18.1   Special Event on the Star of India – San Diego, California – Produced by Cue One Productions

Figure 18.2 Special Event on the deck of the U.S.S Midway – San Diego, California – Produced by Cue One Productions

Credit: Photos by Jay Sheehan

"You don't have to be a great technician to be a successful technical director or production manager in special events ... you do have to be a team-builder and a problem solver."

- Tom Bollard, Technical Director

Once this relationship has been established and the venue has been confirmed, the next relationship that you should establish is with the venue management. At this point, you should also begin to identify who other key players are on the team and start creating those relationships as well. Lighting and audio vendors as well as video and labor providers should all be called and introduced to the production manager.

TIP – In many venues, there may be an "in-house" event and production planning company. These are separate companies from the venue, but they have the "exclusive" contractual rights to provide production-related services and equipment to hotel clients requesting the service. You may also get a list of "preferred" vendors. Preferred vendors are those friendly with the local venue, but the producer does not have to use them. It is important to know and understand the differences between "exclusive" and "preferred" when it comes to working with vendors and venues.

Once you have identified the in-house production contact, connect by phone or e-mail and begin discussions on technical requirements for your event. Let them know the basics, such as what lighting, sound and/or video will be used. Providing in-house contact with a production or load-in schedule is also an important task for the production manager. The venue and in-house production staff are a big part of the production manager's team, and giving them as much information as possible will make your job easier on show day.

> "There are no notes too small to be taken seriously ... attend to EVERYTHING!"
>
> - Tom Bollard, Technical Director

It is important to note that in addition to providing information to the venues, the venues will need to provide information to you. These are called production guidelines. They will tell you the rules and regulations for activities in the venue, such as driving a lift on the floor surfaces, putting tape on the walls, the use of cable ramps, how you order power, and other physical engineering needs you may have. You should take the time to thoroughly read these guidelines. Often, a signature will be required from either the production manager/producer or the client, confirming you will adhere to the information contained. As in the other performing arts, the production manager's checklist is another important part of the pre-production process. Having everything accurately listed on one document will greatly aid you in the planning and laying out of the physical production. The checklist should contain every element (listed below) needed to successfully produce a special event.

Figure 18.3   Special Event in a parking lot - Loading in the lighting truss - San Diego, California – Produced by Cue One Productions

Figure 18.4   Adding the guest tables

Figure 18.5   Ready for guests

Figure 18.6 Behind the tech table
Credit: Photos by Jay Sheehan

VENUE LOGISTICS

Every venue will have its own set of physical attributes that the production manager should be aware of. They will affect the layout and design of the event. The following is an introduction to the production elements used in special events.

One of the first pieces of information that you will need is the height from the floor to the ceiling. This is important information for the production manager to have because many vendors and designers will require it for their pre-production planning. The height of the stage, length of drapes, and size of video screens allowable in the room are just a few of the production elements affected by the height of the ceiling. Once the ceiling height has been measured, the rest of the venue planning can now begin. Careful consideration and collaboration should be taken as you get into the details of laying out the venue with the various team players.

> **TIP** – Not all ceilings are the same shape or size. Many have soffits, chandeliers, or other unique characteristics. Make sure you measure all the various ceiling elements in the room that are relevant to your production. Having a good, reliable, digital tape measure, as well as a 100-foot tape measure or measuring wheel, are essential tools in the toolkit for the successful production manager!

STAGE HEIGHT AND STAGE PLACEMENT

The placement of the stage is one of the first steps in laying out and designing the room. Typical hotel stage platforms are usually 4 foot × 6 foot or 6 foot × 8 foot and are usually set at either 16 inches, 24 inches, or 32 inches in height. In addition to the main stage, there may be other staging requirements for your event, such as risers or platforms for the tech area in front-of-house, IMAG (Image Magnification) cameras, follow spots, or drum risers. The actual size of the stage will be determined by the production's needs, including entertainers and their equipment, presenters or speakers, and décor or other physical equipment needed on the stage for the event.

Stage steps and placement are also an important part of the production manager's checklist. Having proper entrances and exits to the stage is essential to a smooth-flowing traffic pattern on the stage. Make sure that all of these factors, as well as any other flow of people or entertainers on and off stage, are discussed with your design team and hotel or production company representative.

> **TIP** – Stages over 32 inches in height will usually require a safety railing. The production manager should check with the local staging provider or venue for codes in your local area if planning anything taller.

DRAPE LINES – SOFT GOODS – MASKING

Masking and soft goods are a big part of the design in many special events. Some of the uses of drape lines include:

- Entrances and exits to the stage
- Creating backstage spaces such as a green room or performers' waiting area
- Providing masking for equipment, such as rear projectors
- Covering the back of the stage or the back of the entire upstage wall
- Storage for equipment, such as empty road cases
- Decorative covering for interior walls of venue
- Show control drape or "front of house" mix position drape (used to cover up the unsightly look of the backs of audio and lighting boards as well as hide extension cords and other technical equipment at the tech riser, usually located at the back of the venue or ballroom)

> **TIP** – If your event involves food service, verify that you leave large enough openings in your drape line to allow food servers carrying trays to perform their duties throughout the venue. This will help you in creating a good working relationship with the catering team, as well!

STAGE MANAGER/TECHNICAL TABLES LOCATIONS

One of the main differences between regional theatre and special events is where the stage manager is located. Because many special event venues (hotel ballrooms, convention center rooms, backyards etc) do not have a traditional booth for the stage manager one must be created within the venue. Sometimes it is front-of-house, and sometimes it is backstage behind drapes or walls. Wherever it gets located it is important to communicate this with your audio and video team as headset communications and video monitors will need to be run to those locations.

BACKSTAGE SPACES

For a majority of special events, backstage space is usually at a premium. You should make sure that anyone needing backstage space discusses their needs as soon as possible. Many times, "video villages" consisting of playback monitors, switchers, rear projectors, and other video equipment are created from drape or soft goods as part of the backstage set-up. Other uses for backstage space can include a performers' green room. Backstage spaces may require a lot of additional production elements, such as tables, seating, lighting, mirrors, etc., so make sure that you go over any backstage needs in detail.

> **TIP** – Use bright colored tape and make sure you tape out areas that are off limits to guests that might be going onstage. Nothing is worse than having a shadow image cross your video screens because the backstage guest walked through the rear screen projector beam! Also, use white tape to create directional arrows for drape openings, entrances, and exits.

SEATING

Seating can be in many different styles and configurations. For most of the events that happen in hotel and convention-type rooms, the seating will either be "theatre" style, that in which the rows and aisles are lined up neatly, or "banquet seating" where round or square tables with chairs are arranged in the space. "Classroom seating" is another style of seating. As the name indicates, audience members are in a classroom setting with smaller, narrower tables and are usually required to take notes. "Chevron seating," or that in which some of the sections are at an angle to the stage, is also commonly used. No matter which type of seating is used, you should familiarize yourself with the drawing or discuss with the team what type of seating is being used at your event.

SIGHTLINES

The area that the audience sees from their seat to the stage is called the sightlines. Sightlines are sometimes moving objects and will vary from seat to seat. Questions should be asked early in the design process to assure that possible sightline issues have been addressed

Your checklist should look something like this:

- Where is the lectern placed on the stage?
- Does everyone in the seating area have a clear and unobstructed view of the guest speaking at the lectern?
- Does everyone in the seating area have a clear and unobstructed view of the video screens or projection surfaces that need to be visible to all guests?
- Will any sightlines be compromised by other production elements, such as ground-supported trussing, audio speakers, lighting equipment, etc.?

> **TIP** – If the venue sets the tables and chairs ahead of your load-in, which is often the case due to the venue's schedule, make sure you address any potential sightline issues as soon as you arrive at the venue. Be prepared to ask the venue staff to move tables and chairs to accommodate sightlines!

RIGGING

Whenever equipment such as lighting, audio, video, or scenic elements is used, the design team must first decide what is the best way to mount the equipment. Many factors, such as the event design, time, money, and labor, will all affect the decision of how the equipment will be rigged, or set up. Identifying immediately if the show is "ground supported" or has a "flown rig" is the first step in figuring out what production elements will be involved. A ground-supported rig is a structure usually made of trussing and is supported by the ground or floor. A ground-supported rig can be lighting trusses, audio systems, or video screens lifted by ground-supported structures such as Genie Lifts or Sumner Lifts (www.sumner.com). A "flown" rig, as would be indicated, is flown above the stage or above the heads of the audience members. Flying a rig is always more costly, but many times it is the only solution to some of the more challenging production issues, such as the weight of equipment and sightlines for the audience members.

Once the decision has been made to fly the rig, it is the responsibility of the production manager to find out how many riggers are required for the labor call. "Up riggers" (those usually suspended high above the ground) and "down riggers" (those on the ground assisting the up riggers in the air) will be needed to install. These riggers are usually on four- to five-hour minimums for both a load-in and a load-out. This is the beginning of the budgeting process for rigging.

Understanding rigging costs is important for a production manager, as the production manager is usually responsible for keeping track of the overall production budget. Costs per "rigging point" (everywhere the equipment attaches to the ceiling is called a rigging point) and hourly rates are a few of the line items found on the production manager's budget checklist. If you don't know or understand the costs, make sure you

Figure 18.7   Luncheon event with ground-supported drape and soft goods and flown truss for lighting

Credit: Photo by Tom Bollard

find out. Because rigging costs for a simple four-point/two truss install can run a client into thousands of dollars in costs, it is important to make sure you and your client understand that rigging costs are usually added by the venue and are usually above and beyond the normal production costs of using equipment.

LIGHTING

Almost every event you work on will have some sort of lighting. As with the other areas of technical equipment, the production manager should be familiar enough with various types of lighting equipment to be able to speak competently with the lighting designers and technicians about it. Making sure the designer (if there is one) is getting their expectations met is a key component of the production manager's job, and the production manager must assure that the event has the correct resources, such as the right amount of crew and working equipment, for example, aerial work platforms and ladders. If there is no lighting designer, then you, as the production manager, may have to fill in. If you do, here are some other points to consider when thinking about the lighting component of the event:

- When is load-in and load-out?
- If the lighting is ground supported, are there any sightline issues preventing the audience members from seeing a clear picture of the stage?
- If the lighting system is flown, how much does the equipment weigh? This is important information for the rigging company! How many points will be used?

- How far is it from the tech table/front-of-house tech area to the stage? This helps determine the length of control cables needed to run the show from the lighting console.

- How much power is needed for lighting, and where is it located in the venue? How far is it from the power panel to the stage? This information helps your technicians prepare properly with the correct amount of cable.

- Are there follow spots? If so, are they on any type of staging or platform?

- Is additional lighting needed for other areas, such as silent auction tables, food stations, cocktail bars, or dessert stations?

- Will you need cable ramps to cross door openings for food servers or guests?

- How will you focus the lighting rig? Is a lift needed? Is a ladder needed? If so, what is the trim height of the lighting rig?

- Do you have cue sheets or a script for show calling purposes?

All of this information above will need to be reviewed prior to every event, so use your checklist wisely.

AUDIO

In addition to lighting, almost every special event has an audio component. The bigger the event, the bigger the audio package. Variables such as who is speaking at the lectern, what is the entertainment on the stage, and how much stage space is available for equipment all need to be discussed. Every scenario will be different, and careful audio planning is another step in the creation of a successful event. Remember that it is the production manager's responsibility to have all of these questions answered and have the information disseminated as soon as you can, and as is the case with the other design elements, you should work closely with the audio designer or technicians to meet the expectations of the client.

> **TIP** – Many of the answers to your audio preproduction questions may come via the technical rider that is usually supplied by the entertainment. The rider will contain such information as a stage plot, input list, and "hook-up" chart for audio. Having this information handy will aid you greatly in your advance work or pre-production. (More detailed information on the rider and the contract can be found in Chapter 13, Rock and Roll.)

As with lighting, it is imperative to make sure the audio technicians are getting their expectations met. Make sure that the audio team has the correct resources, such as the correct amount of crew and working equipment such as man lifts and access to power. It is also important to note that the production manager should make sure that any sound checks are clearly indicated on the schedule or timeline. Having adequate time in the schedule to address such issues as wireless microphone radio frequency interference (it happens), correct patching of the system and other various tasks is essential.

Like with all of the other equipment being used, the production manager should have a working knowledge and speak the language of the sound designer and technicians. "Front Fills," "Side Fills," "IN ears," and "Monitor wedges" are just a few of the terms that will become part of the everyday language used when discussing audio requirements.

The audio checklist should include the following bullet points, and the production manager is responsible for collecting and disseminating this information:

- Is the audio system flown or ground-supported?
- Are we using wireless microphones or wired microphones?
- If ground supported, what are the speaker cabinet sizes, weights, and locations? Are they on the CAD?
- If the audio system is flown, what are the speaker cabinet sizes and weights?
- Will the entertainment be using monitor wedges or "in ear" monitors?
- Are there multiple speakers at the lectern at once? Will each need their own microphone, or will they share?
- Will the speakers at the lectern use a lapel microphone or an over the ear microphone?
- How far is it from the tech table/front-of-house mixing console to the stage? (This is important to know so you can order the correct length of the audio snake, the cable connecting the stage equipment to the front-of-house sound board.)
- What is the path that the audio "snake" will take? Is it flown? If it is ground supported, will you need cable ramps to cross door openings for food servers or guests?
- Where is power coming from? How far is it to the power panel? How much power is needed for audio?
- Who is supplying source material, such as walk-in music, recorded audio cues, etc.?
- What playback capabilities for source material are needed for audio?
- Are we using an iPod, laptop, cellular device, compact disc? (Yes, they still exist.) Is there a signal or feed from video to audio that needs input on the audio board? Are there cue sheets or a script prepared for the audio portion of the event?

THE SOUND CHECK

The sound check is a very important part of the day's schedule. Sound check details and lengths can vary based on how complicated the event is. If the event has one presenter at the lectern and one microphone, chances are the sound check will take less time. If you have entertainment, such as a musical group, you will need to plan for a longer sound check. The bottom line is that you should always do a sound check and test your microphones and equipment prior to the doors being opened to let guests into the venue.

VIDEO AND IMAGE MAGNIFICATION (IMAG)

Many special events will have some sort of video components such as PowerPoint slides, video clips, and live-action camera shooting (IMAG) that will need to be projected onto large screens. The production manager should be familiar with these components as well as common screen sizes and shapes, projector brightness, throw distances, and rigging options. The discussion of rear vs. front projection should also be clear and thought out properly. Both front and rear projections have special needs with regard to throw distance and placing the projectors on your CAD will help immensely in the process of deciding front vs. rear projections. At this point, you should also determine if the video screens will be ground-supported or rigged, as discussed earlier in this chapter. The most common screen size for larger events are usually 9'x12' and 10 ½' x 14' with the height being the first dimension and the width being the second dimension. This is with the common aspect ratio of 4:3. A 9'x16' is also commonly used when the aspect ratio is 16:9. More and more events are beginning to use LED video walls, consisting of several small panels put together to create one large video wall. The sizes of LED video walls can be from as small as one panel to many hundreds of panels, creating a wall close to 60 feet wide and 20 feet in height. The limitation for the size of the video wall will depend on many factors, such as rigging capabilities, desired size of the screens, locations for the screens, and budgets. LED video walls are significantly more expensive than standard projectors. One of the major benefits of using an LED wall for projections is that, unlike projectors, they work well outdoors and in full daylight.

> **TIP** – Understanding the limitations of video equipment and the surrounding environment is another tool in the production manager's toolkit. Such questions as – are you indoors or outdoors, what time is sunset, if outdoors, and how bright are your projectors? – are all great questions to ask when advancing your event. Having a "Sunrise/Sunset" app on your personal phone or device is a great idea. Oftentimes, this question will come up at a walkthrough, and having this information is a valuable asset to your planning.

Here are some other thoughts about the video and its components:

- What type of playback does the video vendor need to provide? Laptop? DVD Player? What inputs are needed for the video components? HDMI? DVI? SDI?
- Do you have cue sheets or a script for video operators?
- Is there enough electricity at the video front-of-house position or backstage position?
- Are remote control slide advancers needed for the presenter onstage?
- Is a "confidence monitor" needed at the edge of the stage? (This is so the presenter onstage can see what is being shown on the screens.)
- A switcher will be needed for multi-camera setups and multiple graphic sources

Like the audio and lighting components of the event, you should make sure that you have ample time in the schedule to go over the video content and cues.

> **TIP** – Make sure that any video playback that has audio on it (such as film clips) is all tested prior to opening the doors of the venue to the public. You should personally hear the video playback and NOT rely on someone else to tell you "it worked."

For larger scale events, the use of a camera or a multi-camera shoot for image magnification (IMAG) on the large screens within the room is also commonly used. Carefully placing cameras and platforms on the CAD becomes the production manager's responsibility, as well. Deciding what camera shot to bring up at what point during the event is also under the careful eye of the production manager. Also, the production manager should work with the technical director and video lead to determine the best locations for the stage manager's cameras and video monitors. They will need these if there is not a clear view of the stage, or if the stage manager has been allocated somewhere off in the distance.

Many of the events using a video component will need a playback device, and the laptop computer is still the most preferred way. This playback device will almost always need a line input to the audio board in order to hear the dialog on the video. It is important to find out from your client what format the projected media will be coming to you on. This will help in proper planning what equipment will be needed for the event. Video and digital imaging of events are quickly becoming more and more of an integrated design concept, and as with lighting and audio, make sure you know the basic language of the video team. Having this knowledge will make you a valuable asset to the client and the production team.

> **TIP** – If possible, have the show files loaded in and played on the actual laptop that will be at the event. Oftentimes, media can be created on earlier versions of software, and fonts and formats may not match. Having the video played on the actual show laptop will help prevent any last-minute crisis of the media not being played properly.

ORDERING POWER: HARD POWER VS. GENERATOR

Ordering electrical services can be a big responsibility for the production manager to wrangle. The first order of business is to find out what electrical services are available in that particular venue. This can often be found on the venue's website, but a call to the in-house production company or engineering department will provide the most current information and inform you of any other details you need to know with regard to ordering power.

In addition to finding out how much electrical service is available in the venue, you will also want to know what type of connectors the electrical service ends in. Camlock connections are the industry standard for most hotels and major convention centers around the country. You may also find 30 and 50 amp twist lock connections. Make note of what type of connections the hotel has. You will also want to pay attention to the type of power that is needed for the event. It can be called "three phase" or "single phase."

Three phase power is electricity capable of delivering 220 volts, as opposed to single phase, which can only deliver 110 volts. The power the venue provides must match the needs of the equipment. The production manager must ask the various vendors (lights, audio, video, etc.) what their requirements are and carefully order and oversee the distribution of the electrical loads to the various areas by way of breaker panels and large power cables. During this part of the process, the production manager should make sure that there is a separate power service for lighting and a separate power service for audio and video (who usually share power).

> **TIP** – By separating the equipment and power, you greatly reduce the chances of having a "buzz" in the audio system, which usually happens when you share power with lighting and audio. Make sure you fully understand the power requirements and create a final power distribution plan to double check your power loads. You should also keep an eye out so that the audio snake and main power cables are not run next to each other!

For non-traditional venues and events that are held outdoors, large portable generators (usually towed by a truck) are used to get the amount of electricity needed for the event. In this case, the production manager would calculate all of the power needed for the event and contact their local generator provider to discuss the sizes of generators and the amount of cable needed to get the power from the generator to the stage or other areas needing power. The generator company can also provide you with cable ramps for safety, which are used in entrances and exits to prevent people from tripping on the large power cables.

> **TIP** – Once you have established how much power is available in the event space, make sure you know the distance from the power panel to the stage or area containing lighting dimmers or audio amp racks. This information should easily be found on the CAD drawing. This is helpful for the lighting and audio vendors providing the power cables that extend from the power panel to the stage or other distribution points.

WORKING SAFELY WITH ELECTRICITY

Working with live, high-voltage power can be dangerous and very careful considerations should be made when deciding who will be involved in that area. Usually, at most events, there is a designated electrician who either deals with the house power supplied by the venue, or special event generator power, which is used for major events where power must be brought in. The job of the electrician is a serious one and often times, that is the only responsibility for the electrician: To oversee the safe and proper installation of electricity.

> There are many resources available on the topic of electrical safety at special events. One such resource is the **Event Safety Guide created by the Event Safety Alliance.** You can also scan the web for OSHA documents related to electrical safety.

WORKING WITH LABOR

Much of the work of the production manager on show day is about managing the various crews and maintaining the fast pace of the production schedule. You will need to find out if the labor at your event is International Alliance of Theatrical Stage Employees labor (IATSE) or non-union labor. The working conditions and hourly rates will vary based on what city you are in and what labor contract you might be under. You should make sure you understand these hourly rates and working conditions (i.e., overtime hours, meal penalties, etc.) for whatever situation you find yourself working with.

> **TIP** – Not fully understanding your local contract or labor agreement could result in a costly mistake for those paying the bills at the end of the night.

On most events, crews are divided by departments, and the production manager must make sure that each department is adequately staffed with labor. Lighting, audio, video, staging, décor, and rigging crews are all managed by the production manager, and a careful watch should be kept by the production manager to make sure that no area falls behind in the production schedule. At times, you may find yourself having to move labor from one department to another if one falls behind. This is at times challenging if all departments are behind and you have no extra staff.

> "Production Managers should ensure that their team and crew have the resources and support they need to execute their responsibilities. Providing production or event schedules, creative documents, stage plots, audio input

lists etc. on day one will set the team up for success. When the crew is provided with the necessary tools from the beginning, fewer obstacles present themselves. Your success and leadership will truly excel based on the empowerment you provide your crew and the trust you instill in them."

- Juan Torres, Production Manager | Show Production

Keeping a labor checklist will help you as well. Some of the items on this checklist might be:

- Crew call time for load-in – load-out
- Amount of crew needed for truck unloading and loading
- Amount of crew needed for "pushing" the equipment from the dock into the room. (Some IATSE venues will contractually require separate "pushers" from the rest of the crew. Check your local contract!)
- Amount of crew needed for lighting
- Amount of crew needed for audio
- Amount of crew needed for video
- Amount of crew needed for scenery/drapery installation
- If it is a non-IATSE crew, is there a crew chief on the call that you are working with?
- Is crew parking paid for or validated at the hotel or other venue?

As you can see, managing labor is all about time management and people skills. Making everyone feel like they are part of the team and that they contributed to the event's success is all a part of the production manager's job.

TIP – Make sure that you give the crews their proper break periods throughout the day. Some may be contractual, so make sure you know the local rules. Your crew will appreciate this!

THE INITIAL SITE VISIT OR VENUE WALK-THROUGH

Once your team has been identified, use your contact sheet to schedule a venue walk-through. Though the participant list may vary from event to event, generally they will include: the client, venue staff (such as catering managers), and in-house production company representatives, as well as event designers and vendors (décor, lighting, sound, and video). This will often be the first time that everyone is in the room together, so this will provide an opportunity for relationship-building and practicing good communication techniques.

Start with introductions and have your contact sheet ready for distribution. You should have a written agenda and try to stick to it. If too many side discussions are occurring and it overwhelms the meeting, it becomes your job to get the others on task and focused. You should note that not all questions will be answered at the first walk-through. Oftentimes, the walk-through creates more questions than it answers, so be prepared for it to go either way. Make sure you capture the information and notate it either with a pad and paper or a tablet-type device.

ENTRANCE

The walk-through should begin at the entrance of the event. At this point, the production manager should be on the lookout for any design elements discussed. This could include lighting, audio, and/or video elements. You should also determine if there will be a VIP entrance as well as start to determine if way finding signage will be needed.

LOBBY/FOYER

The lobby, foyer, or entrance to the main ballrooms in the hotel is usually the next stop on the site visit. Oftentimes with corporate theatre meetings and conventions, the lobbies and foyers are filled with registration tables, silent auction tables, alcohol bars, or other items that may come as a surprise later. Again, look for electricity needs, lighting needs, and possibly another sound system for production elements such as background music, a live band or auctioneer.

Larger scale and higher budget events often use the foyer as an additional performance space. Bringing in production elements is not an uncommon experience in these spaces.

THE MAIN BALLROOM OR CONVENTION CENTER ROOM

As the site survey moves into the main ballroom, the realization of the physical production should start to take place, and the walk-through will cover a myriad of topics.

Placing the stage at the correct location in the venue is usually the first decision to be made. This can be decided by physical limitations or by the client's specific requests. Once the stage is placed, the rest of the design team can now concentrate on locating other production elements. For the production manager, the questions will start to accumulate. What is the size of the stage? What are the audio, video, and lighting components needed for the event? Where will they go? Where is the tech table set up? Many other discussions will be happening once you get in the ballroom. Seating styles (theatre, banquet, classroom), table sizes and placement, decorations (décor), thematic interpretations of the event – all will start being discussed as it pertains to the main ballroom. Be prepared to listen in to discussions about seating, sightlines, schedules, meal menus, décor, and color themes. Table centerpieces, video elements and talent

Figure 18.8   Snow storm during load in – Minneapolis, Minnesota
Credit: Photo by Jay Sheehan

needs will all be discussed as well. Much like a theatre production meeting, all of the various topics need a place on the agenda.

Once you conclude the meeting, you should find time to walk the venue again either by yourself or with an assistant. Having these details ahead of time will help you be more effective on show day. First, find the loading dock and check how many trucks can unload at once. Check the height of the dock to determine if an additional ramp or forklift is needed. Now check the loading dock door size to make sure your production elements will fit. Also, check the route that the equipment is going to have to follow to get loaded into the room. Are you loading equipment through the hotel kitchen, with many obstacles? Is there a freight elevator near the loading dock if the event is on a different level in the hotel? How tall are the ceilings in freight elevators? Do you have to share elevators with room service staff at hotel venues? You would be surprised how many hotels are not set up for a smooth load-in for the audio-visual crews. By walking the route ahead of time, you will have a head start on show day. With that knowledge, you can inform the stagehands about the various challenges ahead of time, thus saving time and saving money.

WORKING OUTDOORS

Not all events are held indoors, and special attention should be paid to the added challenges and risks that accompany any outdoor event. Outdoor venues can be created almost anywhere you have space. From baseball fields to golf courses, to private backyards, outdoor events are especially popular and production managers should keep an additional checklist of items that will need to be attended to make the event a success. While each outdoor event will have its own special set of circumstances, many will need the same basic production elements as those that are held indoors.

As is the case with indoor venues, the first thing that the production manager should do is schedule a site visit. Outdoor venues need to be visited long before the load-in, so the production manager should schedule this site visit as far in advance as possible. Upon arrival for the site visit, the first item on the list that should be looked at is the load-in process. This includes looking at the path for how the stagehands will bring the production gear to the stage and audience area. Is the ground made of concrete, dirt, soft grass, or perhaps gravel? Remember that heavy road cases and soft surfaces don't get along and wheels will immediately get stuck once they land off the truck. To fix this potential issue, plan on plywood or a decked "road" from the back of the truck to the final destination of the road cases. If this is overlooked, the stagehands may have to hand carry cases and truss pieces and that may exhaust your crew before the load-in is complete.

> **TIP** – Find out where the local crew needs to park for your event. Having this information communicated to the crew prior to the event insures everyone arrives and is ready to work by the call time. You should also determine a break room for meals and let your crew know once they arrive for their calls.

In addition to looking at the path of travel for gear, check where your trucks will have to park after load out as not all outdoor venues will have the luxury of onsite truck and staff parking. Many times, trucks and staff will have to park offsite, and the client or producer will usually have a shuttle system in place to transport the staff back from the offsite parking location to the venue. Figuring this out on the day of load-in wastes valuable time and energy, so make sure this is on your list to check far in advance.

The next item you will need to address is power. Very rarely is there enough electricity to power up your outdoor event? Once this is confirmed and you figure out how large of a generator is needed, figure out where it will be parked. (Some events may need multiple generators so look carefully at the potential placement areas.) Things to keep in mind about placement are numerous. How close will it be to the stage, and will generator engine noise interfere with the performance stage audio? Placing it far enough away to avoid this issue means extra cable lengths to get from the generator to the distribution center, so make sure you measure this out at the walkthrough.

> **TIP** – When using a portable generator, don't forget to check the fuel levels regularly. If you run out of gas, your event is over ... all because of a neglect to watch the fuel tank gauge.

Another thing to confirm at the site visit is the time of the event. Once you have established the start time of the event, check your app for the sunset on your event day. (Make sure you have downloaded a good sunrise/sunset app on your device). Knowing when sunset directly affects production elements like projections and lighting. It makes no sense to start a video when you can't see the screen, so plan these elements with great care.

Each outdoor event, venue, and client will be different, and you will need to keep an accurate checklist of items for consideration. Here are some items to add to your checklist:

- Think in advance about storage. Once road cases are emptied, where will the cases be stored? If there is no ample storage location, then you may have to put the empties back on the truck which will increase the labor needs over the course of the day. Plan ahead!

- Make sure you collaborate with the catering company that will be cooking and serving at the venue. Discussing the days schedule is especially important as the catering company will have trucks that need access, special power requirements, and parking for up to 100 employees, food servers, bartenders, chefs, and other staff. Also, meals are often served at specific times during the events program, and being late or early can make or break the night's success, so, make sure you stay in close contact with the head catering staff on event day!

- Restroom facilities will need to be assessed carefully. Most events will need portable restrooms, so check for the load-in location and placement for these units. Most VIP toilet units will arrive on a large trailer so make sure the drivers can get a large vehicle in and out easily. Pay attention to the details on this. Many of these units will need access to a water source with a hose connection as well as power. This may be a big challenge, depending on the venue's location. A solution may be to ask for self-contained units that have a large capacity of water already in them as well as solar-powered lighting (Make sure you know how many guests are attending so you know if your holding tanks are large enough. If they are not, you are in for trouble as toilet overflow at your event isn't great!)

- Check the local ordinances for late-night curfew and decibel limits and adhere to them. Most cities have strict noise and time curfews and it's important to be good neighbors, so do your due diligence and find out what the local rules are.

- You should also carefully consider accessibility for your guests and crew, and also make sure there are no obstacles to prevent exiting in an emergency.

The other major topic for you to discuss is the backup plan in case of inclement weather.

CONSTANTLY CHECK THE WEATHER! This seems obvious but is a good reminder.

Have a backup plan in case of rain or snow. Have a good weather app on your device and check it every day. If the potential for rain or snow is in the forecast, you may need to plan for putting up a large tent for the event to move into.

This is a very costly item as large tents to house the entire event will be in the tens of thousands of dollars. Additionally, large tents need time to set up. Do you have that time in your Plan B schedule? The decision to put up a tent will need to be made at least 48 hours before the event so that the tenting company can schedule equipment and staff.

Lightning is also a factor, especially if you have people standing on a stage with a steel roof overhead. If lightning gets within a certain distance of your venue, you will have to get everyone off the stage and into a safe location. Your weather app should be able to tell you the distance of recent lightning strikes, so make sure you've downloaded an app that has that feature. The potential of evacuating the venue due to sudden weather should be taken seriously and discussed at the first site visit. Determine at what distance the lightning strikes will cause the stage evacuation to begin and monitor those distances.

> "As a minimum, lightning safety experts strongly recommend that by the time the weather monitor observes 30 seconds between seeing the lightning flash and hearing its associated thunder or by the time the leading edge of the storm is within six miles of the venue, all individuals should have left the venue site and be within a safer structure or location."
>
> - https://www.ncaa.org/health-and-safety/lightning-safety

Weather is going to be one of your biggest challenges and knowing when to put the evacuation plan into action should be taken very seriously. Many tragedies because of weather could have been avoided if weather plans were taken more seriously. Besides rain and lightning, you should also look out for wind. Weigh down items like small tents and tablecloths etc. The wind is especially dangerous if you have constructed a large stage with a roof system. (You should always have a stage technician onsite in case you need to lower the roof due to high winds.)

> **TIP** – Check out the companion website to this book for useful links to help with weather and other outdoor considerations.

The production manager in special events, like the production manager in the other performing arts disciplines, is by no means a small job. As technology advances and productions become more and more complicated, a properly trained production manager may be the difference between a successful event and one that may not go so well. The plethora of details cannot and should not be overlooked, as no detail is too small for the production manager. By using your relationships created along the way as well as your checklist, you, too, can become a successful and competent production manager in the exciting world of special events.

CASE STUDY – ORGANIZING THE CHALLENGES: BIG SHOW, BIG BALLROOM

CONTRIBUTOR: TOM BOLLARD, TECHNICAL DIRECTOR

As is the case in television and film, live theater and the corporate meeting industry, key positions are often titled differently, which can be a bit confusing. For the purposes of this case study, we use the tile of production manager and technical director interchangeably.

This project was a simple enough product launch meeting for a multi-national medical device manufacturer, being produced in an appropriately sized ballroom with a realistic production schedule. I had been working on the drawings with the producers for nearly six months. Three weeks before our move-in the show was in great shape. At that point, the client decided to completely revise the entire show, including the creative treatment, budget, and production schedule without any knowledge of what was physically possible within the space.

When this happens, the first thing the producer does is ask the technical director/production manager if it's even possible and if so, what it will cost. This call triggers the accelerated re-pre-production planning of the project in a predictable, linear fashion. I start by making a list of the details I'll need to confirm and whether the new plan is realistic before worrying about cost. Then I prioritize those action steps and get to work.

In this business, relationships are everything and knowing your designers is critical. I had a good deal of experience with each designer so, instead of asking them to reimagine the show from scratch, I got them to think about possible ideas that would have to work within a revised rigging and truss layout. I would design this new layout based on the realities of the venue and the event's timeline. In one email I had the entire design team and their staffs reorganizing their timelines, thinking creatively, and alerting the shops to stand by.

As a ballroom or convention hall technical director/production manager, a successful venue interface will make or break your project, so I was immediately on the phone with the venue's rigging supervisor. The new plan included turning the stage and audience configuration 45 degrees from what was traditional for a ballroom with a built-in stage. This means that the available rigging points (places and hardware in the ceiling from which to hang trussing) become only marginally useful. Adding to the fun were six huge chandeliers, hanging majestically like mines in a harbor. After several days of back and forth, we were able to get enough points needed to fly a super-structure, from which we actually rigged and flew the show trusses and equipment. We used over 1500' of truss and 92 motors whereas the original plan called for half of that. In the original contracting process, we had a detailed discussion outlining clearly how any changes to the approved scope of work would affect costs and how we would estimate those costs, gain client approval, and track changes, which proved essential for the final billing process.

Once the rigging was sorted out, the design team quickly adjusted, and I turned my attention to the production schedule. In the original plan, we had one full pre-rig

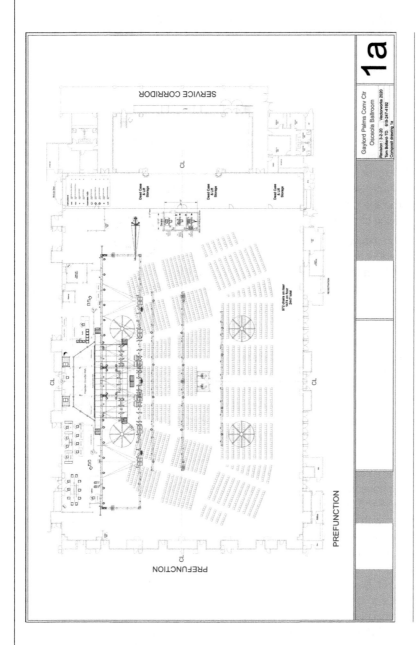

Figure 18.9 Ground plan by Tom Bollard

day, two days of load-in, a day for faxing all systems, focus and programming lighting, working on projector & audio cues, and generally getting ready to hand off the room and crew to the stage manager for rehearsals. From that point, we had 1.5 days for rehearsals before the opening session.

The biggest challenge for our load-in was that the hotel had extended the client before us by a day in the one part of the ballroom where we had the most points. So, instead of getting the entire ballroom at 7:00 am on load-in on day one, I got two-thirds of the ballroom at 7:00 am and the rest at 10:00 pm. Because at least some part of most of the trusses flew in the section of the ballroom that I didn't get until 10:00 pm, I had to add a large overnight rigging crew, which meant I could not realistically begin hanging lights, audio, video, or scenery until 5:00 am the next day.

Our tech day had been cut in half to accommodate client rehearsals so our load-in day two became our focus, program, and tech notes day. Predictably, day one melted into day two and the entire crew was exhausted. I was able to turn the room over to a sympathetic stage manager on time, but I had to come back into the ballroom after rehearsals that night and supervise the installation of seating risers … until 5:00 am. After a quick shower and change of clothes, I met the show operating staff at 6:00 am and we opened on time … barely.

There are, of course, many takeaways from a project like this and although I don't recommend production chaos to anyone, this show did reinforce many essential, key points that every technical director/production manager needs to understand.

- Be adaptable and ready for anything. You never know when a challenge will be presented before you.
- Be crystal clear in your contract, about what hours are included and what constitutes acceptable additional billing. The ballroom industry is built on ten-hour days with all hours after ten billed as overtime. There is flexibility here of course but get paid for your time!
- As the production manager, the buck stops with you. Do the preproduction work, including the drawings and take responsibility when something goes wrong.
- Be respectful of everyone on your team, including and especially the local crew. Advocate strongly for proper breaks, good crew catering, paid parking. Remember that you are only as good as your crew.
- Treat the venue respectfully and professionally. It's amazing what doors will open for you once you gain the trust of the hotel staff. It's no surprise that venue rigging supervisors make up the majority of my holiday card and gift list.
- Remember that ultimately you are in the unique position of being the lead team-builder and problem-solver in what is often a very stressful environment … there is great satisfaction in that!

The possibilities for creativity within what amount to an empty rectangular box make producing industrial theater so satisfying for production managers putting six truckloads of gear into a two-truckload ballroom in half the time needed to do it comfortably is the kind of thing us problem solvers enjoy … right?

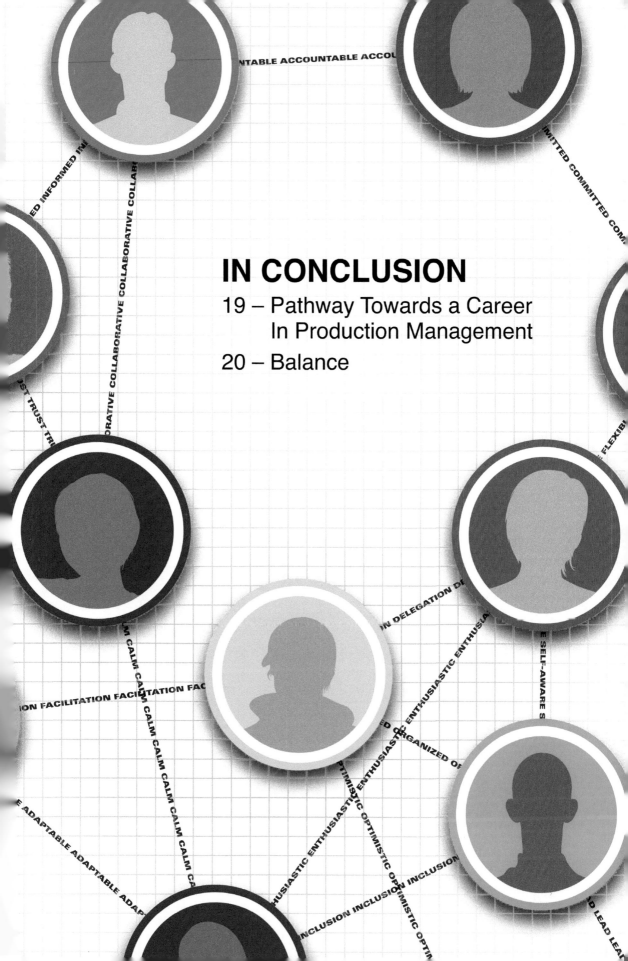

IN CONCLUSION

19 – Pathway Towards a Career In Production Management

20 – Balance

Pathway Toward a Career in Production Management

> "It impresses me so much the quality of people who do our job. The cream really does rise to the top."
>
> - Veronica Bishop, Former Production Manager at Cincinnati Playhouse in the Park

THE BEGINNING OF THE PATH

As with most jobs in the entertainment business, getting a job is often about whom you know and who knows you. Every production manager we spoke with for this book achieved their position by working their way up through other parts of the business. Many production managers got their start as stage managers, a few come through technical direction and there are also some who were designers or performers. If this is a business you want to break into, it is necessary that you have put in time in other positions within an organization. Rarely, if ever, will you be trusted to manage production if you have not already participated at some level within the process and proven yourself to be knowledgeable and capable. People will need to trust in your abilities. Some of the larger performing arts organizations in the country hire fellows or apprentices in production management. These positions are not plentiful, and the hiring process is competitive, however, if you can get an entry-level position, it will be a great stepping-stone that might gain you access to the business.

Education is another path. Graduate training programs in production management can provide early career individuals training in this area and provides an opportunity for career pivots later on if desired. Graduate training gets a bad rap from so many in the industry who worked their way up the ladder and feel everyone else can (and

DOI: 10.4324/9780367808174-24

should) do so too. However, many have used the opportunity to advance their career. It's not for everyone, but it can be right for many, particularly those who have had limited access to advancement opportunities.

> "I look back on my first job working as an education programs coordinator for an opera company. I had just graduated from college and was eager to take my degree for a spin. To be honest I made lots of mistakes, mostly from not having the job skills that others with more experience did. However, with each mistake came an opportunity to grow. By the time I left that job, my base knowledge was so much greater than it was when I arrived. I am so grateful for those who were with me in the early years... and for their patience!"
>
> - Paige Satter, Director of Facility Administration
> at the San Diego Symphony

APPLYING FOR A NEW JOB

Your cover letter is an important tool in the application process. It should be tailored specifically to the job you are applying for. Do not use a generic cover letter; address the letter to the person doing the hiring. Make sure to include why you are applying for the job, why you think you are right for the job and what experience you have that backs up that statement. If you have a personal connection to the job or know someone at the organization, you should mention it in your letter. It's all about relationships! Don't feel you need to list your entire job experience history in the letter; that is what your resume is for. Keep it short and sweet, though make your points and say what you need to say. And always proofread! AND, have someone you trust to proofread it too!

> "Highlight the crossover skills between your last job and the one you are applying for and really pull those to the front of the resume/cover letter."
>
> - Kelsey Sapp, Production Manager at the International
> Festival of Arts and Ideas

When you apply for a job, make sure your resume is in top shape. Your resume should be:

- Easy to read: Do not make the reader search for the information. Make sure your contact information is at the top.
- Pleasing to the eye: People are more likely to read a resume that is clearly laid out, nicely formatted, and with a sense of style.
- Succinct: Include all necessary information, but keep it concise. The resume merely opens the door for you; if interviewed, you will have more opportunities to elaborate on your skills and potential.

- Current: Make sure to update your resume with your most recent employment or training information. Weigh the importance of any credits/jobs and list the ones that show you off best. You may begin with a resume full of the college experience, but once you have enough professional credits, remove the college credits.

- Specific to the job: Your resume should cater to the job for which you are applying. For example, if you are applying for a job in opera, make sure to list your opera credits first.

- Without errors: Do not ever send a resume with a typo or incorrect data. It reflects poorly on your abilities.

- Truthful: Never lie - our world is too small. We all know each other in this business, and a lie might come back to haunt you.

Your Name
Mailing Address/Email address/Phone Number

PROFESSIONAL EXPERIENCE –

2008-Present   Production Manager
The Palace Theatre
- Supervise the production effort for ten shows per season.
- Coordinate the scheduling of performances, production meetings, rehearsals and technical rehearsals as well as pre-show and post-show events during performances.
- Work in association with the Producing Director to hire designers and production personnel.
- Maintain a production budget of $350,000.

2004-2008   Production Manager
Urban Theatre Project
- Oversaw all production for three shows in repertory.
- Worked in association with the Artistic Director to hire all designers and production personnel. Allocated and maintained a production budget, requiring creative use of small funds.
- Supervised the student company, who served as the crew for all production aspects – set construction, set painting, light hang and focus, run crew.
- Coordinated the scheduling of production meetings, rehearsals and technical rehearsals as well as pre-show and post-show events during performances.

2002-2004   Assistant Production Manager
Round the Corner Theatre
- Responsible for all payroll and bills for the production department.
- Facilitated the casting and hiring of actors, designers and production personnel, including negotiating with agents and generating union contracts.
- Assisted in scheduling production meetings, rehearsals and technical rehearsals.
- Maintained a production budget of $500,000.

SPECIAL SKILLS –
- Valid driver's license
- Fluent in American Sign Language
- Proficient at Vectorworks and Adobe Photoshop

EDUCATION –
Bachelor of Arts in Theatre from the Mid-Atlantic University, 2002

REFERENCES –

Anne White	Donald Wilson	Jamaal Mason
Producing Director	Former Managing Director	Production Manager
Urban Theatre project	The Palace Theatre	Round the Corner Theatre
Email/phone number	Email/Phone number	Email/Phone number

Figure 19.1   Resume example

Whether the employer requires it or not, you should list three references on your resume. These should be people you have worked with or worked for, not friends or family. Ideally, the three people would know you in different situations in different organizations. Three professors from the same school, for example, is not the best choice. Some jobs require one or more letters of recommendation. Select your recommenders wisely and, if possible, have a conversation with them about the job and why you think you are right for it. You want recommendation letters to be personalized to you and highlight your strengths and potential.

> **TIP** – always ask people if they are willing to serve as a reference for you. If you have used them in the past and plan to again – ask a second time, and maybe a third. Do not let it be a surprise when a potential employer calls your reference. You do not want them caught unaware. Also, make sure you ask your reference which phone number and/or email address they want you to list.

You got an interview – congratulations! However, the job is not yours yet. Here are some things to consider for your interview:

- Be prepared: How will the interview occur? Phone, video, in person? Attend to whatever details are necessary to make sure you show up ready to go. If it is a video interview on a new software platform you have never used, take care of any necessary downloads in advance and then do a rehearsal with a friend. If the interview is in person, make sure you know where it will be and how you are going to get there.

- Do your homework: Know as much as you can about the organization, the people, the work, etc. Chances are good you might be asked about your thoughts on one or more of those subjects, and you want to be prepared.

- Dress the part: Make sure you dress one step above the people with whom you are interviewing. Know that those working in the performing arts world rarely come to work in three-piece suits and tend to favor more casual attire, but a corporate theatre job could be the opposite. A good rule of thumb is to make sure you are comfortable climbing a ladder in what you are wearing. You never know when you might be offered a tour of the facility and need to do just that!

- Be ready to ask questions: Make sure you get the information you need to accept the job should it be offered to you. You are interviewing them as much as they are interviewing you. Some employers might expect questions as a sign of your job interest, your intelligence, and your engagement. Questions can demonstrate that you have done your research and you are serious about the position. This is also an opportunity to check in on values alignment. How your questions are answered (or not) can provide useful clues to the culture and values of the organization.

- Be on time: Make sure you know where to go and how long it's going to take to get there. If you have any concerns, scope it out ahead of time. Do not be late! In fact, be early.

- Follow up: A small note or email to say "thank you" can show that you are serious and excited about the job. If you do not get the job, do not break the relationship. Maybe you were a close second choice and maintaining a good relationship with the employer could mean a future opportunity. Do not burn any bridges if you can avoid it!

> "When I look for a new job, I know I need to work for a company that cares about me, wants to hear from me and aligns with my values. I take an anti-racist approach to presenting who I am and what my values are. First you have to research the company – what they do and how they do it, and their reputation in the industry. Talk to people who have worked there. Theatre is a small world, you probably know someone who has worked there, could have been 20 years ago. If the position I am applying for has been a revolving door, then I ask about that in the interview process. How have they changed things to make sure this does not keep happening? If they can't answer that, it is an automatic red flag for me. I also ask the person who is interviewing me about their personal anti-racist ethos. If they regurgitate the company statement, then that's another red flag. Now I also ask how their company handled Covid and how they would change things if they had to do it again. If you don't ask about all of this up front, you set yourself up for failure if you end up taking the job."
>
> - Miguel Flores, Associate Director of Production
> at the Huntington Theater

If you are offered the job, it is important to consider your own worth as well as the logistics of taking the job. For example, the job might offer good compensation, but the location of the work will require an expensive commute, negatively impacting your net pay. Make sure you are looking at the big picture. Can you afford to take this job? Are you taking a risk by making this move? You are the only person who can answer these questions. And don't forget – it's perfectly natural to negotiate. Many people, especially those young in their careers, feel odd about doing this, but most employers expect it. Don't be afraid of the process. Taking a new job is an important decision and should not be approached lightly. (Refer back to the Hiring and Casting chapter for more details on negotiations.)

YOU GOT THE JOB!

Time for celebration for sure, but now the real work starts. Whether this is your first or fifth new job as a production manager the onboarding process, duties, and scope of work will be different from what you experienced before. Let us look at how a new production manager joins an organization.

> "Sometimes change comes to us as an opportunity, and sometimes change comes to us as a surprise. Sometimes we are looking for change, other times it's looking for us. With each change I made – in my case not in 'job' but rather in 'organization' – I was able to build on my production management skills. This is an important part of moving from one organization to another."
>
> - Paige Satter, Director of Facility Administration
> at the San Diego Symphony

LEARN ABOUT THE ORGANIZATION

Each organization and therefore each production management position you find your-self in is different. Do not ever make assumptions – be adaptable. Work closely with the people and the systems to best know how you will fit in and what changes you might need to make, but do not rush it. Resist the temptation to make changes right away. Learn the team and how they work. Dig into the who, what, when, and why of how structures and processes were created. Understand why things are the way they are and then decide how you want to leverage these ideas toward change. Also know that change is hard – an organization is sometimes like a large ship. It takes time to turn it around. Check out the book *Switch: How to Change Things When Change is Hard* by Chip and Dan Heath if you find yourself in a position to make a sizable change.

> "Try not to change anything in the first 6 months of the job. That's how long it takes to get a full understanding of the place. Start with small changes up front and then build to larger changes. Challenge the tradition of 'we've always done it this way.' Look for illegality that people might be unaware of. Digging into the details of the historical data of the company or annual projects might unearth things that need to change."
>
> - Miguel Flores, Associate Director of Production
> at the Huntington Theater

WHAT IS MY JOB?

Though you may think you understand what a production manager does and what is expected of you, take the time to investigate your new situation to wisely choose your path forward. Here are some critical questions to ask:

- What is my actual job description? – Luckily for you, you were recently hired and there should have been a job posting that you reviewed when you applied. That is a good place to start. If not, then ask the organization for one. If there is no job description – then you will need to create one. We hope this book has characterized what can and will be expected of most production managers, but as we have said multiple times, each job is different. Take the time early on to understand what you are supposed to be doing. If you have taken on a new position, you have the opportunity to craft your own job description and help create the priorities for your position within the organization.

- What does my boss think my job is? – Sometimes what your job description says might be different or not as inclusive as what the person who hired you (or the person who now supervises you) expects. Make sure there is an opportunity early on to meet one-on-one with your supervisor and begin to learn what they want from you.

- What do my employees expect of me? – As a production manager you are likely supervising staff members. One of the first things you should do upon entering a new organization is meet with staff one-on-one to get to know them and to understand what they need from you. How best you can support them? If they have been with the organization longer than you, they can also provide you with some critical understanding of areas needing your focus. Listen to your employees, don't just hear them.

- What did my predecessor do? – If you are entering a position that was recently vacated then, whether you like it or not, you might be inheriting job expectations. Often the duties are easy to understand but the method might take some time to grasp. You should also be prepared for the fact that people might have really liked, or not liked, your predecessor's job performance and these feelings are now linked to you. You might be in a position to overlap with the previous person or have access to them to ask questions during your transition. This is very useful and should be taken advantage of. However, this might not be the case and you might have to find this information out for yourself.

- Why am I responsible or not for certain things? – Again, if you are taking over the job from someone else then there is much that was decided about your position before you arrived. If there are duties or expectations that seem out of line for you, then ask. There could be a great reason for why you are expected to do something. It could be because your predecessor had a set of skills that lent themselves to a certain task or because no one else in the organization stood up to take something on. Just because the previous production manager did something doesn't automatically mean it's now your responsibility. It might make more sense for a duty to be redistributed to someone with more interest or expertise. Remember to make changes incrementally.

> "During my first month on the job, I expect there to be an onboarding plan that introduces me to the company. The place I have seen this the most is in Academia when the production manager works for a unit that is part of a larger institution already set up with these procedures. Smaller companies or departments that do not onboard people often have more trouble. Unfortunately, there is no standard in our industry, and it is something we need to change."
>
> - Miguel Flores, Associate Director of Production
> at the Huntington Theater

POSITIONAL POWER

Within an organization or on a single project the production manager holds power. Power to make decisions, spend money, influence others, hire and fire people, etc. Learning to be comfortable with that power, and the responsibilities that come with it, can be a challenge, especially if you are new to the job. Remember that you are a product of everything that has happened up until now. Perhaps this is your first time having this much power and influence, but there are certain experiences you can pull from, either those you experienced directly or those you have witnessed.

If you find yourself as a lead production manager for an arts organization then likely you will be invited and/or expected to participate as a senior staff member in conversations about the direction, values, vision, and mission of the organization. If this is your first time having a seat as this table, it can be daunting. Find and build a connection with other senior staff whom you now sit alongside. Learning from them will do three things.

- It will provide you with an understanding of how high-level conversations work at this organization and any previous history that might prove helpful to understand.

- It will help you learn about other departments and contemplate how your department can work collaboratively.

- It will build relationships with other department heads. It can be lonely at the top and having a friend/colleague or two with similar positional power can be helpful as you navigate this new experience.

When in doubt it is always a great idea to connect with a mentor. There are many production managers in this industry that were once in the same position and are willing to give advice. Find someone who can be a sounding board and can provide guidance as you build your confidence. And once you have established yourself, begin to mentor others. There is a famous quote by James Keller that says – "A candle loses nothing by lighting another candle." Find a way to contribute to a student or early career production manager's success and to be the candle that helps light another.

> "In every situation I have found myself, I have picked up a new skill or I realize where some bit of knowledge I have might be useful."
> - Jared Clarkin, Director of Production at Milwaukee Rep

REPUTATION

To lead, we must be adept at influencing others. How do you do that quickly and efficiently? One way is your reputation. Building a reputation starts early in your career. Reputation is about all aspects of your life and career. As we keep saying this is a small world we live and work in, and everyone is connected. Your personal relationships within the business as well as your social media presence have an impact on your reputation. Proceed with care and caution. Do good work always, be consistent, and have a good attitude.

There are two types of people, those who trust immediately and those who need time for trust to be earned. It is often best to fall into the first category. This business is one that necessitates fast relationship building. If you can trust right away, then you can more easily connect with people and the working relationship is stronger. Trust that people are in the positions they are in for a reason. Someone decided they deserve to be there. It is also necessary to be trustworthy. Do not let people down. Remember that Don Miguel Ruiz states in his book *The Four Agreements*, "your word in your vow." Keep your promises and if that is not possible explain why and adequately rectify the situation. Trust others and be trustworthy.

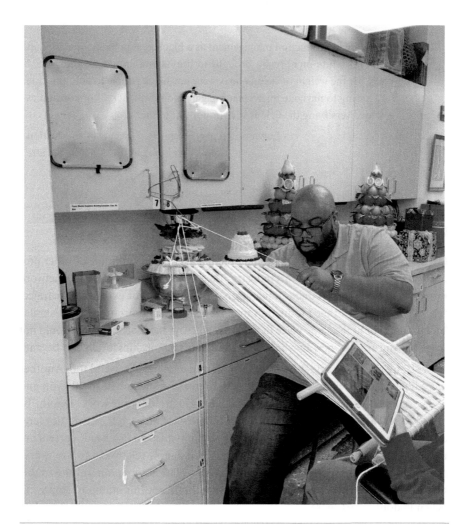

Figure 19.2 Production Manager Lawrence Bennett lends a helping hand with props during a production of *Mojada: a Medea in Los Angeles* at the Repertory Theatre of St Louis

Credit: Photo provided by Lawrence Bennett

IMPOSTER SYNDROME

Impostor syndrome is the feeling that you should not be in this position, that you do not belong there. You will inevitably feel it at some point in your career, if not multiple times. A common time to experience this is with the start of a new job. Did they hire the right person? Do I have the skills to do this? What if I cannot get this job done? Questions like these and more can rattle through your brain during a time of transition. Breathe deep and work through it. Trust your instincts, they are what got you this far in your career. Take solace in the fact that someone chose for you to do this job which means they believe in you. Let that be enough to make you believe in yourself. If you still struggle, then find someone to talk to. It can be hard to be an objective observer when working through something like this yourself. It helps to have another more experienced eye give perspective on your situation.

> "Working in production management as a black person in an industry that is mainly white men, really brought to life having imposter syndrome. I really felt the weight of being one of very few black people to hold this title and having to navigate micro/macro-aggressions and lack of opportunities is why diversifying the field is very important to me."
>
> - Lawrence "Larry" Bennett, Director of Production
> at the Alliance Theatre

CREATING YOUR NETWORK

One incredible benefit to being a production manager is the multitude of other production managers working in this industry. Take the opportunity to build a network for yourself. Look for production managers who parallel your experience or trajectory. This could be other production managers at like organizations, with similar backgrounds, or at the same place in their careers. And these connections should not stop once you are not "new" anymore. Keep building relationships locally and beyond.

A strong network aside from other production managers is useful too. Another incredible group of people to connect with are vendors who will supply you and your organization with tools, knowledge, and skills to do your work. Do not be afraid to reach out to local vendors to get to know them, even if you do not have an immediate need. There may also be large companies whose headquarters are nearby. Reach out and introduce yourself. Once again, relationships are everything. Do not let the work be solely transactional. The companion website to this text lists a variety of vendors in our industry that meet our stamp of approval. When in doubt start there.

> "As you move throughout your career and into different organizations, it is essential to keep your resources and relationships close. Keeping in touch with previous colleagues and vendors can be a lifesaver in certain situations."
>
> - Paige Satter, Director of Facility Administration
> at the San Diego Symphony

Do not focus solely on building your external network. Your internal network is just as important, especially connections with people outside of your unit. Creating bonds and building relationships with people in other departments will allow you to find allies and gatekeepers to navigate the organization. This includes "navigating" the people within the organization. Show respect to those who have been at the organization longer than you, they can teach you things not only about the organization but also about how to thrive in this business.

Figure 19.3 Author Cary Gillett gets back to her stage management roots. As you progress in your career don't be afraid to look or step back from time to time

Credit: Photo by Jay Sheehan

MOVING UP WITHIN THE ORGANIZATION

It is not uncommon to see a member of the production team move up into a production management position. Often the hiring authority will prioritize institutional knowledge and employee growth opportunities by promoting from within. The guidance in this chapter will apply to you if you find yourself in this position, however, there are some additional things to be aware of –

- The people you are working with will not change, but your relationship with them will. People who were your peers are now your employees. Those who were steps above you in the hierarchy are now your direct supervisors. This is not necessarily a challenge, but it is something to be critically aware of. You may need to build new or different relationships with all of these people. It is also important to acknowledge that they may shift their relationships with you too. Someone who might have been your friend may take a step back if they are now your employee.

- Because people already know you, they may feel more comfortable coming to you right away with thoughts on changes to how things should work. They may also have a list of things they never got from your predecessor that they are eager to get from you.

- You will already have an in-depth knowledge of the production department. You will know, for example, the problematic staff members and who needs pushing. You will also know the exemplary staff and what support they need to continue doing great work.
- There will be things you do not know, so a period of learning and comprehending will still be necessary.

> "I knew I would be in an entry level position for a brief period before I would transition into another position. I needed this step to get to the next one, to keep the trajectory going."
>
> - Kelsey Sapp, Production Manager at the International Festival of Arts and Ideas

TAKING THE NEXT STEP IN YOUR CAREER

Your first production management job does not need to be your last. It is okay to love the work, but not the organization or the people you are currently working with. It is also okay to recognize that your current situation is not the challenge you crave. Whatever the reason, if you feel the urge to search for new work you should. The live entertainment field is filled with people who change jobs more frequently than in other fields. Being in a job 3–4 years and feeling ready to move on is not uncommon, especially if you are in an assistant or associate production management position. We applaud the desire to keep growing and learning and often with that comes new opportunities.

The next step in your career does not always need to be another production management job. The skills and temperament that this job requires are applicable in so many other positions and fields. Do not ever let yourself feel limited by the uncertainty of what comes next. Keep growing and learning!

TOP THREE TAKEAWAYS

- Any path to production management is the right path. Learn as you go, and it will serve you well.
- Build your networks – internally, externally, within the industry and outside of it. All of this will benefit you immensely.
- Continue to build and refine who you are – your reputation, your style, your brand, etc.

Balance

> "Walking the tightrope of being a human in the workforce is a balancing act of the highest degree. We need to invest in ourselves first to be able to invest in things outside of ourselves later."
>
> > - Parker Detchon, Life Coach

The preceding chapters have all been about the job of the production manager. What does it take to network, to make the client or director happy, and to have a successful production? The bottom line is that it takes hard work, long hours, and extreme dedication to the art form in which you are working. The job of the production manager is not for the faint of heart or for those seeking out some excitement in their everyday job. Careful thought should be given before taking on this career. One must think of balance, define it for oneself, and decide how to achieve that in each circumstance.

> "Balance to me means everything. Being able to do what you love while raising a family, having great friends, enjoying good food and living life with fun and laughter is the balance I strive to achieve."
>
> > - Christy Ney, Stage Manager for Wicked on Broadway

BALANCE? WHAT IS THAT?

Balance, equivalence, equity, proportion, harmony, and evenness are words that the production manager may hear in a design meeting. While these words do help us to describe design thoughts and ideas, it is also important to think of these words as the

DOI: 10.4324/9780367808174-25

Figure 20.1   Finding balance in all of our work
Credit: Photo by Jay Sheehan

way we should strive to run our busy production manager lives. Every one of these harmonious-sounding words has a counterpart though, and the wise production manager should also be on the lookout for such things as imbalance, inequality, inequity, disproportion, discord, and unevenness. If you start to recognize that this is starting to happen to you, it may be time to try and regain your equilibrium and start to seek some much-needed balance.

"We can only give to our passions with any degree of longevity when our proverbial cup is running over. Overflowing with energy that we derive through the various practices of balance in our lives. This balance is an ongoing juggling act of physical maintenance, mental/emotional stability, and spiritual/community connection. When any one of these legs goes weak the whole system can go down, which means your availability to provide creative energy goes offline as well. In a practical sense, work to life balance is like farming. You are nurturing your body, mind and soul so that you have energy to bring to market. If you don't water the plants, care for their bodies, and have adequate nutrients from connection to the Earth, well then you won't have anything to sell at the end of the day. We sometimes believe that we can carry-on without one or another of these elements, however we consistently find that the hard lesson is that even though it's possible for a short time to continue, that we inevitably break under the stress of acting in this way. Once our energetic cup runs dry in any sector of our lives by failing to nurture ourselves physically, mentally, or spiritually, we snap back and can no longer give to any other project until balance is restored in that area. It's a fail-safe built into our systems. The key to success in the practice of balance is to maintain a caliber of abundance in an ongoing way so that we can provide energy output for others, our creative projects, and the world at large. Basically, we need to invest in ourselves first in order to be able to invest in things outside of ourselves later. Remain sensitively attuned to how each major element is balancing its weight on the scales of your life and you'll be able to communicate and execute upon what maintenance you need before it becomes a problem. Walking the tightrope of being a human in the workforce is a balancing act of the highest degree. We must remain well fed, watered, socialized, loved, stretched, strengthened, rested, all to be able to maintain the degree of balance required to perform in this circus."

- Parker Detchon, Life Coach

PAIN IS INEVITABLE, SUFFERING IS OPTIONAL

What exactly happens when we get out of balance? What can suffer? The answers will vary from person to person but for many of us, being out of balance can have some serious consequences. Let's look at a simple example of what happens when we get stressed and out of balance:

- We lose focus on the projects
- We lose interest in the work
- We make simple mistakes
- Our work doesn't get done

- We get depressed
- We become introverted
- We distance ourselves in our relationships

None of these things are helpful for a production manager in show mode. We must be able to think clearly and effectively, and to do that we must be able to handle stress well. The fact is that it's not about the stressful job, but how you handle the stress. That's what is meant by suffering as optional. We can help control this by looking at ways to reduce our stress and limit our "suffering."

According to researchers at San Diego State University, an eight-level approach to wellness is best. Here are some ways in which you can reduce your stress and have a healthier, happier life:

- Physically: Caring for your body to stay healthy now and in the future, eating well and being active.
- Socially: Maintaining healthy relationships, enjoying being with others, developing strong friendships and intimate relationships, caring about others, and letting others care about you.
- Emotionally: Managing your emotions in a constructive way, understanding, and respecting your own feelings, values, and attitudes; appreciating the feelings of others.
- Occupationally: Developing a sense of your strengths, skills, values, and interests in your career; maintaining a balanced life between work, family, play, and taking care of yourself.
- Multicultural: Being aware of your own cultural background and becoming knowledgeable about, respectful of and sensitive to the culture of others.
- Environmentally: Awareness of how your behavior impacts the earth, as well as how the physical world impacts you, demonstrating a commitment to a healthy planet.
- Spiritually: Finding purpose, value, and meaning in your life with or without organized religion.
- Intellectually: Growing and maintaining curiosity about all there is to learn, valuing life-long learning, and responding positively to intellectual challenges.

There are many other ways in which you could approach your own stress management. The bottom line is to be aware of how you feel and adjust as necessary.

FREELANCING AND STRESS

The freelance production manager gets an added layer of stress that they must contend with, and that is always keeping an eye out for work. Looking for your next gig can be a full-time job, and the freelancer must carefully balance the search for future work with the demands of current work. While it is often advised for young production managers to take on every opportunity presented before them, the fact is that overextending and taking on too many projects becomes stressful. One way to reduce

Figure 20.2 Painting by Parker Detchon

stress is to understand your limits and learn how to say "no" when necessary. When you become overextended, all of your clients start to suffer as you become less and less available due to the many projects you have taken on. Most of your work becomes mediocre instead of all your work being excellent. All of this equates to unhappiness. Your work suffers, and you suffer.

"As a young professional in entertainment I often found myself naively sacrificing my bodily and mental health for a paycheck. I would work long hours using coffee to stay up and alcohol to come down from the stress. It inevitably caught up with me by way of simply being unfit for work. Missing early call times from lack of sleep or just having low mental capacity available to problem solve would abruptly end work opportunities. I realized this was my body's way of saying, "I've had enough and it's time to re-balance." Once I was out of work, I would get healthy, get rested, and hopefully get a new job. I quickly realized that an unbalanced lifestyle was unsustainable and have since made corrections to support a more balanced way of working through healthier alternatives."

- Parker Detchon – Life Coach

KNOW YOUR SHOW TO REDUCE STRESS

What are some other ways that we can control stress? The fact is that production management is all about how we handle the unknown factors that pop up in our daily production lives. By limiting the number of unknown factors, we immediately start to eliminate some of our day-of-show or everyday stresses. Bottom line is to know your show or your event and to really know it inside out. By knowing your show, you are investing your time into balance without even knowing it. By knowing your show, you are properly planning for limiting your exposure to stress. Remember what Perry Silvey said in the touring chapter – "by knowing your show, you can save time by making correct decisions." Making correct decisions reduces stress.

HAVE A FULL LIFE

What does it mean to have a full life? It means balancing your work life with your personal life. Take time to be with your family and friends. Go experience museums, movies, music, and art, or take your dog for a walk. And when we say, "be with your family and friends," it means be WITH them. Be present and be focused on what is happening at that moment where you are. Use your production management skills that you use with your clients at home as well. Make your family member the most important person you are talking to at that moment. Turn off the phone and put down the email device. Be present.

"As I've matured, I've realized that although my professional life has provided many gifts, it is a relatively small part of who I am. Work is a 'means to an end' but the end is so much more. I'm a production manager and technical director and love that...but being a father, husband, artist,

> philanthropist, gardener, volunteer and mentor is what colors my life and provides the balance I need. My approach to balance is to integrate all these things into my work life because it makes me real. I wish I had learned this lesson as a younger man."
>
> > - Tom Bollard, Production Manager/Technical Director
> > for Meeting Services Inc.

Many production managers have greatly benefited by finding advice and support through organizations such as the United States Institute for Theatre Technology (USITT) and the Production Managers' Forum. It is important to recognize that if you are feeling stressed out, these groups can help to bring balance by connecting you with people who have gone through many of the same things and if nothing else, can help to reassure you – you are not alone. Additionally, there are organizations that you can reach out to if you are in immediate need of counseling. One such organization is the 24/7 Crisis Text Line. If talking to someone isn't comfortable for you, please try this text helpline. https://www.crisistextline.org/ – Text HOME to 741741 to reach a volunteer Crisis Counselor.

We hope that all of you can take some time to think about your life/work balance and to try and make some needed changes, then go out and live life! Use the tools you have learned in this book to fill your toolkit and production manage to the best of your ability. Work hard, build confidence, find balance, and enjoy the ride. Production management is like nothing else you will ever experience.

> "I did then what I knew how to do. Now that I know better, I do better."
>
> > - Maya Angelou[1]

NOTE

1 Quote courtesy of Caged Bird Legacy, LLC.

Index

Note: Page references in *italics* denote figures.

accountability, and anti-racist production managers 44
Abrons Arts Center 157–159
Actor's Equity Association (AEA) 99, 101, 102, 220
adaptability 32–33
advance checklists 175
advancing the show 167, *168*, 202
agendas for production meetings 67–68, 71
American Federation of Musicians (AFM) 103, 196
American Federation of Television and Radio Artists (AFTRA) 102
American Guild of Musical Artists (AGMA) 102
Angelou, Maya 285
Anna Karenina 154–156, *155*
anti-racism 43
anti-racist production managers 41–46; accountability 44; decentralized leadership 42–43; showing up 41–42, *42*; working together 43; *see also* production managers
The Artist Is Always Right 196–198, *197*
artist fees 77–78
artistic director 34, 102, 125, 192
assessing: safety 109–110, *109*; shops 112–113
assistant stage manager (ASM) 52, 72
audio at special events 249–250
auditions 95–98, *96*, *97*
Aurora Productions 130–132
Ayala, Itzel 41

background checks 93
backstage spaces 246
balance considerations 279–285, *280*, *283*
ballet 147–151, *148*, *151*
Basarab, Heather Rose 236–238
Bennett, Lawrence "Larry" 219–223, *275*, 276
Bishop, Veronica 223–226, *225*, 267
body language *see* non-verbal communication
Bollard, Tom 261–263
breakout sessions 71
Broadway theatre 128–129
Brooklyn Academy of Music (BAM) *233*
budgeting/money concerns: artist fees 77–78; communication of 82; co-productions 214–215; creation of budget 77–78, *79–81*; income sources 75–76; introduction 75; management 82–83; paying people their worth 81–82; purchasing 85–86, *86*; in schedule management 56; tracking 83–85, *84*; understanding overall budget 76–77

Cady, Drew 196–198
California State University Summer Arts 210–212
callbacks 98
Campbell, Catherine 43
Canadian Opera Company 145–146, *146*
casting *see* hiring/casting
checking employment references 93
Chen, Cody 154–156
child guardians 100
children, hiring of 100
Clarkin, Jared 223–226, *225*, 274
collaborative team in performing arts 31
communication 133–134; budgeting 82; difficult conversations 17, *18*; during hiring process 93; face-to-face communication 8; introduction 7–8; non-verbal communication 7, 8, 9–12, *10*, *12*; phone communication 12–13; saying no 16; saying yes 14–15, *15*; schedule management 55–56; written communication 13–14
community building 134
compensation considerations 101
comp time 105
computer assisted drafting (CAD) drawings 239
concept meeting 65
conference calls 61–70
contemporary dance 152, 153, 154
contingency fund 78
continual learning 38
contracts: hiring 100–102; independent contractors 94–95; legal language in 101; pink contracts 129, 235; presenting theater and 202–203; rock and roll 169; technical riders 168–169, 229
contributed income 76
Coppaway, Autumn 144–146
co-pro document 222–223
co-productions: after closing 219; budget 214–215; cooperative productions 219–223; goal of 213; introduction

213; physical production *216*, 216–217; production manager relations 214, 223–226; schedule management 215; staffing 217–219; transportation 217
cost out meeting 65
costume design deadlines 56
cover letters 268
COVID-19 pandemic 13, 69, 117–118, 134–135, 226
creation services 142
crew empowerment 29–30

dance: Abrons Arts Center 157–159; ballet 147–151, *148*, *151*; festivals 154; introduction 147; The Joffrey Ballet 154–156; modern/contemporary 152, *153*; site-specific work 153; solo *vs.* shared dance concerts 153–154; specific theaters for 152; training 149
deadlines, in planning and scheduling 56–58, *58*
debrief meeting 66
decentralized leadership 42–43
delegating in production management 37
Destiny of Desire 223
development department 126
difficult conversations 17, *18*
diplomacy in touring 232
dispute resolution 105
donation sources 76
drape lines 245–246
dressing rooms 172–174, 206
dress rehearsals 60
Drive: The Surprising Truth About What Motivates Us (Pink) 35
drug testing 93
during rehearsal meetings 66

earned income sources 75
education department 127
email communication 13–14
emergency plans 116–117
empathy in communication 8
employment references 93
enjoyment of opera programs 142
esteem needs 36
event budget 206–207
The (r)Evolution of Steve Jobs 142–144, *144*
eye contact during communication 8

face-to-face communication 8
facilitation 33, 70–72
Fair Use Privilege 54
final design meeting 57, 65
fire marshals 113–116, *115*
"fire watch" staff person 114, *115*
Fisk, Kimberly 118–121
flexibility in schedule management 56
flexible theatre 51
Flores, Miguel 271, 272, 273
found-space venue 51

The Four Agreements (Ruiz) 8, 27, 274
freelancing and stress 282–284, *283*
fulltime workers 94, 105, 128, 130, 149–150
future performances 62

"General Industry Standards 1910" guidelines 107–108
general management companies 128
genuineness in communication 8
Glimmerglass Opera 27, 138
Götterdämmerung 144–146, *146*

Hamilton 118–121
Harper, Jon 157–159
Heath, Chip 272
Heath, Dan 272
Hierarchy of Needs (Maslow) 35–36, *36*
hiring/casting: auditions 95–98, *96*, *97*; of children 100; contracts and riders 100–102; fulltime *vs.* seasonal workers 94; negotiations 98–99; personnel management 104–106; principal singers, opera 138; process of 89–93, *91*; of production managers 267–271, *269*; responsibility for 89; unions 102–104; vendors/independent contractors 94–95
Horpedahl, Paul 142–144
hospitality needs, rock and roll productions 171–174
human resource department 106

image magnification (IMAG) 193, 245, 251–252
impostor syndrome 275–276
income sources 75–76
independent contractors 94–95
International Alliance of Theatrical Stage Employees (IATSE) 26, 103, 129, 204, 231, 232, 235, 254, 255
interview considerations 270–271
interview plan 92–93, 270
In the Heights 223–226, *225*
Izzard, Suzy Eddie 207–209

job description 272–273
job description wording 89–90
The Joffrey Ballet 154–156
John F. Kennedy Center *200*

labor: calls and management 204–205; laws 106; needs, in rock and roll productions 170–171; over-hire labor costs 78; rules for venues 231–232; special events 254–255
La Jolla Playhouse 22, 38
leadership: decentralizing 42–43; skills 31–32
League of Resident Theatres (LORT) 101, 220
LED video walls 251
legal language in contracts 101
lighting needs 248–249

listening: active 71; during communication
    13; with intention 23–24
load-in schedule 59, 61, 66
love/belonging needs 36
Luxenberg, Liza 130–132

managing by walking around (MBWA) 34
marketing/public relations department
    125–126
Maslow, Abraham H. 35–36, *36*
modern dace 152, *153*
Montero, Herman 207–209
motivation 35
music needs 149

negotiations, in hiring 98–99
network building 276
New Pickle Circus 236–238, *237*
New York City Ballet 35, 49, 150, 227,
    230, 232
"No More 10 out of 12s" 44–46
non-profit organizations 86
non-theatrical venue 51
non-verbal communication 8, 9–12, *10*, *12*
notes period 60

Oates, Tajh 44–46
occupational safety 107–108, *108*
Occupational Safety and Health Act (1970)
    107–108
Occupational Safety and Health
    Administration (OSHA) 107–108,
    110–113
onstage rehearsals 60
open-door policy 43
open flame safety 114
opera 137–142; The *(r)Evolution of Steve
    Jobs* 142–144; *Götterdämmerung*
    144–146, *146*; technical/production
    forum 140
OPERA America 142
orchestra operations 192–193, *193*
orientation of employees 104
outdoor venue 51
outdoor work 257–260
overall budget understanding 76–77
overhire labor costs 78

performance reviews 105
personal protective equipment (PPE) 112
personal space 11–12
personnel management 104–106
petty cash tracking 85, *86*
Philharmonic Society of Orange County
    196–198
phone communication 12–13
physical production 216–217
physical resources management 62, *63*
pink contracts 129, 235
planning and schedule management:
    building schedule 59; co-productions
    215; creating schedule 56; deadlines

56–58; future performances 62;
    load-in schedule 59, 61, 66; overview
    55–56; production meetings 57,
    65–66; rehearsal schedule 57–58, *58*;
    rights and permissions 53–54; safety
    concerns and 116–121, *119*; schedule
    creation 56; script/project analysis
    52–53; season selection 49–51,
    50; show treatments 54–55; strike
    schedule 61–62; tech schedule 59–60;
    venues 51–52
Plott, Glenn 77
positional power 273–274
post-tech meeting 66
The Power of a Positive No (Ury) 16
preliminary design meeting 65
pre-rehearsal meeting 65
presenting theater: advancing the show
    202; contracts and riders 202–203;
    dressing rooms 206; event budget/
    show settlement 206–207;
    introduction 199–202, *200*, *201*; John
    F. Kennedy Center *200*; labor calls
    and management 204–205; technical
    equipment needs 205; ticketing needs/
    production holds 205
principal singers, hiring 138
Pringle, Shannon 210–212
production holds 179, 205
production management: adaptability 32–33;
    applying for new job 268–271, *269*;
    beginning of career in 267–268;
    career in 267–278; continual learning
    38; creating network 276; delegating
    37; facilitation 33; impostor
    syndrome 275–276; introduction 1–3;
    job description 272–273; learning
    about organization 272; managing
    boss 34; managing by walking
    around (MBWA) 34; motivation 35;
    next step in career 278; positional
    power 273–274; promotion 277–278;
    psychology of 35–37, *36*; reputation
    274; schedule management 55–56;
    venue 167; walking among staff 34
production managers: anti-racist 41–46;
    artistic director and 34; challenges
    for 261–263, *262*; co-productions
    and 214; creative designer and 33,
    33; crew and 29–30; director and
    34; fixing poor relationships 28–29;
    hiring of 104–106; as psychologist
    35–37, *36*; rules, knowledge of
    26–27; season selection 49–51; shop
    supervisors/production staff 35–36;
    stage manager and 35–36; symphony
    music and 194–196, *195*; team and
    24–25; understanding everyone's role
    25; working with another 223–226
production meetings: conference calls 69–70;
    facilitating of 70–72; follow-up to
    72–73; introduction 65; preparation

for 67–68; remote attendance 69; room for 69; scheduling of 57, 66; types of 65–66; video conferencing *60*, 69–70; walk-throughs/site visits *73*, 74

production right costs 78

production staff and production manager 35–36

professional development 104

project manager relationships: artistic director 34; creative designer 33, *33*; the crew 29–30; director 34; fixing poor relationships 28–29; introduction 21; listening to others with intention 23–24, *23*; not taking things personally 27; observation 26; rules, knowledge of 26–27; shop supervisors/production staff 35–36; stage manager 35–36; team and 24–25; trust and 21–22, *22*; understanding everyone's role 25

promotion 277–278

proscenium theatre 51

psychological needs 35–36

psychology of production management 35–37, *36*

purchasing concerns 85–86, *86*

regional theatre 125–128, *126*, *127*; Broadway theatre *vs.* 128–129 ; development 126; education 127; introduction 125, 126; marketing/public relations 125–126; *She Kills Monsters* 132–135, *133*; summer stock theatres 129–130; *To Kill a Mockingbird* 130–132, *131*

rehearsal schedule *58*, 57–58

reimbursement tracking 85

rental costs 78, 150

reputation 274

respect in communication 8

resume review 92

riders in hiring contracts 100–102

rigging costs 247–248

rigging special events 247–248, *248*

rights and permissions 53–54

"right to work" law 103

Ringle, Jennifer 190

rock and roll: advance checklists 176–177; advancing a show 167, *168*; contract/technical rider 167–168; hospitality needs 171–174; introduction 161–163, *162*; labor needs 170–171; local ground transportation 180–183; putting on show 178–179; security needs 174–175; technical needs 168–169, *170*; ticket holds/production kills 179–180; touring advance checklists 177, *178*; touring needs *vs.* venues 163–166, *163–166*; venue production management 167; venue technical packet 175–176

Ruiz, Don Miguel 274

safety concerns: assessments 109–110; case study 118–121, *119*; and COVID 117–118; documentation for 110–112, *112*; fire marshals 113–116, *115*; hierarchy of needs 35–36; introduction 107; occupational safety 107–108, *108*, *109*; planning and schedule management 116–117; in the shops 112–113; training 110

Sanders, John 161–163, 183–187

San Diego Symphony 189, 190, 268, 271, 276

Santa Fe Opera 141, 142–144, *144*

Sapp, Kelsey 269

Satter, Carolyn 27, 199–202, 204–205, 207

Satter, Paige 189, 190, 268, 271, 276

saying no 16

saying yes 14–15, *15*

SCARF (Status, Certainty, Autonomy, Relatedness, Fairness) tool 17

schedule building/creation 56, 59, 95

schedule management 55–56; *see also* planning and schedule management

Schwartz, Jennifer 132–135

Screen Actors Guild (SAG) 102

script/project analysis 52–53

seasonal workers 85, 130

seating at special events 246

Seattle Opera 34, 140, *141*, 143

security needs, rock and roll productions 174–175

shared dance concerts 153–154

She Kills Monsters 132–135, *133*

shop supervisors and production manager 35–36

show settlement 206–207

show treatments 54–55

sightlines at special events 246–247

Silvey, Perry 35, 49, 150–151, 227, 230, 232, 284

Sister's Follies 157–159, *158*

site-specific work in dance 153, *153*

site visits 74, 255–256

sitzprobe rehearsal 140

Skype interviews 69

smiling during communication 13

social networking communication 14

soft goods 245–246, *248*

solo dance concerts 153–154

sound attenuator 116

sound checks 249, 250

special events: audio 249–250; backstage spaces 246; ballroom/convention center room 256–257, *257*; case study 261–263; drape lines/soft goods 245–246; entrance 256; hard power *vs.* generator 252–253; introduction 239–244, *240–244*; labor 254–255; lighting 248–249; lobby/foyer 256; masking 245–246; production manager checklists for 240; rigging 247–248, *248*; seating 246; sightlines 246–247; sound checks 233; stage

height/placement 245; stage manager 246; storage 259; technical tables locations 246; venue logistics 244; video/image magnification 251–252; walk-throughs 255–256; working outdoors 257–260; working safely with electricity 254
specificity element in communication 7
staffing co-productions 217–219
Stage Directors and Choreographers Society (SDC) 102
stage height/placement 245
stage manager (SM) 35, 52, 246
The Stage Manager's Toolkit (Kincman) 7
standard operating procedures (SOP) manual 113
storage at special events 259
stress: and freelancing 282–283, *283*; reducing 284
strike schedule 60–61
summer stock theatres 129–130
supply costs 78
Switch: How to Change Things When Change is Hard (Heath and Heath) 272
symphony music: case study 196–198, *197*; introduction 189–191, *191*; orchestra operations 192–193, *193*; production managers and 193–196, *195*

tactful element in communication 7
tax exempt status 86
team work in production management 24–25
technical contract riders 202, 229
technical director, challenges for 261–263, *262*
technical equipment needs 205, *206*
tech rehearsals 60, 234
tech schedule 59–60
territory space 11–12
Theatre Communications Group (TCG) 90

ticket holds 179–180
ticketing needs 205
timely element in communication 7
To Kill a Mockingbird 130–132, *131*
touring: advance checklists 177, *178*; needs *vs.* venues 163–166, *163–166*; overview 227–235, *228*, *230*, *233*
tracking budgeting 83–85, *84*
training: and dance 149; of employees 104; graduate 267–268; in safety concerns 110
trust and relationships 21–22, *22*
Two Trains Running 223–224

union concerns 77, 78, 102–103
United Scenic Artists (USA) 103
United States Institute of Theatre Technology (USITT) 1–2, 91, 226, 285
Unmasking the Face (Ekman) 9
US Department of Labor 100
Utzmyers, Tracy 104, 130

vendor hires 94–95
venues: logistics for special events 244; planning/scheduling 51–52; production management 167; technical packet 175–176; touring needs *vs.* 163–166, *163–166*; walk-throughs 255–256
video conferencing 13, 69–70
video production 251–252

walk-throughs 74, 255–256
wandleprobe rehearsal 140
weather 183–187, *185*, *186*
work-life balance 284–285
written communication 13–14

yellow cards 231, 235

9780367406363